Principles of Economics: Micro

THE IRWIN SERIES IN ECONOMICS

CONSULTING EDITOR   LLOYD G. REYNOLDS   *Yale University*

Principles of
ECONOMICS
Micro

WILLIS L. PETERSON, Ph.D.
University of Minnesota

1974   Revised Edition

 RICHARD D. IRWIN, INC.   *Homewood, Illinois 60430*
Irwin-Dorsey International   *London, England WC2H 9NJ*
Irwin-Dorsey Limited   *Georgetown, Ontario L7G 4B3*

Revised Edition
First Printing, January 1974
Second Printing, May 1974
Third Printing, November 1974
Fourth Printing, January 1975
Fifth Printing, April 1975

ISBN 0–256–01508–2
Library of Congress Catalog Card No. 73–84296

Printed in the United States of America

LEARNING SYSTEMS COMPANY—
a division of Richard D. Irwin, Inc.—has developed a
PROGRAMMED LEARNING AID
to accompany texts in this subject area.
Copies can be purchased through your bookstore
or by writing PLAIDS,
1818 Ridge Road, Homewood, Illinois 60430.

Preface

As is all too evident to students during examinations, knowledge has a tendency to slip away with the passage of time. Not only do we forget a substantial amount of what we learn but part of what we do retain is likely to become obsolete in future years. It is important, therefore, that education be of a nature that facilitates retention of acquired knowledge and that this knowledge have a long lasting value. The kind of education that provides durability and lasting value is perhaps best described by Alfred North Whitehead in *The Aims of Education and Other Essays:* "Whatever be the detail with which you cram your student, the chances of his meeting in afterlife exactly that detail is almost infinitesimal; and if he does meet it, he will probably have forgotten what you taught him about it. The really useful training yields a comprehension of a few general principles with a thorough grounding in the way they apply to a variety of concrete details. In subsequent practice the men will have forgotten your particular details; but they will remember by an unconscious common sense how to apply principles to immediate circumstances."

In keeping with this philosophy of education, this text strives to strike a balance between principles and their application to current economic problems and decisions. Although circumstances will change with the passage of time, the principles contained in this volume should remain applicable to problems and decisions faced during a person's entire lifetime.

This book is a twin. It is linked to my *Principles of Economics: Macro* in style and is complementary in content. Yet either can stand alone or be used with another text. As is the case for the macro volume, this text is designed to be used in either the macro-micro or reverse sequence. The introductory material on demand and supply that has been added to chapter one of this revised edition of the micro text should provide a clearer perspective of what is to be covered during the first six chapters, regardless of the sequence employed.

Among other changes that I believe make this a better book, it has been "fleshed out" in many areas (without becoming obese) and hopefully all the bugs of the first edition have been removed. Much of the credit for the improvement should go to those who have offered detailed comments and suggestions on the first edition and on the first draft of the revised edition: Barbara Henneberry and James Witte of Indiana University, Lloyd Reynolds of Yale, and Frank Tansey of Baruch College of the City University of New York. In addition I am indebted to many users of the first edition who have taken the time to offer comments and suggestions, many of which they will recognize in this revised volume. Special thanks also goes to Dorothy Peterson who probably learned more economics than she really wanted to know while assisting me with the proofreading.

December 1973   WILLIS L. PETERSON

Contents

1

Introduction to microeconomics

"Micro" versus "Macro" economics

As economics developed into a discipline, two major areas in the study of the subject emerged: micro and macro. Microeconomics is concerned mainly with the economic activities of individual consumers and producers, or groups of consumers and producers known as markets. Macroeconomics, on the other hand, is concerned with economic aggregates, or the economy as a whole. The two major problem areas of macroeconomics are unemployment and inflation. To be sure, these are of great concern to individuals, but they are also problems over which the individual has relatively little control. Both the cause and the solutions to these problems lie in the realm of governmental action, which affects the entire economy.

It would be a mistake, however, to conclude that the micro and macro areas are distinct or unrelated fields of study. There is a certain amount of overlap between the two. For example, we will see in later chapters that much of what the government does in terms of enacting laws or levying taxes directly affects individuals and markets, and these effects can be analyzed with the tools of microeconomics. By the same token, the actions of large groups of consumers or producers, such as the increased desire to save on the part of many people, are analyzed with macroeconomic tools.

Because of the impossibility of completely separating the micro

1

from the macro, some economists argue that a more appropriate division would be price theory versus monetary and income and employment theory. In more advanced courses, particularly at the graduate level, microeconomic principles are generally referred to as price theory, mainly because the material deals with the determination of prices and their effect on the output and input mix in the economy.

The problem of scarcity

In studying economics, as in any other activity, we like to have some reason for exerting effort. We attend the theater or go to a ball game because it is enjoyable. We attend school to learn or to make it possible to hold down a job and earn a living. But why study economics?

There may be a few people who would be willing to study economics purely for the enjoyment it brings. For most, however, learning economics is not 100 percent entertainment. To be sure, mastering a subject provides a certain amount of intellectual satisfaction, but it is hard to justify economics only on this basis. Crossword puzzles or chess might do just as well (or better) on this score. The social science of economics must rest on a different foundation. I have posed this question to my students and so far all have been too kind (or too smart) to say that we study economics because it is a required subject. But this would beg the question: Why is it required?

The answer we are looking for can be simplified to a single word —scarcity. Human wants are greater than the resources available to satisfy them. In fact, economists traditionally have argued that human wants are unlimited or insatiable. At first you may find this hard to believe. Surely, you might argue, there is some level of income or standard of living where one would be completely satiated. But if you spend a few hours, or even a few minutes, making a list of the goods and services that you wouldn't mind having, chances are their purchase would put a millionaire in a financial bind. Of course, you need not limit your list to the familiar "private" goods and services, such as housing, cars, or vacation trips. You might want to include cleaner air and water, or a comfortable and convenient public transportation system.

Suppose by some stroke of magic all the items on your list were supplied. Would you then be completely satisfied or satiated? Probably not, especially if everyone else also were granted their fondest wishes. Human nature being what it is, we always seem to be just a little dissatisfied with what we have. A new VW, Pinto, or Vega may satisfy for a time, but eventually we would be giving admiring glances to a Mark IV or an "El D." In addition, we must remember that entirely new goods and services, many of which are not even in the realm of our present imagination, will be developed and come on the market in the future, as they have in the past. A "dream list" prepared by your great-grandparents certainly would not have contained many of the items on your own list, simply because they were not even imagined at the time.

It is less difficult to envision the scarcity of resources at our disposal. In recent years attention has been drawn to the day our non-renewable natural resources, especially fossil fuels, will be exhausted. Although less newsworthy, it is important to realize that *all* resources, including land area, labor, and manmade capital such as buildings and machines, are in limited supply. Being finite in number, these resources can produce only a finite amount of goods and services. Since human wants appear to be infinite, or at least much larger than the resources to satisfy these wants, people must decide what they will produce and what they will have to forego. In other words, we are forced to make economic decisions.

Economic decisions

We must make these decisions (or, if you wish, economize) from the time we are aware of the world around us. This harsh reality becomes apparent the first time a child stands in front of a candy counter clutching a nickel or a dime. The coin might buy a candy bar, a package of gum, or a roll of Lifesavers, but not all three. An economic decision must be made.

It would be misleading, though, to conclude that economic decisions all involve money. They do not. Probably the best example of a nonmonetary economic decision is how we allocate our time— a scarce resource that seems to become scarcer the older we become. The student must decide if he will spend the evening studying, say, mathematics or history, or, perhaps even more fundamentally, whether he will devote it to study or to leisure. Allocating our time to the best use is one of the most important economic decisions we have to make. It could well be one of the most important things learned in school.

More traditional types of economic decisions involve the operations of households and firms. For the household, a continuing array of economic decisions must be made on how to allocate the weekly or semimonthly paycheck. How much goes to housing, how much to food, clothing, transportation, entertainment, and so forth? Managing just a modest income for a family requires thousands of economic decisions each year.

Considering the complexity of a household's economic decisions, we can appreciate the decisions that must be made in managing a business firm. What kind of things should the firm produce? Should it specialize or diversify? Should it produce a large volume and sell at a low price or produce less and charge more? How do the decisions of rival firms affect each firm? Should the firm employ more labor and save on machines, or should it substitute machines for labor? These are some examples of economic decisions each manager must make. How well he makes them largely determines the success or failure of his firm.

The need to make economic decisions, of course, does not stop at the level of the household or firm. Economic decisions must be made at all governmental levels, ranging from local governments such as townships and municipalities to the states and federal government. Perhaps the most basic of these economic decisions concerns how much of the total production of society shall be provided through the public sector and how much through the private sector. In a democracy, governmental decisions tend to reflect the broad wishes of society, but, of course, they cannot please everyone. People of a more conservative philosophy tend to desire a greater share of production in the private sector, while those of a more liberal bent stress the need for more public goods and services.

Once society settles on a mix between public and private goods, it must decide what kinds of public goods and services should be produced. For example, what is the appropriate mix between military and nonmilitary public goods? Should we have fewer weapons and greater public expenditures for slum clearance, public parks, pollution control, and so forth? Economic decisions involving governments or nations have this in common with those made by the child at the candy counter: Both require making a choice among alternatives, although one involves a nickel or dime, while the other may run into billions of dollars.

The usefulness of theory

Economic theory has suffered from a bad press for many years, not entirely without justification. Students tend to be turned off by theory because they visualize dry, abstract material that has little relevance to their world. But theory does not have to be dry or irrelevant. In fact, little is to be gained by theory if it cannot be of help in making day-to-day economic decisions or resolving economic problems.

The main value of theory is that it provides a framework for thinking. We need such a framework because the world is by far too complex to take into account every bit of information that bears upon a decision or problem, and we have to sort out the important from the unimportant. But information does not come in neat categories labeled "important" and "unimportant," nor is it always obvious which is which. For example, some goods or services increase in price during their peak seasons, such as Christmas cards and hotel rooms on Miami Beach. Other products decrease in price during the time of the year they are most actively bought and sold, such as fresh fruits and vegetables in the northern states. Without an understanding of economics, particularly demand and supply, it might appear that price and quantity have very little relation to each other. For some commodities price rises when quantity exchanged increases; for others, it declines when quantity increases. To the person untrained in economics, there may appear to be very little order in markets. But after gaining an understanding of the theories of demand and supply (hopefully by the end of Chapter 6), you should be able to explain such phenomena and even predict future changes in price and quantity of goods and services. In the latter sense, theory serves as a sort of "crystal ball."

Theory has come to be known by a number of names. One synonym is "principle," as in the title of this book. A theory is also sometimes referred to as a "model," probably because theory represents and predicts reality without necessarily duplicating it exactly or in detail.

Production possibilities

We have established that economics exists because we cannot have everything we would like, and thus we are forced to make economic decisions. These decisions take the form of choosing among alternative goods or services that will best satisfy our wants. Thus society must decide what to produce out of an almost infinite range of possibilities. Economists have traditionally represented this range of choices by what they call a "production possibilities schedule" (Table 1–1). This schedule can also be represented by a diagram (Figure 1–1) called a "production possibilities curve." Figure 1–1 is a representation or picture of the relationship expressed by the numbers in Table 1–1. Economics uses diagrams a great deal to present pictures of ideas, because a diagram is a relatively efficient and concise way of explaining an idea or concept.

TABLE 1–1
Production possibilities schedule

Wheat (million bushels)	Corn (million bushels)
0	80
10	75
20	65
30	50
40	30
50	0

The production possibilities schedule or curve is a way of illustrating the idea that a nation or individual faces limits on what can be produced and must make choices between many possible combinations of goods or services. In the simple example used here, if this nation devoted all its resources to the production of corn it could produce 80 million bushels of corn and nothing else. Or if all resources were devoted to wheat, 50 million bushels could be produced but no corn. It may like to have 50 million bushels of wheat *and* 80 million bushels of corn, but this combination is not

FIGURE 1–1
Production possibilities curve

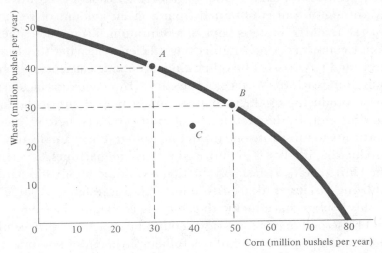

possible because the nation does not have the resources to produce both. It would be more realistic, of course, for the country to choose some combination between the two extremes, say 40 million wheat and 30 million corn, or 20 million wheat and 65 million corn. We will postpone for now just how a country goes about making this choice. The important point here is that such a choice must be made.

Efficiency and full employment

The very best economic condition that can be achieved is to be on the surface of the production possibilities curve. Any point outside the curve is by definition not possible. Essentially the curve bounds or defines what it is possible to achieve, but it would be a mistake to believe that a nation or an economy always achieves the possible. To be on the surface of the curve, say at point *A* or *B*, requires two conditions: (1) all production is carried on in the most efficient manner possible and (2) all resources are fully employed.

You might ask what we mean by efficiency. Essentially there are two types, and both are required to be on the surface of the production possibilities curve. One, engineering efficiency, requires that maximum output is obtained from a given amount of resources; that is, resource waste is kept to a minimum. Economics generally is not concerned with engineering efficiency, leaving this to engineers and physicists. The other kind, economic efficiency, also is required to reach the surface of the curve. By economic efficiency we mean producing products that consumers most desire at the lowest possible cost. In the production of most products there is some opportunity to substitute one input for another. For example, in wheat production, if labor is high priced relative to machines, as is true in the United States, wheat production should be highly mechanized, utilizing machines to substitute for high-priced labor. A large part of this book is concerned with achieving economic efficiency.

The second major condition required to reach the surface of the production possibilities curve is full employment of resources. The resource that we are most concerned with is the human resource. If there are people who are unemployed but would like to be working, the economy is not getting the goods or services these people could produce. Thus unemployment is wasteful for society, and, of course, for the individual who is unemployed the loss of income is a critical problem. Much of the material in macroeconomics deals with achieving full employment.

It would be an extremely unusual economy that would be able to achieve both maximum efficiency and full employment. Most economies probably operate somewhat below the surface of the production possibilities curve. This does not prevent them, however, from striving to reach the maximum production possible, subject to environmental constraints and conservation needs. Many economists are concerned primarily with helping society move toward its maximum possible output.

Opportunity cost

Assume that a simple economy is achieving maximum production so that it is now on the surface of the curve, say at point *A* in Figure 1–1. At this point it is producing 40 million bushels of wheat and 30 million bushels of corn per year. Suppose it wished to increase its production of corn, say up to 50 million bushels per year. To do this the nation would have to reduce its production of wheat from 40 to 30 million bushels. In other words, it would have to give up 10 million bushels of wheat to obtain the extra 20 million bushels of corn. This 10 million bushels of wheat, then, is the opportunity cost of the extra corn. Thus we can define opportunity cost as the amount of a good or service that must be given up to obtain more of another good or service.

Numerous combinations of goods or services might be used to illustrate opportunity cost. The only restriction is that two goods or groups of goods be considered at a time because of the two-dimensional nature of the diagram. This does not in any way make the idea less relevant or useful.

An important decision facing the United States at the present concerns the choice between military and nonmilitary goods and services. A decision to maintain a large military establishment means that the nation must forego a certain amount of nonmilitary goods and services, such as housing, transportation, a cleaner environment, and so forth. These goods and services represent the opportunity cost of military goods. (You might want to illustrate this choice with a production possibilities curve. What happens to a nation's position on the curve when it goes to war, assuming it is on or near the surface of the curve?)

Every economy must make a decision on the choice between consumption goods (items consumed to satisfy present wants) and investment goods (items such as machines and structures that increase future output). A nation that decides to devote a large share of its output to investment goods must give up some consumption goods. The Soviet Union provides a good example of this case. Another choice that must be made is between agricultural and nonagricultural products. Nations that must devote a large share of their resources to produce food because of a relatively unproductive agriculture by necessity must give up the production of other things such as housing, transportation, and medical care. The so-called underdeveloped nations of the world illustrate this case.

So far the examples of opportunity cost have focused on the national level, but the opportunity cost concept applies as well to the individual firm, household, or person. The firm that uses its plant to produce shoes cannot produce belts or basketballs. The family that spends its vacation at the seashore must forego the opportunity to spend this time in the mountains. When you are reading this book you cannot be doing something else, such as reading a novel, studying mathematics, or sleeping. Thus the opportunity cost of studying economics is the novel you did not enjoy, the mathematics you did not learn, or the sleep you lost. Everything you do has a cost; nothing is absolutely free.

The idea of opportunity cost applies particularly to the choice between labor and leisure. For a person paid by the hour, the opportunity cost of going fishing or to a baseball game on a weekday afternoon is the wages foregone from a job. There is little chance that a person who values his income highly or what it will buy will take off to go fishing, because the opportunity cost would be too high. Another individual might place a high value on leisure, and the person who not only values freedom and leisure highly but, through lack of skills, can earn only a low wage will probably choose more leisure. Of course, wage earners who support a family generally take their welfare into account when deciding whether the value of their leisure is greater than the income foregone.

We should stress again the importance of being on or near the surface of the production possibilities curve. If a nation is experiencing substantial unemployment, it may be able to increase its output of all goods and services simultaneously. This can be illustrated by Figure 1–1 above. If the nation is at point C, the movement to point B results in more of both corn and wheat. The same applies to an individual. Given the "gray matter" at your disposal, are you learning as much as possible during the hours you spend in class and studying on your own?

Public versus private goods

The production possibilities curve is useful to illustrate that total output for a nation is limited and that choices must be made among alternatives. In the previous section we mentioned the choices between military and nonmilitary goods and between consumption and investment goods as examples. Another classification that is useful to make is between public and private goods. It is perhaps simplest to think of public goods as goods which society buys collectively, such as public parks, highways, national defense, law enforcement, and public education. Typically these goods are not bought and sold in the marketplace but financed through taxes or special fees and distributed through a governmental agency. Public goods can be further classified as consumption goods (public parks) or investment goods (hydroelectric dams), or some combination of the two.

Society finds it necessary to produce public goods because it would be largely impossible, or at least uneconomic, for individuals to acquire these goods for personal use. You could not afford to build the highways and streets you use each day. It would be a mistake to conclude, however, that public goods are produced by governments. Although these goods generally are financed through public funds, the actual production is carried on largely by private firms under contract to the government.

In a democracy the amount of public goods produced depends largely on the wishes of society. Almost everyone would agree on the need for at least a minimum amount of public goods and services, such as law enforcement and highways. But the optimum amount of public goods and services to be provided is not so universally agreed upon. Conservative members of society stress the ability of the individual to provide for himself what he deems best. More liberal individuals acknowledge the dependence of people on one another and support the need for more public goods and services. The actual amount of public goods is therefore a compromise between the wishes of different groups in society.

Private goods, the other major classification, include the items we purchase and use in our daily lives; food, clothing, shelter, and entertainment are a few standard examples. It is, of course, possible for some of these goods to be provided by the government (such as public housing and food stamps). Nevertheless, if society decides to increase the amount of public goods, or goods provided by the government, it must in most cases be willing to decrease the amount of goods and services purchased privately and vice versa. Such is the nature of opportunity cost.

Public utilities

There is a class of goods and services that falls somewhere between the public and private goods categories. These are called public utilities; examples include local power and light or telephone companies. Goods and services provided by these companies generally are purchased by individuals in the marketplace, so in this sense they resemble private goods. But for reasons that will become clear in a moment, society has decided that the normal production of these goods by many firms in each area would not be desirable. Thus the government regulates their production, and in this sense public utilities resemble public goods.

The main reason for public utilities is to avoid a costly duplication of facilities and services. Suppose, for example, there were ten telephone companies serving your area instead of one. Each of these companies would require its own lines, telephones, and so forth. Assuming comparable efficiency, the cost under this system would be high compared to that for one set of lines and one telephone per subscriber. It is also easy to imagine how difficult it would be to make calls; for example, you might buy telephone service from a different company than the person you wish to call. Thus in order to avoid duplication and unnecessary confusion, the government gives exclusive right to just one company to operate in each city or area.

By giving a firm exclusive right to operate, however, the government makes a public utility a virtual monopoly, free from the competitive forces in the market. In order to guard against excessive prices or inferior service to the public, the government also regulates these firms by setting the prices they charge and establishing standards of performance.[1]

Increasing opportunity cost

Increasing opportunity cost refers to a situation in which increasing amounts of one good or service must be given up to obtain additional increments of another good or service. This idea is illustrated by the example in Table 1-1, but to illustrate it a bit more clearly, we have computed the cost of additional increments of wheat in terms of corn given up. These costs are presented in Table 1-2.

---

[1] Telephone and electricity users in the northeastern part of the country probably have good reason to doubt whether the government can in fact enforce the standards.

TABLE 1–2
Cost of wheat in terms of corn*

Increment of wheat (bushels)	Corn given up (bushels)	
	Total	Per bushel of wheat
First 10 million	5 million	½
Second 10 million	10 million	1
Third 10 million	15 million	1½
Fourth 10 million	20 million	2
Fifth 10 million	30 million	3

* Computed from Table 1–1.

Notice that in order to obtain the first 10 million bushels of wheat, this country had to give up 5 million bushels of corn (80 down to 75). Or, for each extra bushel of wheat obtained, one-half bushel of corn was given up. Suppose we go one step further and see what happens when this economy increases its wheat production from 10 to 20 million. Now corn production is reduced from 75 down to 65 million. In this step, for each extra bushel of wheat obtained, 1 bushel of corn was given up. At the range where we approach the maximum wheat, 3 bushels of corn are given up for each bushel of wheat obtained. Thus we see that the opportunity cost of a bushel of wheat increases from one-half bushel of corn to 3 bushels of corn .

The same thing would be true if we start at the bottom and move up. At first only one third of a bushel of wheat is given up per bushel of corn. At the top two bushels of wheat must be sacrificed to obtain an extra bushel of corn.

This idea of increasing costs also is illustrated by the concave nature of the production possibilities curve shown in Figure 1–2. Note that when the curve is concave to the origin, the lower right-hand segment is relatively steep. This means that the first ten-million-bushel increment to wheat output takes us back along the corn axis a relatively short distance. But as we approach the maximum possible wheat output, corn output is reduced by a large amount, and the curve becomes flat. The increasing amounts of corn given up in order to obtain the successive ten-million-bushel increments of wheat are illustrated by the larger and larger distances *between* the vertical broken lines, moving from right to left.

The same result would occur if we started with all wheat and zero corn and moved down the vertical axis and out along the hori-

FIGURE 1-2
Production possibilities curve illustrating increasing opportunity cost

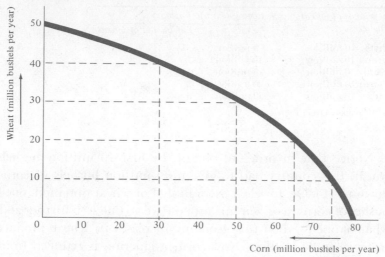

zontal axis. Now with additional ten-million-bushel increments to corn output, wheat output would decline by progressively larger amounts. (It will be helpful to prove this to yourself with a diagram of your own.)

The slope of this curve tells us, therefore, how easy or how difficult it is to transform one good into another. For this reason the production possibilities curve is sometimes called the "transformation curve." In this example, when we move down the curve we transform wheat into corn, or moving up, we transform corn into wheat. As we move along the curve, the rate of transformation changes because of increasing costs. With little or no corn, it is easy to transform wheat into corn; with almost all corn it becomes more difficult to make this transformation.

Does it make sense to believe that the idea of increasing costs fits reality? Economists have argued that it does because they believe that resources are more productive in some uses than in others. In our example, it is reasonable to believe that some land is better suited for wheat than for corn. In the United States the arid Great Plains area would provide an example. If all of this land were planted to corn it would not yield very much. Taking the land out of corn and replacing it with wheat would not reduce corn production very much because of the low corn yield in this area, but it would increase wheat production considerably because wheat grows relatively well there.

In the production of other products, the idea of increasing costs is less clear. For example, if all our resources were devoted to the production of either automobiles or airplanes, would you expect increasing costs? Both use steel, aluminum, plastic, rubber, and semiskilled and skilled labor. In this case the rate of transformation probably would not change very much as you moved down along the transformation curve, and we would come closer to case of constant costs. In the case of constant costs, the opportunity cost of one good in terms of the other does not change at the various combinations of output. In this example, the opportunity cost of an additional airplane (in terms of automobiles given up) would not be expected to change very much over the range of production.

But, you might argue, if the point of all airplanes and zero automobiles is reached, surely there will be a shortage of specialized people such as test pilots or aeronautical engineers, which will lead to increasing costs because less qualified people will have to do these tasks. True. And this brings up an important point. If resources are *rapidly* shifted from automobiles to airplanes, we would likely run into increasing costs of airplanes. On the other hand, if the move was very gradual and people anticipated the shift so that more would receive training in the needed skills, there would be less evidence of increasing costs.

This example brings out the importance of time for adjustment. Allowing little or no time for adjustment, a large-scale and rapid change to a different combination of products means that many resources will have to be employed for other than their intended purpose. Automotive factories must be turned into airplane factories, mechanical engineers into aeronautical engineers, and so forth. Allowing a longer time to adjust will permit resources to become better adapted to new uses. New factories that are built will be designed for airplane production, and more people will train as aeronautical engineers. Thus the transformation curve would not exhibit as much curvature when a longer time is allowed for resources to adjust as when a more rapid adjustment is forced. Figures 1–3 and 1–4 illustrate this difference.

A related point, but important, is the need to realize that no

FIGURE 1–3
Transformation curve allowing one year to adjust

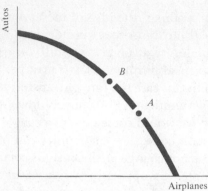

FIGURE 1–4
Transformation curve allowing ten years to adjust

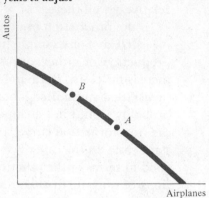

economy ever moves the entire distance along the transformation curve from one axis to another. Most changes are relatively small, say from *A* to *B* or *B* to *A* in Figures 1–3 and 1–4. And note that even though the transformation curve has a pronounced curvature, especially in Figure 1–3, the segment of the line between points *A* and *B* is close to a straight line. (You might check this by running a straight edge through points *A* and *B*.) A perfectly straight line represents constant costs throughout.

Thus it is reasonable to believe that in the range where you would expect changes to take place, there would not be as much evidence of increasing costs as over the entire range of the transformation curve. And the more time allowed for adjustment, the closer this segment would come to a straight line, as illustrated by segment of the line between *A* and *B* in Figure 1–4.

Economic growth

So far we have been concerned mainly with moving along the surface of a given production possibilities curve. As long as all resources are fully employed, an increase in the production of one category of goods must be accompanied by a decrease in the output of the other category. Yet we observe in developed nations such as the United States, Canada, Japan, or the Western European countries an increase over time in the production of most broad categories of goods and services. For example, it is evident that during the current year the United States has produced more of both private and public goods and services than it did during 1930.

An increase in the total output of goods and services over time is referred to as economic growth. Economic growth can be attained by an increase in the total quantity of resources, such as population or capital goods, or by an increase in resource productivity. Strictly speaking, the latter also amounts to an increase in quantity of resources, since a more productive resource provides more resources than a less productive one. A man-day of skilled labor provides more labor than a man-day of unskilled labor. The idea of productivity differences between resources is discussed more thoroughly in the chapter on economic growth and development in the companion volume to this text, *Principles of Economics: Macro*. The main objective here is to recognize that nations need not be constrained to a given level of output for all time.

The phenomenon of economic growth can be illustrated by a shifting to the right of the production possibilities or transformation curve, as shown in Figure 1–5. At any point in time, such as 1930 or 1973, more of one kind of good entails less of the other. Over time, however, more of both kinds of goods can be attained by economic growth.

We should point out that the production possibilities curve we

FIGURE 1–5
Production possibilities curve illustrating economic growth

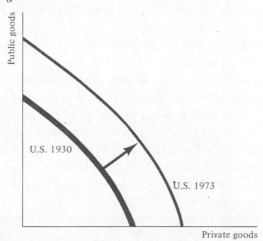

Public goods

U.S. 1930

U.S. 1973

Private goods

have been discussing refers to total output rather than output per person. If population growth equals output growth, the individual really is no better off, even though the total output of the economy is growing. This phenomenon characterizes many underdeveloped countries. In the developed nations, output has grown more rapidly than population, giving each individual increasing amounts of goods and services.

Introduction to demand and supply

Since price plays such an important role in a market economy, it will be useful at this point to probe just a bit deeper into the price-making process. Basically we can say that price is determined by the forces of demand and supply. Much of Chapters 2 and 3 will deal with the derivation of demand, while Chapters 4 and 5 will build up the concept of supply, and Chapter 6 will consider in some detail how these forces interact to determine price. But just as a builder must see a picture or blueprint of what he is going to build before he begins, it will be useful to sketch a picture of demand and supply to see what we will end up with in Chapter 6.

We can define *demand* as a relationship between price and quantity. For most goods and services, there is an *inverse* relationship between price and quantity demanded. That is, when price is relatively high, the quantity of an item that people buy per week, per month, or per year will tend to be relatively low. Conversely, if price is relatively low, the amount that people buy tends to be somewhat greater.

The idea that people buy less of an item when its price is relatively high and more when price is relatively low has a certain intuitive appeal. Generally what happens is that a high price prompts people to look for less expensive substitutes that will satisfy their wants. For example, when beef is high, people tend to cut back on beef consumption and eat more pork, chicken, or fish. Conversely, when the price of an item is relatively low, it becomes the substitute for other more expensive items. The inverse relationship between price and quantity demanded is merely a reflection of people trying to get the most for their money.

Economists will often illustrate this relationship with a diagram, placing price on the vertical axis and quantity on the horizontal axis. By choosing various possible prices and observing the amounts people will buy at these prices, it is possible to trace a downward-sloping line, as illustrated by Figure 1–6. For example, if price is

FIGURE 1–6
A demand curve

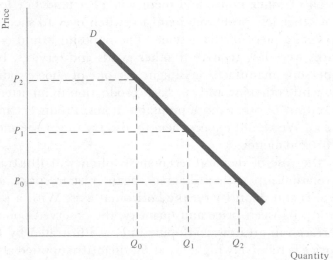

relatively high, say at P_2, quantity will be small, say at Q_0. As price declines to P_1 and P_0, quantity increases to Q_1 and Q_2. If we assume that the same relationship holds *between* these points as on them, we can connect the points and obtain a downward-sloping line. Economists call this a "demand curve," even though it is often drawn as a straight, downward-sloping line.

We also can define *supply* as a relationship between price and quantity. For most goods and services, there is a *positive* relationship between price and quantity supplied. That is, when price is relatively high the quantity of an item that producers will place on the market per unit of time will tend to be relatively large. Conversely, if price is relatively low, the quantity that producers are willing to make available for sale tends to be smaller.

The idea that producers will produce more when price is relatively high and less when price is lower also is intuitively appealing. In this case, a high price provides an incentive for producers to increase output because their profits will be greater than when price is low, other things equal. The prospects of relatively high profits for an item tends to cause producers to cut back on less profitable activities and increase the output of the high-priced item. If shoes are high priced, leather-goods manufacturers may build more manufacturing capacity for shoes and cut back on the production of other items, and there will be a tendency for producers of other less profitable items to switch over to shoes in an effort to "get a piece of the action." The opposite would occur if shoe prices were low relative to other goods and services. In that case some shoe manufacturers might get out of shoe production entirely, while others would cut back production in an attempt to expand output of other more profitable items. Producers are consumers too. We would expect them to also try to get the most for their effort and money.

As in the case of demand, economists often will illustrate the supply relationship with a diagram, again placing price on the vertical axis and quantity on the horizontal axis. With a positive relationship between price and quantity, the observed points will tend to trace out an upward-sloping line, as illustrated by Figure 1–7. If price is relatively high, say at P_2, quantity supplied also will be relatively large, as indicated by Q_2. As price declines to P_1 and P_0, quantity supplied also declines to Q_1 and Q_0 respectively. Econ-

FIGURE 1–7
A supply curve

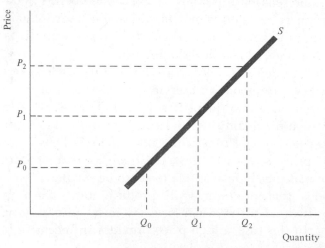

omists call the line that is traced out by this price-quantity relationship a "supply curve," although it is often drawn as a straight,
upward-sloping line.

It should be emphasized that demand alone, or supply alone,
cannot tell us which price or quantity will prevail in a market. They
only indicate various possible prices and quantities that *might*
prevail. But when we combine the two concepts, the market price
and quantity can readily be determined. The demand and supply
curves are something like two blades of a scissors; both are necessary
to do the job.

The process of price and quantity determination can best be
understood by superimposing the demand and supply curves on
the same diagram, as shown by Figure 1–8. This is possible because
both have price on the vertical axis and quantity on the horizontal
axis.

Perhaps the easiest way to determine which price will prevail is
to begin with a price that would *not* be likely to prevail, at least for
long, say a relatively high price, P_2. At this price, consumers buy a
relatively small amount, Q_1^d, but producers supply a relatively large
amount, Q_2^s. The outcome of this situation would be a buildup of

FIGURE 1–8
Determination of equilibrium price and quantity

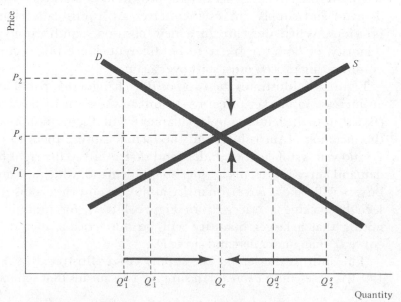

unsold goods or services, which would tend to result in a downward pressure on price. Some buyers, seeing the glut in the market, might press sellers to lower the price, and some sellers, seeing the buildup of inventories, might initiate price reductions in an effort to entice buyers to take a larger amount of their output.

As another possibility, consider price P_1. At this relatively low price, buyers are willing to take a relatively large amount off the market, whereas sellers are less anxious to produce because of the low price. In this case, we would observe a shortage and a drawing down of inventories. Some buyers, rather than go without, would offer sellers a higher price, and some sellers, seeing that they could sell their entire output for a higher price, would likely begin to hold out for it.

There is only one price, P_e, and one quantity, Q_e, that will tend to prevail. Economists refer to these as "equilibrium price" and "equilibrium quantity," respectively. P_e corresponds to the intersection of the demand and supply curves. At price P_e, buyers are willing to take off the market the exact same quantity sellers are willing to offer. There is no pressure, therefore, for price to move down or up. We can say that the market is in equilibrium.

One might conclude at this point that once a market gets into equilibrium, price and quantity should remain unchanged forever. Right? Wrong! What generally happens in most markets is that the demand and supply curves themselves are continually changing positions. When they are in a new position, equilibrium price, quantity, or both are likely to be different. Once this occurs the equilibrating process must start over again.

Figure 1–9 illustrates the two possible changes that could lead to an increase in market price: (A) a shift to the right by demand, or (B) a shift to the left by supply. Chapter 6 will discuss in more detail the meaning of such shifts and the factors causing them to occur. For now, it is sufficient to understand that a shift to the right by the demand curve represents an *increase* in demand, which means that buyers will take a *larger* quantity at any given price. This can be seen by picking a price, P_e' in Figure 1–9(A), for example, and noting that a larger quantity will be purchased under demand curve D' than under demand curve D.

The shift to the left in the supply curve illustrated by Figure 1–9(B) represents a *decrease* in supply. This means that sellers offer

FIGURE 1–9
Changes in demand and supply causing an increase in equilibrium price

(A) Shift to the right by demand   *(B) Shift to the left by supply*

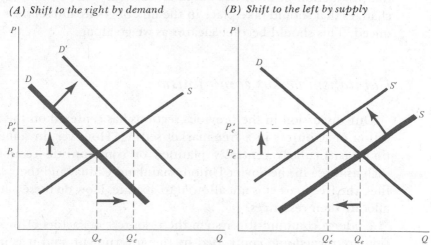

a *smaller* quantity on the market at any given price. Again this is easiest to see by picking any price, P_e' for example, and noting that a smaller quantity will be forthcoming under S' than under S.

Basically it is these shifts that cause adjustments to take place in the allocation of the nation's resources. The good illustrated by Figure 1–9(A) would exhibit an increase in quantity as producers responded to the increase in price caused by the increase in demand. The good illustrated by Figure 1–9(B) would exhibit a decrease in quantity as consumers responded to the increase in price caused by the decrease in supply. We should also point out that such demand and supply shifts can take place simultaneously, but this possibility will be discussed in Chapter 6.

Similarly, there are two kinds of shifts that can cause a *decrease* in equilibrium price: (1) a shift to the left by demand and (2) and a shift to the right by supply. In the first case there is a *decrease* in quantity as producers respond to the *decrease* in price caused by the *decrease* in demand. In the second, quantity would *increase* as consumers respond to the *decrease* in price caused by the *increase* in supply. (You might want to illustrate these two cases with diagrams.)

Hopefully you now have a somewhat clearer picture of how resources are allocated in a free market economy. These demand-supply interactions can be thought of as determining (1) where on the production possibilities curve an economy will be and (2) the changes that should take place in the mix of goods and services produced. This should become clearer as we go along.

Capitalism versus communism

Our discussion in the previous sections has centered on the allocation of resources in a free market setting. However, in some nations, particularly centrally planned or communistic economies such as those in the Soviet Union, mainland China, and their satellites, the free market is not allowed to operate. How do these nations allocate their resources?

Under a communistic system the resources or factors of production are owned and controlled by the government, and it is up to the government to decide where and how the nation's available resources are to be employed. For the most part these allocative decisions reflect what the authorities have decided is "best" for the country, at least at the macro level. For example, the Soviet planners have traditionally devoted a larger share of their resources to investment goods than has been the case in the U.S. economy. Although Soviet consumers have at times voiced a desire for more consumer goods, the authorities have in large part followed their long-run plans. At the micro level, however, the wishes of consumers appear to carry a bit more weight. For example, if the people desire less bread and more meat, there will be a tendency for some bread to go unsold and the meat shelves to empty quickly. As a result, the authorities may attempt to increase meat production while cutting back on bread production.

In recent years, the Soviet Union has begun to utilize prices a bit more in attempts to modify consumer behavior. If the authorities think the people should continue to eat a large amount of bread and very little meat, they will tend to lower the price of bread and raise the price of meat. Even though prices are set by the government, people in these countries respond to price changes just as people do everywhere, buying less of the item increased in price and more of the item that is less expensive.

The ability to set price is a powerful force in the hands of these governments. By manipulating price the authorities can often get people to do things voluntarily that they might otherwise not do, even under direct orders. For example, in order to reduce the consumption of cocoa the Soviet authorities set the price of chocolate candy bars at about 60 cents. Needless to say, not many people buy chocolate candy bars in the Soviet Union. Similarly, the price of vodka was increased a few years ago in order to reduce the consumption of that beverage.

Bear in mind, though, that price manipulation doesn't solve all problems. If the price that is set for an item does not correspond to the price people wish to pay for the quantity produced, there will tend to be either a shortage or a surplus of the item. If price is set lower than would exist in a free market for this quantity, there will be a shortage; long lines of prospective buyers will be observed and "black market" activities or bribing will tend to emerge, usually unobserved. If price is higher than what people would be willing to pay to buy all that is produced, unsold stocks will begin to pile up.

To summarize briefly, capitalism and communism share a common characteristic in that both have a finite capacity to produce; that is, both are constrained by a production possibilities curve. Under capitalism or a free market economy, the mix of goods is determined in large part by the forces of demand and supply. Under communism, the mix is largely influenced by the decisions of a small number of authorities in the government. There are other differences, of course, such as in the amount of personal, political, and religious freedom that the people can enjoy, but that is another story that would take us out of the realm of economics.

Preview

We have set the stage for a detailed look at the basic ideas and concepts in microeconomics. We will begin by focusing on the individual consumer or household to see how each can obtain the most satisfaction from the things he buys. We then extend what we know about consumer behavior to derive the concept of consumer demand. Next we take a similar look at the production side, first studying how resources can be combined in the most efficient manner and then extending our knowledge to derive producer supply.

Then we combine the concepts of demand and supply to see how they interact in the market to determine the price paid and quantity sold of a good or service.

After becoming acquainted with demand and supply and how they work in the market, we take a more detailed look at different kinds of product markets from the standpoint of the degree of competition present. Specifically we will see why some firms have price determined for them by the market while others have some power to determine the price they charge. We will then turn to a discussion of the labor and capital markets, finding that these markets have much in common with the markets for consumer goods and services. Finally, we will consider the topics of education and science and attempt to determine whether or not they represent a good investment for the individual or for society.

Main points of Chapter 1

1. Economics has evolved into two major fields of study: macroeconomics and microeconomics, although there is considerable overlap between the two.
2. Economics exists because of the basic problem of scarcity. Human wants are greater than the resources available to satisfy these wants.
3. Because resources are scarce, individuals, households, firms, and governments must choose among alternative goods or services. Everyone from small children to the largest governments must make economic decisions. Not all economic decisions involve money; allocating time is an important nonmonetary economic decision.
4. Economic theory is useful because it provides a framework for thinking, enabling us to separate important from unimportant information in making economic decisions or solving problems.
5. The production possibilities curve represents the idea that total output of goods and services is limited by the resources

available, and choices must be made among possible alternatives.

6. The surface of the production possibilities curve is reached only with maximum engineering and economic efficiency, and full employment of resources.

7. With maximum efficiency and full employment of resources, more of one good or service can be obtained only by giving up a certain amount of another good or service. This is called opportunity cost.

8. Every advanced society produces both private and public goods. In general, public goods are those bought and used collectively by society, although in the United States most of the public goods are actually produced by private firms.

9. Increasing costs occur if resources that are less well suited to the production of a good or service are shifted into its production from more suitable alternative employment.

10. Increasing costs become less prevalent when more time is allowed for resources to adjust to new uses.

11. By economic growth a nation is able to increase its total output of goods and services over time.

12. Demand is defined as an inverse relationship between price and quantity. When price is high, quantity demanded is low; when price is low, quantity demanded is high.

13. Supply is defined as a positive relationship between price and quantity. When price is high, quantity supplied is high; when price is low, quantity supplied is low.

14. Equilibrium price is defined as that price at which quantity demanded is exactly equal to quantity supplied. It corresponds to the intersection of the demand and supply curves.

15. Changes in equilibrium price and quantity occur because of shifts in demand, supply, or both. An increase in price results from an increase in demand and/or a decrease in supply. In the first case quantity exchanged in the market will increase; in the latter case quantity will decline.

16. Capitalism and communism share the common characteristic of being constrained by a production possibilities curve. Under capitalism, or a free market, the mix of private goods and services is determined largely by the forces of demand and

supply. Under communism, governmental decisions determine in large part what is produced.

Questions for thought and discussion

1. Once upon a time a wise king instructed one of the most learned men in his kingdom to teach him the most important concept in economics. The king's only condition was that the lesson had to consist of ten words or less (the king was a very busy man). After months of deliberation, the sage approached the king and was heard to say, "There is no such thing as a free lunch." What do you suppose the sage meant by this statement?

2. Is it possible to economize on time? Explain.

3. List some economic decisions you made in the past few days. Include some that involved money and some that did not.

4. What does a movie or stage play have in common with an economic theory?

5. What is the opportunity cost of the time you have devoted to the study of economics so far this week?

6. Does "playing hooky" from school have anything to do with opportunity cost? Explain.

7. Consider the following production possibilities schedule.

Points on economics quiz	Points on math quiz
0	200
25	180
50	140
75	80
100	0

    a) What is the opportunity cost of increasing economics points from 25 to 50? From 75 to 100?

    b) Does this example represent constant or increasing opportunity cost between economics and mathematics? Explain.

    c) Represent this production possibilities schedule by a production possibilities curve.

8. Suppose you decide to spend five more hours per week studying economics, starting with the second week of classes. From what activity would you take this time? Why?

9.   Would you expect increasing opportunity cost to be important in your allocation of time? Consider, for example, spending most of your time on economics versus spending a small amount on economics and the remainder on other subjects and leisure.

10.   At the beginning of the Vietnam military buildup a high government official stated that the United States can have more of both "guns" and "butter," meaning more of both military and nonmilitary goods. From what you know about a production possibilities curve, indicate under what conditions this statement would be valid. Under what conditions would it be false?

11.   *(a)* What is demand? *(b)*   What is supply?

12.   Explain what happens if the market price of an item is above the equilibrium price. What happens when price is below the equilibrium?

13.   What can cause a rise in the equilibrium price in a market? What can cause a fall in this price? Illustrate with diagrams.

14.   Does a rise in price in a market always lead to a reduction in quantity exchanged? Why or why not?

15.   Suppose you worked in the economic planning office of a communist nation and your job was to set the price of beef for the coming year. How would you determine the price that would make people want to buy just the exact amount that is scheduled to be produced?

16.   Referring to question 15, how might you discourage the consumption of beef?

2

Consumer choice

Consumer sovereignty

It is fitting to begin the study of microeconomics with the individual consumer, because without consumption there would be no justification for production. The ultimate aim of all production is to satisfy the desires of consumers.

In the U.S. economy and in all other reasonably free market economies, the consumer is king. It is in the interest of each producer to cater to the wishes of consumers because if he produces what is most highly demanded, he is rewarded by higher profits and a better living for himself and his family; producers are consumers too. Economists refer to an economic system where production is carried on to satisfy the wishes of consumers as one characterized by "consumer sovereignty."

Society has found it necessary to restrict the sovereignty of the individual consumer somewhat, however. If consumption of a good is thought to be harmful to either the consumer himself or to others around him, society may pass a law against it. The use of habit-forming drugs is one example. The individual, as well as harming his own health, may also harm others if he drives an automobile under the influence of these drugs or turns to crime to obtain money for their purchase. Laws regulating consumption of alcoholic beverages are another example of restricting consumer sovereignty to a certain degree. Society might prefer that consumers have cornflakes for breakfast rather than bourbon, but in general consumers are free to choose what they most desire, and producers respond to their wants.

In recent years, however, some people, including some economists, have begun to question whether the idea of consumer sovereignty accurately depicts our current economic system. They argue that today's giant corporations, with their multimillion-dollar annual advertising budgets, are able to persuade consumers to buy what the corporations want to produce, and this is not necessarily the same as what consumers would buy in the absence of such advertising. If the basic wants of consumers are in fact altered or determined by the advertising campaigns of corporations, it might be more accurate to refer to "producer sovereignty" rather than consumer sovereignty.

Economists who maintain that consumer sovereignty still reigns in our economic system argue that it would be unprofitable, hence irrational, for corporations to spend millions of dollars to change the basic wants of consumers. Rather, they maintain, it is much more profitable for producers to find out what the basic consumer wants are, to cater to these wants, and then to advertise in order to expand the sales of their particular brand of that product. It must be granted that the ultimate sovereignty of consumers has been illustrated in past years by their reception of such products as the Edsel and the midi-skirt. The producers of these products misjudged consumer wants and suffered the consequences. The current anti-cigarette campaign also illustrates the difficulty of changing consumer wants. In spite of warnings on the cigarette packages and the prohibition of cigarette commercials, people are smoking more than ever.

This is not to say, of course, that all consumers want the same thing or that these wants remain unchanged over time. The discussion to follow will stress the diversity of consumer wants.

Tastes

Since the consumer is such an important part of our economic system, it will be useful to study him in some detail. The first thing to be realized is that no two consumers are exactly the same in terms of their likes and dislikes. One may like to spend his leisure time watching baseball on television while drinking beer and eating pretzels; another may prefer to attend the opera or a symphony concert and dine on champagne and caviar.

Even though it is generally recognized that tastes differ between people, we have a tendency to forget this when we criticize others for liking things that do not appeal to us or for spending their income on a different mix of goods and services than we do. One person may place an expensive home high on his list of priorities, while another prefers to spend more on travel or a more expensive automobile. But who is to say which is the superior taste—the expensive home or the expensive auto? If a person were forced to sell his expensive auto and buy a higher priced home, his total satisfaction might well be decreased considerably. For this person, the superior taste is represented by the automobile. The main point to remember about taste is that there is no absolute standard—each person decides what he likes best and then tries to satisfy his wants.

Utility

Although tastes and satisfaction are familiar ideas, it is difficult to express them in concrete terms. Suppose you had just eaten an apple and a candy bar. Could you tell someone how much satisfaction you received from each of these items? Possibly you could tell which item you liked best, but could you tell how much better you liked one over the other? You might say "quite a bit" or "just a little" or some such vague descriptive term. But how much is "just a little" or "quite a bit"?

It is evident, then, that we need a more quantitative measure of satisfaction. For this reason economists have developed the concept of utility. The word "utility" means about the same thing as satisfaction. For illustrative purposes, however, economists have created the concept of a "util," which is a unit measure of utility. In the previous example, suppose you agreed to arbitrarily assign 100 utils as the satisfaction or utility you received from the apple. If you liked the candy bar less you would then assign it a number smaller than 100, or if you liked it more you would give it a number greater than 100. If, for example, you assigned a 50 to the candy bar, we could then say that you liked the apple about twice as much as the candy bar.

Conceivably, if you wanted to take the time, you could assign utils to all of the things you consume or might possibly consume, using one of the items as a reference point. The important thing in assigning utils to each item is not the absolute size of the util measure of each item but its size relative to the other items. Because tastes are an individual matter, utility is not something that can be compared from person to person. An individual might assign numbers to a partial list of the things consumed during one week in the following manner:

Items consumed per week	No. of utils
Two pounds of steak	100
One-fourth pound of coffee	30
Two quarts of milk	60
Shelter of house	300
Transportation by auto	200

This example brings out two points that should be emphasized. First, consumption is measured as an amount per unit of time. In this example, we used one week. It does not make any sense to say two pounds of meat were consumed if you do not specify per day, per week, per year, or per lifetime. The time dimension is necessary in order to know how much is being consumed relatively. The second point is that we consume services as well as goods. In the above example house shelter and transportation are services. We could list many more, such as services purchased from a doctor, lawyer, dentist, barber, or beauty shop operator. In economics a service is treated just as if it were a good. For our purposes they are essentially the same; both yield satisfaction or utility to the buyer.

The marginal unit

A concept that is used a great deal in economics is the marginal unit. Perhaps the easiest way to grasp this idea is to think of "marginal" as being the same thing as "extra" or "additional." If you have 10 units of something, say 10 pencils, and you acquire 1 more, then the 11th one is the marginal pencil. The marginal unit is the one that is added to or subtracted from the top of whatever you have.

The idea of the marginal unit is one of the most important and useful of those employed in economics. This is because most economic decisions involve relatively small (or marginal) changes. For example, you do not decide whether to spend all your income on steak or none on steak. Rather you decide if you should buy a little more steak and a little less hamburger, or vice versa. Thus the decisions you make generally involve the marginal or extra unit.

Marginal utility

Marginal utility is the extra or additional utility you obtain consuming one more unit of a good or service per unit of time. It can also be the utility you lose by reducing your consumption by one unit. In the utility example in the previous section, 100 utils were obtained by consuming two pounds of steak per week. Now suppose you were to increase your steak consumption to three pounds per week and receive 140 utils from this amount. The utility received from the third, or marginal, pound of steak in this case would be 40 utils. We could take the same example and subtract one pound of steak from weekly consumption. If, for example, we received 55 utils from one pound, then the marginal utility of the second pound is 45 utils. The following table summarizes what total and marginal utility might be for zero, one, two, and three pounds of steak consumed per week:

Pounds of steak consumed per week	Total utility (utils)	Marginal utility (utils)
0	0	—
1	55	55
2	100	45
3	140	40

You will note that the utility added by the marginal unit (the marginal utility) can be calculated by subtracting the total utility obtained *before* the marginal unit is added from the total utility obtained *including* that unit. Another method of calculating marginal utility is to divide the *change* in total utility by the *change* in number of units consumed:

$$\text{Marginal utility} = \frac{\text{Change in total utility}}{\text{Change in units consumed}}$$

You might also note that the total utility of any given unit is the sum of all the marginal utilities up through and including that unit.

Diminishing marginal utility

The preceding example also illustrates the idea of diminishing marginal utility. This means that as you increase your consumption of one good or service, say steak, holding constant the other things you consume, beyond some point the extra or marginal utility you obtain from the last unit will begin to decline. The intuitive appeal of diminishing marginal utility stems largely from our own personal experience. If we consume more and more of something, even steak, we soon tire of it and desire more variety.

The idea of diminishing marginal utility also is supported by lack of evidence of "monomania" among people, even among heroin addicts. If diminishing marginal utility did not prevail, there is no reason why some people would not spend all their income on one thing. In that case, you might as well choose an item that gives you the most satisfaction for the first dollar spent and then devote your entire income to it.

Marginal utility and price

The utility or satisfaction we receive from a good or service is, of course, a major reason why we buy the things we do. Generally if we do not like a product we do not buy it. But it is not quite this simple. For one thing, likes or dislikes are not all-or-nothing concepts. We all have varying degrees of likes and dislikes, as indicated by the diminishing marginal utility concept. And there is another problem we all have to face: the problem of price.

When faced with a choice between two or more items that we

could buy, we often deliberately choose the item we like the least. Looking over a menu in a restaurant, for example, you may prefer the $5 T-bone steak to the $2 chopped beef, but you choose the latter. Or, when buying a car, you may like the $5,000 sports car better than any car in the showroom, but you end up buying the $2,500 sedan. Is your behavior irrational or inconsistent with the concept of utility? Not at all. In your purchasing decisions you must consider price as well as utility.

When you choose an item that is less desirable but also less costly, you are implicitly deciding that the extra cost is not worth the extra satisfaction it brings. You decide, for example, that the additional satisfaction from the steak over the hamburger is not worth $3 to you. There are other things you can buy with the $3 that will give you more utility. In deciding what things to spend your money on, you really look at marginal utility per dollar rather than marginal utility alone. Using the chopped beef–T-bone steak example, suppose the marginal utility, price, and marginal utility per dollar (marginal utility divided by price) are as follows:

	Marginal utility (utils)	Price	Marginal utility per dollar
Chopped beef	30	$2	15
T-bone	50	$5	10

This example illustrates that choosing chopped beef over T-bone is indeed a rational choice. The marginal utility per dollar of the cheaper cut (15) exceeds the marginal utility per dollar obtained from the T-bone (10). Now, of course, this is only an example. We could have as easily created an example in which T-bone would have been the best choice, by raising its marginal utility or lowering its price. The point is that it is not always best to buy the cheaper item. But it can be.

Maximizing satisfaction: Marginal utility over price approach

So far we have considered choosing between only two items. We know, however, that life is a good deal more complex than this. During a normal shopping trip to the supermarket, for example, we have literally thousands of items to choose from. How do we decide what to buy?

The first thing we must realize is that our budget is limited; we just have so much to spend. Given this constraint, our objective is to maximize our satisfaction or utility. The basic rule is to equalize, as much as possible, the marginal utility per dollar for all the goods and services we buy. Recall that marginal utility per dollar is obtained by dividing marginal utility by price. For example, if the marginal utility (MU) of good A is 30 and its price is $5, then its marginal utility per dollar is 6. The general rule to follow for all goods and services A through Z is:

$$\frac{\text{MU of A}}{\text{Price of A}} = \frac{\text{MU of B}}{\text{Price of B}} = \cdots = \frac{\text{MU of Z}}{\text{Price of Z}}$$

Thus to maximize utility, we should try to make the marginal utility per dollar of good or service A equal to that of good or service B, and make these equal to all the other things we consume.

Why does an equalization of the marginal utility per dollar for all goods we consume result in maximum satisfaction for us? This is perhaps easiest to see if we look at a situation where they are not equal. Suppose the marginal utility per dollar you spend on housing per month is 50 but the marginal utility per dollar spent on the automobile per month is only 30. Consider what would happen if you spent one less dollar on your automobile and one more dollar on housing. Your total utility from the auto would decline by 30 utils, but your total utility from housing would increase by 50 utils. Thus you would give up 30 but gain 50, for a net gain of 20 utils, and you could gain 20 utils per month simply by rearranging your purchases. This same idea applies to everything you buy. If certain goods or services are not giving you as much marginal utility per dollar as other goods or services are providing, reduce your purchases of the low-return items and increase your spending on those that give you a higher marginal utility per dollar. By doing so, you can increase your total satisfaction without spending an extra cent.

Some complications

Although the preceding rule for maximizing utility cannot be questioned from the standpoint of pure logic, one might question its practical usefulness. Surely, you might argue, no one takes the time to think of the utils he obtains from consuming an item, much less writing them down and dividing by price. It might come as a surprise to learn that most people implicitly follow such a rule in their daily purchases. Most of us have felt at one time or another that an item was a "good buy" or that it "wasn't worth it." In doing so, we have indeed made an implicit calculation of the item's marginal utility per dollar. If we decide that an item is a "good buy," it is an indication that its marginal utility per dollar is large relative to other things we could buy. If an item "isn't worth it," its marginal utility per dollar for us is relatively low. We have also often purchased items that we could not be sure were good buys; in these cases the items provided a marginal utility per dollar that was just about equal to that of the other things we buy.

Even though we may try to maximize our satisfaction by striving to equalize the marginal utility per dollar for all our purchases, we are not likely to ever reach that theoretical maximum and stay there. One main reason is that our estimates of utility or satisfaction from each good and service are likely to be changing all the time, because of several factors. First, we may just grow tired of something that we have consumed for a long while; most of us like some variety in our lives. Thus the marginal utility of what we consume today depends somewhat on what we consumed yesterday. Second, new products or services may appear on the market that make old ones less desirable to us. This phenomenon is most evident in products that change in fashion or style. How many times have we admired a certain model of automobile only to have a new model come out that made our former dream car seem ugly and old-fashioned? Third, our tastes or estimates of utility may be changed by advertising. If a popular movie star or athlete uses a product, for example, it might become more appealing.

A second major reason to change the mix of goods we consume is because prices are always changing. If the price of one item rises relative to other alternatives, its marginal utility per dollar will decrease relative to other things. We would then want to buy less of it.

As a final complicating factor, the marginal utility of each good or service we consume may well depend on the other things consumed along with it. Economists call this interdependence of utilities. Interdependence between goods can take the form of either a complementary or a substitute relationship. Two goods are complements to each other if consuming one enhances the marginal utility of the other. Bacon and eggs are a good example. Most people find eggs more appealing at breakfast when accompanied by a strip or two of bacon. Or, take the woman who has purchased a new dress; a new handbag, gloves, and shoes, generally will make the dress more desirable, and the dress also complements the accessories. On the other hand, a substitute relationship between goods exists if consuming one good reduces the marginal utility of another. For instance, the marginal utility you obtain from consuming a glass of orange juice at breakfast would decline if you also had a glass of grapefruit juice at the same meal.

Because of the many complications which have the effect of changing the marginal utility of each good or service we buy, or consider buying, the optimum bundle of goods and services that will maximize utility is constantly changing. Therefore it is necessary to continually reevaluate purchase decisions if we hope to get the most for our money.

Consumption versus saving

Although we must decide what mix of goods and services will give the most utility for a given expenditure, this does not imply that all income is spent. Most people attempt to save at least a small portion of their current income, for various reasons. We may save "for a rainy day" in order to have something to fall back on in case we cannot work, or for retirement to supplement a pension. Most people save in order to make a large purchase, such as a car or a downpayment on a house. Others may wish to leave an estate for their heirs or some institution.

The decisions to save or not to save and what to save for are very much like the expenditure decisions we have just considered. The marginal utility of saving is the satisfaction we can expect to obtain when we eventually spend that extra dollar, or the satisfaction we now obtain from knowing that someone else will be able to spend it.

The marginal utility obtained from an extra dollar saved varies among individuals. Some people like to spend what they earn relatively quickly and do not place a high value on saving. Economists would say that these people have a high rate of time preference. They prefer to consume now rather than later. The stereotyped soldier or sailor who epitomizes the "eat, drink, and be merry" attitude is a good example of someone with a high rate of time preference. His marginal utility of future consumption is low relative to current consumption.

Other people, being perhaps more patient, are willing to devote a relatively large share of their current income to saving, with the idea of adding to their consumption in the future. These people could be said to have a low rate of time preference. The miser represents the extreme case of a person with a low rate of time preference, although it is doubtful that most misers ever envison spending the entire amount of their savings at some future date. Of course, even the miser has some degree of time preference. No one can postpone all consumption for the future; if he tried, there would be no future.

Most of us fall somewhere between the spendthrift and the miser with regard to time preference. Those who have a low rate of time preference tend to obtain relatively more utility from future consumption than their high-time-preference counterparts. Hence they will be likely to have a larger fraction of their income, other things equal.

In estimating the marginal utility of future consumption, it is also necessary to take into account the interest or dividends received on savings. If the rate of interest received on savings is, say, 5 percent, $1.00 saved today will be worth $1.05 one year from now. Assuming no increase in prices,[1] the extra dollar saved will buy somewhat more in the future than it will buy today. Hence the interest return on savings compensates us for waiting to consume in the future. The higher the interest or dividend returns on our savings, the more each dollar saved at the present will buy in the future. In other words, a higher interest rate increases the price of present consumption compared to future consumption.

The price of present consumption

The basic idea that the combination of goods we presently consume depends on both marginal utility and price also applies to

---

[1] A stable price level is assumed for purposes of illustration. The effect of inflation on the interest rate is discussed in Chapter 10. The effect of inflation on consumption is discussed in Chapter 2 of the companion macro book.

decisions to consume now or in the future. The price or opportunity cost of present consumption is what must be given up in the future. The higher the rate of interest, the more a dollar saved will buy in the future, and consequently the higher the cost or price of present consumption.

We can therefore consider the price of one dollar in present consumption as the dollar plus the interest return. If we specify the marginal utility that an extra dollar of present consumption will provide, we can divide this by price to obtain marginal utility per dollar. As an example, consider two individuals, one a spendthrift, the other a miser. In situation 1 both receive a 5 percent rate of interest on their savings; in situation 2 the rate is 10 percent. The two situations are shown in Table 2–1.

TABLE 2–1
Price of present consumption and marginal utility

	Marginal utility of an extra dollar consumed at present	*Interest rate*	*Price of present consumption*	*Marginal utility per dollar*
Situation 1				
Spendthrift 20		0.05%	$1.05	19.05
Miser 10		0.05	1.05	9.52
Situation 2				
Spendthrift 20		0.10	1.10	18.18
Miser 10		0.10	1.10	9.09

Because the spendthrift in this example enjoys spending his money in the present more than does the miser, whatever the rate of interest, the marginal utility per dollar of present consumption is higher for him than for the miser. But at higher rates of interest the price of present consumption rises, which results in a reduction in marginal utility per dollar of present consumption for both individuals.

The decision to save or to consume at the present, therefore, is very similar to the decision on what mix of goods to buy, also depending on taste and price. Theoretically a low rate of time preference and a high price (high interest) should be associated with a high rate of saving, and vice versa. Empirically, however, economists have found it very difficult to measure the relative importance of each of these factors in people's decisions to save or to spend. For

one thing an independent, quantitative measure of time preference is lacking. Although there seems to be general agreement that
the rate of time preference does affect the proportion of income
saved, there is much less agreement on the importance of the rate of
interest. The measurement of the impact of the interest rate on saving is complicated by a number of other factors that also are expected to influence saving. These include the level of income,
changes in the general price level (mainly inflation), and expectations of future economic conditions. The probable impact of these
factors on saving is discussed more thoroughly in the macro book
that supplements this text.

Short-run versus long-run saving

The rate at which an individual saves can fluctuate a considerable amount over time. Suppose you want to purchase a new car
next year. During the present year you will probably attempt to
save enough at least for the down payment and possibly for the
entire car. During the time you save for the car the proportion of
your income saved may be quite large—say 40 percent. But as soon
as you buy the car, all this is spent. Thus the length of time for saving generally influences the rate of saving.

The important point is that saving during a short period such as
a month or even a year may not at all reflect long-run saving habits.
The seafaring man may save almost 100 percent of his wage during
a six-month voyage but spend every cent when he arrives in port. It
would be very misleading to measure the sailor's saving during the
voyage and assume this is what he will save in the long run.

A similar situation exists with people whose incomes fluctuate
a great deal; farmers are a good example. It is sometimes argued
that farmers are thrifty folk who save much of their income. But the
real reason might well be that farm incomes tend to fluctuate more
than other people's, and when farm income is high much of it is
saved to provide for times when it is very low or even zero.

With college students it is not unusual to find a negative rate of
saving; they consume more than their income. The difference is
made up either by consuming out of past saving, borrowing, or gifts
from relatives, friends, or benevolent institutions. There is nothing

wrong with this behavior; indeed it is to be expected. In the long run (a decade or more) the percentage of income saved by these same people may well be substantial.

Indifference curves

We have shown that the consumer maximizes utility, or gets the most for his money, by equalizing as much as possible the marginal utility per dollar of all goods and services he consumes, as well as his saving. A slightly different approach utilizes the concept of the indifference curve, which is another way of representing consumer choice. (In the next chapter we will employ indifference curves to develop the concept of product demand.)

Assume that you are given a collection of two different goods, say ten tickets to see your favorite football team and ten tickets to the theater of your choice. We can represent this combination by point *A* in Figure 2–1. Now ask yourself this question: If two football tickets were taken away from me, how many additional theater

FIGURE 2–1
An indifference curve

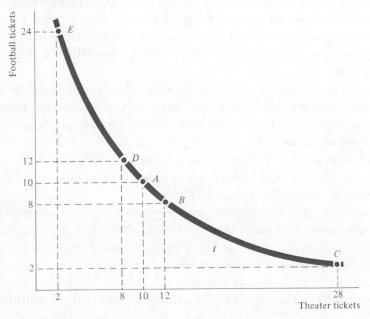

FIGURE 2–2
An indifference map

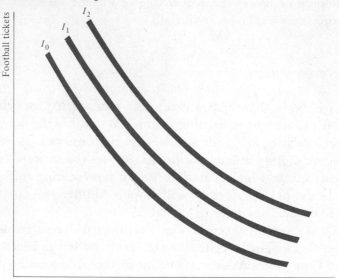

tickets would I have to be given in order to remain equally satisfied? Assume there is no chance to sell the tickets, so you cannot exchange the extra theater tickets for football tickets. Also do not be concerned, at least for the moment, about the price of the tickets. Assume they are being given to you or taken away without charge or compensation.

Your answer to this question will depend, of course, on how well you like football and the theater. Suppose you decide that two additional theater tickets would compensate you for the loss of the two football tickets. In other words, you are indifferent between the combination of 10 football and 10 theater tickets and the combination of 8 football and 12 theater tickets. Let this second combination be point *B* in Figure 2–1.

We might go through the same procedure again, this time taking away a total of eight football tickets. Now you only have two football tickets left. How many theater tickets would you have to be given to remain equally satisfied as with the original combination of ten of each kind of tickets?

According to the idea of diminishing marginal utility, additional nights at the theater will provide less and less satisfaction. More-over, the closer you come to zero football tickets, the loss of football tickets will mean increasingly less satisfaction. It seems reasonable to believe, therefore, that you will require more than eight additional theater tickets to compensate for the loss of eight football tickets. Suppose you want 18 more theater tickets. We could say that you are indifferent to the following combinations:

Combination	Theater	Football
A	10	10
B	12	8
C	28	2

Thus we are tracing out alternative combinations that would make you equally well off. We could also trace out points on the upper part of the curve by taking away theater tickets in exchange for football tickets. For example, you might choose 8 theater and 12 football, or 2 theater and 24 football tickets as additional combinations, labeling these points D and E.

Assuming that the same general relationship holds between the points as on them, we can connect points A through E. We have now constructed what economists call an "indifference curve." From the standpoint of total satisfaction you are indifferent at all points along this curve.

Of course, any number of curves can be drawn, as shown in Figure 2–2. We started out with ten tickets of each but we might have started with six. If you prefer more tickets to less, then the smaller combination would be on a lower indifference curve, such as I_0 in Figure 2–2. Similarly, a larger combination, such as 14 of each, would be on a higher curve, say I_2. Economists call many such curves on a single diagram an "indifference map." In a sense the in-difference map is a picture of your preferences, much like a con-tour map is a picture of the landscape. Curves further away from the origin represent higher levels of satisfaction.

Note something about the shape of these curves. In this particu-lar example, we have drawn them with a slight curvature, convex to the origin. This indicates that you consider football and theater tickets substitutes for one another, although imperfect substitutes. To see why, look again at the curve in Figure 2–1. Moving down the football axis and out along the theater axis, note that additional theater tickets will compensate you for increasingly fewer football tickets. The further you proceed, the greater the number of theater tickets it takes to make you willing to give up another football ticket.

If the two items were perfect substitutes for each other, then the rate at which you give up one in exchange for the other would be constant at all possible combinations. For example, white and brown eggs (except perhaps in Boston) or varying amounts of nickels and dimes would be perfect substitutes. The indifference curve for perfect substitutes is illustrated in Figure 2–3. Economists

FIGURE 2–3
Indifference curves for perfect substitutes

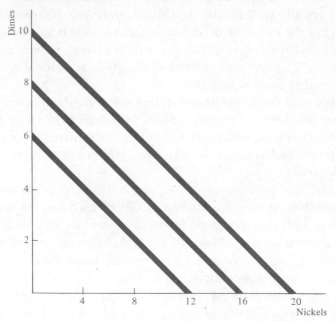

are generally not very interested in goods that are perfect substitutes because, for all practical matters, they are the same good. That is, nickels and dimes are coins, or white and brown eggs are just eggs.

At the other extreme we have what we call perfect complements. These are goods that can only be used in fixed proportions with one another. The classic example is right and left shoes. Presumably you would not be any better off with one right and two left shoes than with just one of each. Thus the indifference curves for such products are represented by 90-degree angles, as in Figure 2–4.

Most of the items consumed everyday are neither perfect substitutes nor perfect complements but the in-between case—imperfect substitutes. Note in Figures 2–3 and 2–4 that these indifference curves (lines) are parallel. In the case of imperfect substitutes, how-

FIGURE 2–4
Indifference curves for perfect complements

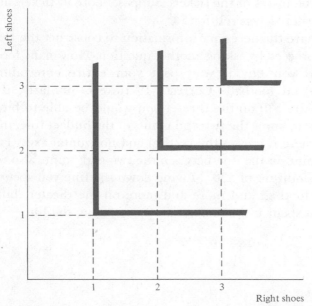

ever, the curves do not have to run parallel to each other. The only restriction is that they do not cross, for if they did they could not be indifference curves. Think about it.

The budget line

In a sense the indifference curve is somewhat like the production possibilities curve. Both show alternative combinations of goods or services, but neither indicates which alternative will be preferred. After we develop the concept of the budget line it will be possible to determine which of the many combinations shown on an indifference map will actually be chosen. The two items that enable such a choice are the individuals income or budget and the prices of the goods represented.

To keep it simple, yet fairly realistic, let us continue to use the football and theater ticket example. We will assume you decide to spend $30 on a month's entertainment (football and the theater). How should you spend this $30 to maximize your satisfaction, that is, to get the most for your money? To answer this question we must know the prices of the tickets. Suppose football tickets are $2 each and theater tickets sell for $3.

We now have the necessary information to construct the budget line. Let us proceed by asking another question. How many football tickets could you buy if you spent your entire entertainment budget ($30) on football? Correct—15 tickets. Similarly, if you spent the entire $30 on the theater you would be able to buy ten tickets. Now we know the two end points of the budget line, that is, the points where it crosses the vertical and horizontal axes (Figure 2–5). Any point on the line between the two end points also represents an expenditure of $30. Moving down the line you spend less and less on football and more and more on the theater, but the total amount spent is the same at all points along the line.

FIGURE 2–5
A budget line

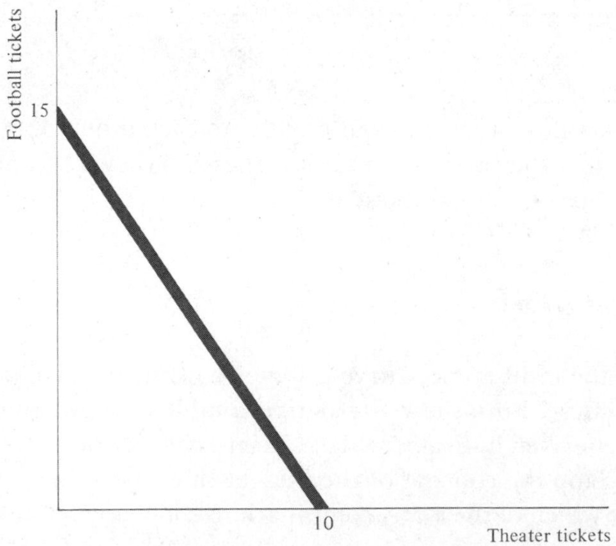

FIGURE 2–6
Budget line on indifference map

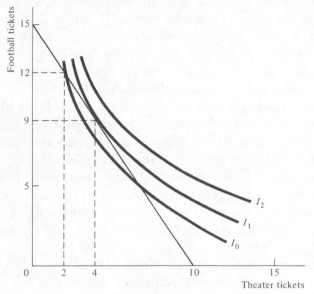

To construct a continuous straight budget line, however, it would have to be possible to buy a fraction of a ticket. At first this may not seem realistic, but keep in mind that we are talking about consumption per unit of time. For example, 3⅓ tickets per month would be equal to 40 tickets per year. Thus most items become divisible when you bring in the time dimension.

Maximizing satisfaction: Indifference curve–budget line approach

We are now ready to combine indifference curves with the budget line to find out what combination of tickets would give you the most satisfaction for your $30. In Figure 2–6 we have imposed an indifference map on the budget line from Figure 2–5. As a first step let us choose any combination of tickets that totals $30, for example 12 football and 2 theater tickets. Will this combination give you the most satisfaction for your money? This question can be answered by looking at Figure 2–6. You will note that the highest indifference curve that can be reached with the 12–2 football-theater combination is I_0. But you will note also that a higher indifference curve can be reached by moving down the budget line, that is, by choosing a different combination of tickets that will be worth $30 (say nine football and four theater tickets). As you move down the budget line you reduce your purchase of football tickets and increase the number of theater tickets you buy.

Keep in mind that your overall objective is to reach the highest possible indifference curve within the constraint of the $30 you have to spend. The highest possible indifference curve you can reach is the one just tangent to the budget line, I_1 in Figure 2–6. Indifference curve I_2 could not be reached unless you wanted to spend more than $30. Thus the general rule to bear in mind is that your satisfaction will be maximized when you select that mix of goods on the budget line that enables you to reach the highest possible indifference curve.

In the example above, the combination that maximizes your satisfaction is nine football and four theater tickets. The cost of this combination, $30, is the same as any other combination on the budget line, such as 12 football and 2 theater, or 3 football and 8 theater, but your level of satisfaction is the greatest only at the 9 football–4 theater ticket combination.

Thus we see that even though we may be able to purchase any one of a number of different combinations of goods and services for a given expenditure, there is only one combination that will maximize our satisfaction. That is the combination which corresponds to the point of tangency between the budget line and the indifference curve.

Main points of Chapter 2

1. In a free market economy, production is carried on solely to satisfy the wants of consumers. This is known as a system of consumer sovereignty.
2. Since each person tends to have unique tastes, it is perhaps more accurate to talk about "different" tastes than "good" or

"bad" taste, at least in regard to a person's choice of goods and services.

3. Utility is a measure of satisfaction. Utils enable us to rank goods or services according to the satisfaction they provide.

4. The marginal unit is the last unit added to or subtracted from the top of whatever we are measuring.

5. Marginal utility is the utility or satisfaction provided by the marginal unit consumed.

6. Diminishing marginal utility means that as you consume more and more of a good or service, holding constant the consumption of other goods and services, the amount of satisfaction obtained from each additional unit consumed will, after a point, begin to decline.

7. When considering whether or not to buy an item, we should consider both its marginal utility and its price.

8. In order to maximize satisfaction for the money we spend, we should equalize as much as possible the marginal utility per dollar of all the things we consume. Marginal utility per dollar is obtained by dividing the utility of the marginal unit by its price.

9. The combination of goods and services that will maximize our utility for a given expenditure is constantly changing, for a variety of reasons. These include: *(a)* changes in how much we like the things we presently consume because of what we consumed in the past, what others are consuming, advertising, and new products appearing on the market, and *(b)* changes in prices of goods or services.

10. The decision to consume now or save for future consumption depends on both the utility of present consumption and the price of present consumption.

11. The price of present consumption increases with an increase in the interest rate because with higher rates of interest each dollar saved at the present will buy more in the future—if prices remain unchanged.

12. The true picture of a person's saving habits is best reflected in his long-run behavior, because much short-run saving may just be an accumulation of money to spend in a large lump sum.

13. An indifference curve traces out alternative combinations of two goods, all of which would make you equally satisfied.
14. An indifference map is a collection of indifference curves. Curves further away from the origin represent higher levels of satisfaction.
15. The shape of indifference curves depends upon the degree of substitutability between the products considered. Indifference curves for perfect substitutes are straight, downward-sloping lines; those for perfect complements (no substitution possible) are right angles. Most combinations of goods fall somewhere between these two extremes.
16. A budget line traces out alternative combinations of two goods that cost a given amount.
17. To maximize satisfaction for a given expenditure, it is necessary to move along the budget line until you reach the highest possible indifference curve. This will be the curve that is tangent to the budget line.

Questions for thought and discussion

1. It has been argued that consumer sovereignty is a thing of the past in the United States because the advertising media in large part determine what consumers want to buy. Do you agree? Explain.
2. Do you believe that society should have laws prohibiting the consumption of certain goods and services, such as laws against mind-distorting drugs? Why or why not?
3. Explain as you would to a friend or relative who has had no economics what a "marginal unit" is. Why is the marginal unit so important in economics?
4. Explain why a person is not maximizing his satisfaction from a given expenditure if he is not equalizing the marginal utility per dollar across his entire range of purchases.
5. Most women prefer mink coats to cloth coats, yet most women buy cloth coats. This just goes to show that most women are irrational. Comment.
6. Suppose you are considering the purchase of a new car. One

of the things you are undecided about is whether or not you should select the factory air-conditioning option. How might you use the concept of marginal utility to help you make this decision?

7. Suppose you are in the market for a new bicycle. A salesman shows you a smart 10-speed model for $95. You say the bike is very nice, but you cannot afford such an expensive model. What do you really mean when you say you cannot "afford" this bicycle? Surely you should be able to put your hands on $95 somewhere, either from your savings or a small loan.

8. Let's say that the combination of food that maximizes your satisfaction for lunch consists of one cheeseburger, one slice of apple pie, and one cup of coffee. According to the marginal-utility-over-price approach to making consumer decisions, you should continue to consume this mix of foods for lunch the rest of your life. True or false? Explain.

9. "The more the merrier" contradicts the concept of diminishing marginal utility. True, false, or uncertain? Explain.

10. Some people have advocated that medical care be made free to all Americans. From what you know about the rule for maximizing satisfaction, what does this imply about the amount of medical services people would want to consume in relation to other goods and services?

11. As a group, do you think college students have a higher or lower rate of time preference in comparison to young people their age who do not go to college? Explain.

12. How does the shape of an indifference curve for two goods reflect the substitution possibilities between these two goods?

13. *a)* Name two goods or services you would consider as perfect substitutes for each other. Name two you consider as imperfect substitutes. Name two you consider as perfect complements.

    b) Draw an indifference curve for each of these three sets of goods or services.

14. Consider a sailor on shore leave who has $300 to spend. He decides that he will spend $200 on wine and women and the remainder foolishly.

    a) Draw the sailor's budget line for wine and women. (For prices you might use the price of a bottle of wine and the cost of an average date.)

    b) Add some indifference curves to the budget line diagram to indicate the mix of goods (or services) that will maximize his satisfaction. Assume in this case that the sailor considers wine and women as very imperfect substitutes, but he is a bit more of a "ladies' man" than a "wino."

c) Next assume that the sailor considers wine and women as good substitutes for each other and, if given a choice, he prefers alcohol to romance. Now draw his indifference curves.

3

Product demand

The concept of demand

Because "demand" is a word that most everyone has used to convey one meaning or another, there tend to be many interpretations of it. It will be useful at this stage, therefore, to define rather rigorously the concept of demand as used by economists. You will probably find that the economist's concept of demand differs at least somewhat from the way it is used in everyday conversation and communication.

The first and perhaps most important thing to recognize about demand as used by economists is that it is not a set or fixed quantity but a relationship between price and quantity. In order to know what quantity a person or group of persons will demand, we must first know what price they will have to pay. For example, if you were asked what your demand is for football tickets, you would probably be reluctant to answer unless you knew what price you had to pay. As we saw in the preceding chapter, the number of tickets you would buy likely would be quite different if you had to pay $10 per ticket than if the price were $1. In this chapter we will organize our thinking about the relationship between the price of an item and the quantity people buy. We will begin by reviewing the concept of the demand curve as presented in Chapter 1, but using the football ticket example established above.

Figure 3–1 provides an example in which only two football

FIGURE 3–1
The concept of demand (football ticket example)

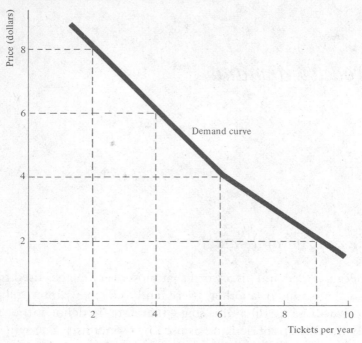

tickets are demanded per season if the price is $8 per ticket. At a $4 price, six tickets are demanded; and at the bargain price of $2, nine tickets are demanded per season. By connecting the series of points on the graph, we obtain a curve which is known as a demand curve. Essentially a demand curve describes a relationship between price and quantity. If we establish a price, the demand curve will tell us what quantity will be demanded. Or if we specify a quantity, the curve will tell us what price will be paid.

It is important to distinguish between demand and quantity demanded. Demand, as we have noted, refers to the relationship between price and quantity. However, quantity demanded refers to a particular quantity or point on the demand curve. Thus when you wish to stipulate a particular quantity you will avoid confusion by calling it "quantity demanded" rather than "demand."

A second important characteristic to note about the concept of demand is that it reflects *wants,* not *needs.* If you tell me that you need six football tickets if the price is $4 per ticket, it would be easy to take issue with your statement. That is, it could be argued that you do not need *any* football tickets because watching football is not necessary to sustain life. Or you might say you need a new car or a vacation trip to a distant city. Again, neither is necessary to sustain life. On the other hand, if you said you wanted six football tickets or a vacation trip, this could not be disputed. Only you can determine what you want, and these wants are at least partly satisfied by the things you buy.

A third item to note about demand is that quantity is measured as an amount per unit of time. In Figure 3–1, the quantity of football tickets is measured in number of tickets per year. However, there is no set time period that is always used. We can measure quantity as amount per week, per month, per year, and so forth. The time dimension that is chosen is often the one that is most useful in analyzing the problem at hand. It must be recognized that when you change the time period you also change the scale on the quantity axis.

A fourth point to note about a demand curve is that it reflects what people actually would do if faced by certain prices rather than what they would like to do. Your favorite make of automobile may sell for $6,000, and you might like a new one every year, but that does not mean you would actually purchase one of these cars every year or even one in a lifetime. Demand only is useful if it reflects the actions of people, not what they would *like* to do.

It should be kept in mind, as well, that the demand curve shown in Figure 3–1 is only an example. In this diagram the demand curve is drawn with a slight curvature. This is not meant to imply that demand curves for all products look this way. Some may be straight, downward-sloping lines; others may have more curvature. For the present our main concern will be with the downward-sloping characteristic rather than with the extent of curvature of the line.

Marginal utility and demand

Although the downward-sloping nature of a demand curve has a certain intuitive appeal, we can establish this characteristic in a more rigorous fashion using what we learned about marginal utility and price in the previous chapter. Recall that a consumer maximizes satisfaction when the marginal utility (MU) per dollar is equal for all the goods and services he buys. The following expression summarizes this idea:

$$\frac{\text{MU of good A}}{\text{Price of good A}} = \frac{\text{MU of good B}}{\text{Price of good B}} = \cdots = \frac{\text{MU of good Z}}{\text{Price of good Z}}$$

Recall also that marginal utility per dollar depends on both marginal utility and price. For a given marginal utility, the higher the price, the lower is the marginal utility per dollar. As a very simple example, suppose a consumer is initially maximizing utility, as is illustrated in the expression above. Now consider that just one of these goods, say good A, changes in price as shown below:

	Initial situation	Price of A rises	Price of A falls
Marginal utility of A	20	20	20
Marginal utility per dollar	5	4	10
Price of A	$4	$5	$2

In the initial situation, all goods consumed by this person yield a marginal utility per dollar of five utils. When the price of good A rises, this good only yields four utils per dollar. In this case it will pay the consumer to reduce his purchases of good A. One dollar less spent on A will reduce his satisfaction by four utils, but spending this dollar on something else that has not risen in price will yield close to five utils. Thus the consumer can gain one util of net satisfaction by spending one less dollar on good A and one more dollar on one or more other goods.

As he continues to reduce the consumption of A, the marginal utility of A will increase (increasing the marginal utility per dollar of A) and as other goods are consumed, the marginal utilities of these goods will decrease. Eventually the consumer will reach a new equilibrium where marginal utility per dollar is again equal for all goods. The important thing to note here is that as the price of a good rises, marginal utility per dollar declines, and this creates an incentive for the consumer to reduce his purchases of the good. The end result, then, is consistent with the idea of a downward-sloping demand curve, such as that constructed in the preceding section, in which a higher price leads to a decreased rate of purchase.

Exactly the same reasoning applies for a decrease in the price of

A. Here marginal utility per dollar increases, which in turn provides an incentive for the consumer to increase his purchase of A at the expense of other goods. Again this is consistent with the concept of demand.

Indifference curves and demand

Having shown that the concept of a downward-sloping demand curve is consistent with the concept of marginal utility, we will go one step further to derive a demand curve from an indifference map.

Using the football-theater ticket example of the preceding chapter, consider what happens when the price of theater tickets is lowered, say from the original $3.00 price to $2.00, and then to $1.50 apiece. With the given $30 budget, the budget lines rotate in a counterclockwise fashion, as illustrated in Figure 3–2. The points of intersection on the horizontal axis now increase to 15 and 20 units, respectively, for the $2.00 and $1.50 prices. The three indif-

FIGURE 3–2
Indifference map and budget lines illustrating changes in the price of theater tickets

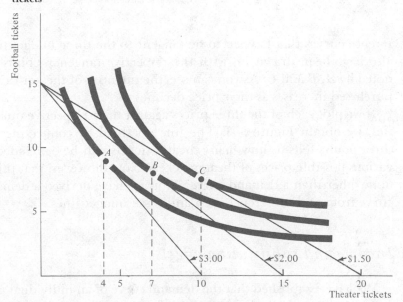

FIGURE 3–3
Demand curve for theater tickets, as derived from Figure 3–2

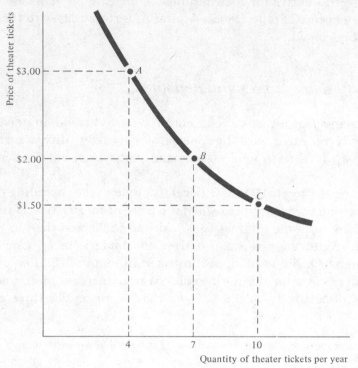

ference curves that happen to be tangent to the three budget lines also have been drawn in, with the respective tangency points denoted by *A, B* and *C*. As you can see, the quantity of theater tickets purchased increases as their price declines.

If we plot each of the three prices against their respective quantities, we obtain Figure 3–3. The line obtained by connecting the three points tells us how many theater tickets will be demanded at various possible prices of theater tickets. Note, however, that this is none other than a demand curve. Thus we have derived a demand curve from an indifference map and some budget lines.

Income and substitution effects

We have established that the demand curve of an individual consumer for a good is a downward-sloping line. To analyze this relationship more carefully, we might begin by asking why people buy more of a good when its price falls. We are quite sure they do, but why?

Economists have identified two major factors or effects that can help explain why people behave this way: (1) the income effect and (2) the substitution effect. The income effect accounts for the fact that a change in the price of a good you buy changes the purchasing power of your income. It has the same effect as if you had experienced a change in income. For example, as the price of theater tickets declines, your $30 entertainment budget could buy a larger number of tickets. It is as if your income had been increased. The opposite occurs, of course, if the ticket price would have risen; then the $30 would have bought fewer tickets, so it would be just like a decrease in your budget or income.

The substitution effect occurs because when the price of one good changes *relative* to another there is the incentive to buy more of the lower priced good and less of the higher priced one. In other words, you try to substitute the good that is relatively inexpensive for the one that is relatively more expensive. But to really understand what the substitution effect is, we first must understand what is meant by relative prices. In the example used to construct the demand curve, the price of theater tickets fell relative to the price of football tickets. This is one example of a change in relative prices, but there are others. If both prices had declined but theater ticket prices had declined the most, then theater prices would still have declined relative to football prices. Or if both prices had increased but football ticket prices had increased the most, there would again be a relative decline in theater prices. The four situations below illustrate a relative decline in theater ticket prices or a relative increase in football ticket prices.

1. Football ticket price the same, theater ticket price declines.
2. Football ticket price declines, theater ticket price declines more.
3. Football ticket price increases, theater ticket price increases less.
4. Football ticket price increases, theater ticket price the same.

Thus the income effect occurs because a price change has the effect of changing the purchasing power of income. The substitution effect occurs because a price change has the effect of changing relative prices, which in turn provides an incentive to buy more of the relatively lower priced good. A somewhat more exact definition of these two effects can be obtained using indifference curves and budget lines.

Figure 3–4 duplicates the information given on Figure 3–2, ex-

FIGURE 3–4
Illustration of the income and substitution effects

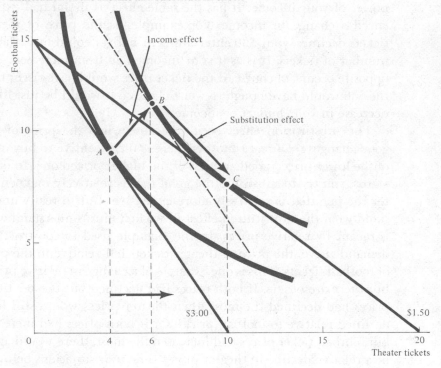

cept the $2.00 theater ticket price line has been deleted. At the $3.00 price, 4 theater tickets are demanded, and at the $1.50 price, 10 tickets are demanded. The question we can now ask is: How many of these six additional tickets demanded because of the price reduction are attributable to the income effect and how many to the substitution effect?

We can measure the income effect by drawing in a hypothetical budget line parallel to the original budget line but tangent to the new indifference curve (the diagonal broken line in Figure 3–4). This budget line illustrates the income effect because the price reduction provides the same effect as an increase in income or budget. Thus the hypothetical budget line will measure the increase in quantity that is due to the income effect. In Figure 3–4, the income effect accounts for two additional tickets, that is, the horizontal distance between A and B. The remaining four additional units of quantity demanded, shown by the horizontal distance between B and C, is accounted for by the substitution effect. The substitution effect is always measured by moving along a given indifference curve, whereas the income effect is measured by moving from one indifference curve to another.[1]

The income and substitution effects provide the formal economic rationale for the downward-sloping characteristic of the demand curve of a consumer. Notice that the quantities measured along a demand curve are those that maximize the utility of a consumer for various prices of the good and the available budget.

Market demand

While we have been concerned with the demand curve of an individual consumer, the concept of demand is most useful when applied to a market situation—an entire group of consumers. We began our discussion of demand at the level of the individual consumer, however, in order to derive the concept of a demand curve from the closely related concept of consumer indifference curves.

It is relatively simple to develop the idea of a market demand from the demand of individual consumers. First, suppose that every consumer has a demand for every product. For some consumers, of course, the demand will be large at a given price; for others, the demand might be zero at the same price. No two consumers need have the same demand for a given product. All we need to do to visualize the idea of market demand is to add up, at each possible price, the quantity demanded by all consumers in the market. In other words, we obtain a horizontal summation of the demand curves of individual consumers. Figure 3–5 provides an example of how this can be done.

---

[1] It is, of course, possible and equally correct to show the substitution effect along the original indifference curve by drawing the hypothetical budget line parallel to the new budget line and tangent to the original indifference curve.

FIGURE 3–5
Constructing market demand from individual demand (theater ticket example)

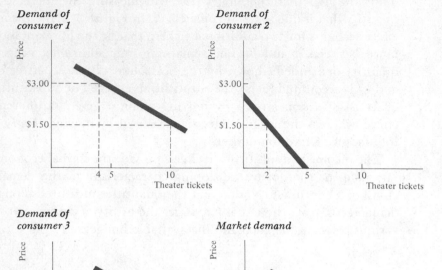

You might recognize the demand of consumer 1 in the first diagram as the same demand as constructed in Figures 3–3 and 3–4. At $3.00 per ticket he demands 4 tickets per season, and at $1.50 per ticket he will buy 10 tickets. Consumer 2 is less of a theater fan. At $3.00 per ticket he would not attend the theater at all, and at the $1.50 price he will buy two tickets. Consumer 3 is a more ardent theatergoer than both 1 and 2. He demands 5 and 11 tickets at the $3.00 and $1.50 prices, respectively.

To keep the example manageable, suppose the market consists of these three demanders. At the $3.00 price, the market demand is found by the quantities demanded by consumers 1, 2, and 3: four, zero, and five, respectively, making a total of nine. At the $1.50 price the quantity demanded by consumers 1, 2, and 3 are 10, 2, and 11, respectively, making a total of 23 tickets. Both these totals are shown on the market demand diagram.

Now, of course, it is not realistic to believe that just three consumers will make up a market. For more realism you might visualize a market where there are 1,000 people like consumer 1, 1,000 like consumer 2, and 1,000 like consumer 3. In this case, at the $3 price, 9,000 tickets would be demanded. (How many would be demanded at the $1.50 price?)

The example we have presented represents a theoretical construction of a market demand curve. Such a theoretical market demand curve is a useful tool in explaining economic phenomena and analyzing economic problems. Economists have also estimated the actual market demand curve for many products on the market today. The estimation is done by statistical techniques studied in intermediate-level statistics courses.

We have been rather vague about the meaning of a market except to say that it is made up of many consumers. The main reason for this vagueness is that markets themselves are rather vague. The number of consumers and the geographic area encompassed by a market will vary from product to product. For new automobiles it seems to be nationwide, or even worldwide. For perishable foods, such as fresh milk, the market is much smaller, many times encompassing only a city. The market for the entertainment services provided by a football team will vary from several states for a professional team to only a part of a city for a high school team. It is impossible to define the boundaries of what is called a market, because they will vary according to the product under consideration, as well as the transportation and communication facilities available.

Price elasticity of demand

Thus far we have characterized the shape of the demand curve (individual or market) as downward sloping. It is important that we become more specific about this, because the shape of the demand curve tells us a great deal about how consumers react to a price change. A demand curve that is very steep, for example, implies that consumers will not change their purchases very much in response to a price change, as shown in Figure 3–6. On the other

FIGURE 3–6
Demand for theater tickets, consumers
unresponsive to price

FIGURE 3–7
Demand for theater tickets, consumers
more responsive to price

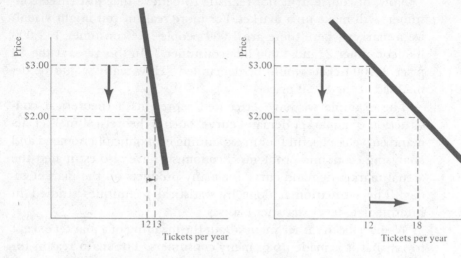

hand a very flat curve implies that a price change will cause consumers to change their purchasing habits greatly (Figure 3–7).

In Figure 3–6, a reduction in price from $3 to $2 increases quantity demanded by just one unit (from 12 to 13). But in Figure 3–7,
the same $1 reduction in price brings forth a six-unit increase in
quantity demanded. A consumer with a demand for theater tickets
(Figure 3–7) would be more responsive to a change in price of theater tickets than one whose demand is characterized by Figure 3–6.

Judging the responsiveness of consumers to a price change by
the mere slope of the demand curve involves one major problem,
however: The slope of any curve can be changed simply by changing the units of measure on either the horizontal or vertical axis.
For example, we could make the curve in Figure 3–7 look very steep
simply by changing the unit of measure from tickets per year to
tickets per month. The change in the shape of the curve brought on
by changing the quantity measure in this way is illustrated in Figures 3–8 and 3–9.

There are, of course, other ways to change the shape of the curve.
We could have changed the physical dimension of the quantity
measure, assigning each ticket a larger or smaller distance on the
quantity axis. The same manipulations could be performed on the
price axis, which would also change the shape of the curve. It is al-

FIGURE 3–8
Demand for theater tickets (tickets per year)

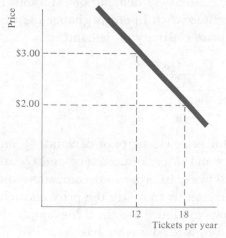

FIGURE 3–9
Demand for theater tickets (tickets per month)

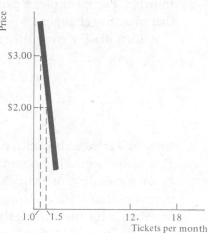

ways well to keep in mind the possibilities for changing the shape of a curve whenever diagrams are used to illustrate some concept.

One way to avoid the problems encountered by choosing different units of measure is to employ percentage changes. The percentage change in a number will not be altered by choosing different units of measure. This is illustrated below where the percentage change in quantity of tickets demanded because of the $1 change in price is calculated, first on a per-year basis and then on a per-month basis. Both result in the same percentage change, even though the absolute changes differ.

$$\text{Percentage change in quantity of tickets per year} = \frac{12 - 18}{12} = \frac{-6}{12} = -50\%$$

$$\text{Percentage change in quantity of tickets per month} = \frac{1.0 - 1.5}{1.0} = \frac{-0.5}{1} = -50\%$$

In order to utilize the advantage of using percentage changes in describing changes in price and quantity, economists have developed the concept of "price elasticity of demand." It is defined as follows:

$$\text{Price elasticity of demand} = \frac{\text{Percentage change in quantity}}{\text{Percentage change in price}}$$

Price elasticity of demand is a number that indicates the percentage change in quantity demanded corresponding to a 1 percent change in price. For example, a price elasticity of demand of -1.5 tells us that quantity changes 1.5 percent for each 1 percent change in price.

A formula for computing price elasticity of demand is:

$$E_d = \frac{\dfrac{Q_0 - Q_1}{Q_0}}{\dfrac{P_0 - P_1}{P_0}},$$

where E_d is an abbreviation for price elasticity of demand, Q_0 and P_0 are the beginning quantity and price, respectively, and Q_1 and P_1 are the ending quantity and price. In order to become somewhat more familiar with the formula, let us compute the price elasticity of demand for the change shown in Figure 3–8. In this example the Q_0 is 12, Q_1 is 18, P_0 is \$3, and P_1 is \$2. Thus we have

$$E_d = \frac{\dfrac{12 - 18}{12}}{\dfrac{3.00 - 2.00}{3.00}} = \frac{\dfrac{-6}{12}}{\dfrac{1.00}{3.00}} = \frac{-0.50}{0.33} = -1.5.$$

In this example, then, a 1 percent decrease in price is associated with a 1.5 percent increase in quantity. You will note that the price elasticity of demand is a negative number. This occurs because as we move along a demand curve, quantity and price change in opposite directions; when price goes down, quantity goes up, and vice versa.

Although the price elasticity measure is a negative number, as we have just indicated, when economists refer to a specific elasticity measure they will often drop the negative sign and designate the number as an absolute value. For example, a price elasticity measure of -1.5 generally will be referred to as 1.5. Once one is aware that the negative sign is implicit in the discussion, it becomes redundant to keep repeating it.

In order to further facilitate discussion, economists have grouped the price elasticity measure, or coefficient, as it is often called, into three categories. Generally the groupings are made according to the absolute size of the coefficient (minus sign dropped). These categories are:

Elasticity coefficient:

Less than 1   = Inelastic
Equal to 1   = Unitary elastic
Greater than 1 = Elastic

When the price elasticity of demand for a product is inelastic, we say that consumers are relatively unresponsive to a price change. In this case the percentage change in quantity is always smaller than the corresponding percentage change in price. If demand is elastic, on the other hand, we say that consumers are quite responsive to a price change. Here the percentage change in quantity is greater than the percentage change in price. In the intermediate case of a unitary elastic demand, price and quantity both change in the same proportions.

The smallest possible value of the elasticity coefficient is zero. If E_d is zero, a change in price will not result in any change in quantity whatever. In this case demand is said to be "perfectly" inelastic. Demand that is perfectly inelastic is represented by a demand curve that is perfectly vertical (Figure 3–10).

The largest possible value of the elasticity coefficient is infinity. Here a very slight change in price corresponds to an infinitely large change in quantity. In this situation demand is said to be "perfectly" elastic and is characterized by a demand curve that is perfectly horizontal (Figure 3–11).

FIGURE 3–10
Perfectly inelastic demand

FIGURE 3–11
Perfectly elastic demand

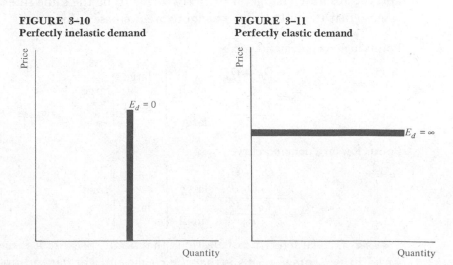

Economists sometimes illustrate demand that is highly inelastic by a very "steep" demand curve, whereas demand that is very elastic will be represented by a relatively "flat" demand curve. However, keep in mind that the slope of a demand curve depends on the units on both axes, except in the two extreme cases of perfectly inelastic or perfectly elastic demand.

Two characteristics of the elasticity coefficient ought to be mentioned at this point. Both stem from the fact that elasticity deals with percentage changes. The first characteristic is that the size of the elasticity coefficient will become larger the higher up we move on a downward-sloping, straight-line demand curve. This phenomenon occurs because the base or beginning values change at different points along the demand curve. At points high on the curve the beginning price will be high. Thus for a given dollar change in price the percentage change will be relatively small. For example, a $1 change in price will only be 10 percent if the beginning price is $10, whereas the same $1 change in price would represent a 100 percent change in price if beginning price is only $1. The same reasoning applies to different points along the quantity axis. The beginning or base quantity will be small at points high on the demand curve (small quantity demanded), which in turn results in large percentage changes for a given absolute change in quantity. The effect of a change in base values on E_d is illustrated in the elasticity formulas below. Consider the absolute change in quantity $(Q_0 - Q_1)$ and the absolute change in price $(P_0 - P_1)$ to be the same in each case, so that the only things changing are the base values.

Points high on a demand curve:

$$E_d = \dfrac{\dfrac{Q_0 - Q_1}{Q_0} \quad \text{small}}{\dfrac{P_0 - P_1}{P_0} \quad \text{large}} \quad \left| \begin{array}{c} \text{large} \\ \\ \text{small} \end{array} \right| \text{large}$$

Points low on a demand curve:

$$E_d = \dfrac{\dfrac{Q_0 - Q_1}{Q_0} \quad \text{large}}{\dfrac{P_0 - P_1}{P_0} \quad \text{small}} \quad \left| \begin{array}{c} \text{small} \\ \\ \text{large} \end{array} \right| \text{small}$$

A second characteristic of elasticity that occurs because it is measured in percentage terms is that the coefficient will depend upon the direction of a given absolute change in price and quantity. In the example for computing price elasticity of demand used above, the beginning or base quantity and price were 12 and \$3 respectively. But if we had started at the \$2 price and moved up along the demand curve, the elasticity coefficient obtained would have been different. This is because the base values would have changed to 18 and \$2 for quantity and price. The larger base value for quantity would have made the percentage change in quantity smaller (-33 percent), whereas the percentage change in price would have increased to 50 percent. The overall elasticity coefficient would have declined to 0.66.

Because different answers are obtained for different directions of movement, the elasticity coefficient is only accurate if it is computed over relatively small changes in price and quantity. Economists measuring price elasticity of demand for actual products utilize statistical tools that measure only very small movements in price and quantity.

For teaching purposes, economists have modified the elasticity formula slightly, using both beginning and ending values of price and quantity for the base in the numerator and denominator. Here the formula becomes:

$$E_d = \frac{\dfrac{Q_0 - Q_1}{Q_0 + Q_1}}{\dfrac{P_0 - P_1}{P_0 + P_1}}.$$

This formula[2] measures the "average" elasticity between two points, and it results in the same answer regardless of the direction of movement. The formula discussed first is sometimes known as the "point elasticity" formula, whereas the second expression has come to be known as the "arc elasticity" formula. Notice that the elasticity coefficient for the example we have been working with would be 1.0, using this second formula.

In an effort to master the mechanics of price elasticity, one

---

2 The above formula also is commonly expressed as $\dfrac{\dfrac{Q_0 - Q_1}{(Q_0 + Q_1)/2}}{\dfrac{P_0 - P_1}{(P_0 + P_1)/2}}$ and referred to as the "mid-points" formula. In this case the base values are taken as halfway between the beginning and ending quantities and prices. However, because the 2's cancel, the same answer is obtained as in the above expression.

should not lose sight of its economic meaning. Keep in mind that price elasticity of demand measures the responsiveness of consumers to changes in price. An inelastic demand means that consumers are not very responsive to price, whereas an elastic demand means that they will be quite responsive to price changes. The elasticity coefficient tells us the percentage change in quantity demanded for a 1 percent change in price.

Price elasticity and total revenue

One of the most valuable uses of the price elasticity concept is that it enables us to predict what will happen to the total expenditure on a product by consumers, or the total revenue going to the sellers of the product, when its price changes. To understand how elasticity is related to changes in total expenditure or revenue, it is necessary to first understand that a price change has two offsetting effects on total revenue or expenditure. Consider the case of a decline in price. Before the price falls, total revenue is given by:

$$TR = P_0 \times Q_0,$$

where TR is total revenue and P_0 and Q_0 are beginning price and quantity. After the price falls, total revenue is given by:

$$TR = P_1 \times Q_1,$$

where P_1 and Q_1 are the new price and quantity, respectively.

The reduction in price, of course, has the effect of reducing total consumer expenditures, or revenue. If the demand curve is downward sloping, however, the reduction in price will lead to an increase in quantity sold, and the increase in quantity will have the effect of pulling total revenue back up. If demand is elastic, quantity increases by a larger percentage than price decreases; in this case total revenue will increase with a price reduction. The opposite occurs when demand is inelastic. In that case, a price reduction results in a decrease in total revenue because quantity increases by a smaller percentage than price decreases.

Figures 3–12 and 3–13 illustrate the relationship between price elasticity and total revenue or expenditure by means of demand

FIGURE 3–12
Price reduction with inelastic demand

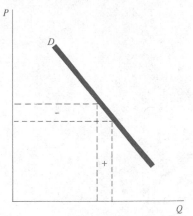

FIGURE 3–13
Price reduction with elastic demand

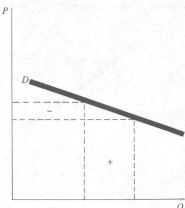

curves. The area denoted by a minus sign represents a pulling down of total revenue, whereas the plus area represents the augmentation of total revenue due to the price fall. In Figure 3–12, a representation of an inelastic demand, the minus area outweighs the plus area, resulting in a reduction in total revenue. The opposite occurs in Figure 3–13, where the plus area outweighs the minus area because of the elastic demand.

Of course, we would observe just the opposite change in total revenue if we considered a price increase. Here an inelastic demand would give rise to an increase in total revenue because price would increase more than quantity would decrease. By the same token, a price rise with elastic demand results in a decrease in total revenue.

In discussing price elasticity of demand, you will recall that elasticity changes as we move along a straight-line, downward-sloping demand curve. At points high on the curve, price elasticity is a larger absolute number than at points low on the curve. We might expect, therefore, that for most downward-sloping, straight-line demand curves, points high on the curve will be elastic, whereas points far down the curve will be inelastic. Moreover, there will be a point somewhere in the middle of the curve where the price elasticity will be 1.

The relationship between total revenue or expenditure and price elasticity of demand is illustrated in Figure 3–14. Starting at a high

FIGURE 3–14
**Relationship between price elasticity of demand and total
revenue or expenditure**

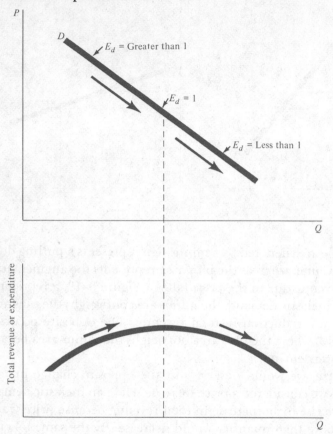

price (a point high on the demand curve) and moving down the curve results in an increase in total revenue or expenditure, until the point is reached where price elasticity is 1. Below this point, price elasticity becomes less than 1, and total revenue declines with a fall in price.

The relationship between price elasticity of demand and total revenue or expenditure is summarized below. This summary applies to both situations mentioned above: (1) a totally elastic or inelastic demand curve and (2) elastic and inelastic segments of a given demand curve.

	Change in total revenue or expenditure
1. Elastic demand:	
a) Price fall	Increase
b) Price rise	Decrease
2. Inelastic demand:	
a) Price fall	Decrease
b) Price rise	Increase

This illustrates that for an elastic demand, price and total revenue or expenditure change in opposite directions, whereas for an inelastic demand they change in the same direction.

Economic factors affecting price elasticity of demand

We have seen that price elasticity is affected by the point we happen to choose along a demand curve. But this is strictly an algebraic phenomenon that occurs because of the way we calculate price elasticity. We now want to explore briefly the economic factors that affect the size of a product's price elasticity of demand. The demand for some goods is elastic, and the demand for other goods is inelastic. Why does this occur?

The first, and perhaps most important, factor influencing the price elasticity of a good is the degree of substitution between it and other goods. The larger the number and the better the substitutes that exist for a good or service, the more elastic will be that particular good or service.

To understand the economic rationale of this generalization, consider a product that has many substitutes, pork chops, for example. When the price of pork chops goes up, consumers have many other alternative products to choose from—other cuts of pork; all other meat, such as beef, poultry, and fish; as well as other protein foods that can be eaten in place of meat, such as cheese or the new meat analogs. A rise in the price of pork chops, then, will provide an incentive for consumers to reduce pork chop consumption and increase consumption of these alternative products. When pork chop consumption declines, it is an indication that consumers are being responsive to the rising price of pork chops. You will recall that this is the meaning of an elastic demand.

Products that have few or very poor substitutes, on the other hand, tend to have an inelastic demand. Salt is the classic example of such a good. If the price of salt should rise, consumers would still have to buy it in about the same amounts, since it has no satisfactory substitute. This means that consumers are not very responsive to a change in the price of salt, which is just another way of saying that salt has an inelastic demand.

It is important to recognize as well that the definition of a product will influence its elasticity. In general, the more broadly we define a product, the lower will be its price elasticity. This is because there are fewer substitutes for a broadly defined product than for one that is narrowly defined. For example, the price elasticity for all pork would be smaller (less elastic or more inelastic) than it is for only pork chops. The substitutes for pork chops include pork loins and pork roasts, as well as the pork substitutes, whereas the substitutes for all pork include only the other meats or meat substitutes. Similarly, the demand for a particular brand of salt would be more elastic than for all salt, because brand X, for example, has substitutes in the form of the other brands of salt on the market.

The second major factor influencing the elasticity of a product is the proportion of the consumer's budget accounted for by the product. Products that take up a very small proportion of the budget tend to be more inelastic than those that rank relatively large in the budget. For example, if the price of paper clips doubles, the impact on your budget would be imperceptible; hence there would not be a strong incentive to reduce your use of paper clips. Yet if something like dormitory room rent rises considerably, you might be forced to find an alternative place to stay, such as an apartment or in a private home, and you might even have to leave school. Thus we would expect the demand for dormitory rooms to be more elastic than the demand for paper clips.

A summary of the effect of these two factors on the size of the price elasticity of demand would be as follows:

Factor	*Effect on price elasticity*
1. Many good substitutes	Increase
2. Large item in budget	Increase

It is not unusual to find cases, however, where each of these two factors has an opposite influence on the elasticity of a product. That is, a product may have many good substitutes, making for an elastic demand, but at the same time it may be a small item in the budget, which makes for an inelastic demand. The resulting price elasticity, therefore, is a summation of these two factors; both must be considered when attempting to assess the elasticity of such a product.

You might have noticed that the two factors named above as influencing the price elasticity of a product closely parallel the two effects, discussed previously in this chapter, that account for the downward-sloping characteristic of the demand curve—the substitution and income effects. This is not just a coincidence. The first factor, the degree of substitution possible, assesses the strength of the substitution effect; and the second factor, the importance of the item in the budget, assesses the strength of the income effect. The stronger or more significant these two effects are, the more responsive consumers are to a price change, which in turn implies a more elastic demand.

Income elasticity of demand

A concept closely related to price elasticity is income elasticity of demand. Income elasticity is defined as the percentage change in quantity demanded resulting from a 1 percent change in income. The formula for computing income elasticity (E_y) is very similar to the price elasticity formula.[3] The only difference is that in this case we divide by the percentage in income rather than the percentage change in price.

$$E_y = \frac{\dfrac{Q_0 - Q_1}{Q_0}}{\dfrac{I_0 - I_1}{I_0}}$$

We will postpone a more detailed explanation of income elasticity, along with a specific computational example, until Chapter 6, where we will discuss the effect of changes in income on quantity demanded. Here we have been chiefly concerned with the effect of changes in *price* on quantity demanded.

---

[3] Economists often use the symbol "y" to denote income.

Main points of Chapter 3

1. Demand is a relationship between price and quantity rather than a fixed amount. Quantity demanded, on the other hand, refers to a fixed amount—a point on the demand curve.

2. Demand reflects wants of consumers, not needs. Demand also reflects what consumers actually do when faced with certain prices rather than what they would like to do.

3. The downward-sloping characteristic of a consumer's demand curve for a product is consistent with diminishing marginal utility because with an increase in the price of a product, marginal utility per dollar declines. This in turn makes it worthwhile for the consumer to reduce consumption of the product.

4. A downward-sloping demand curve is also obtained when it is derived from an indifference map and alternative budget lines. Each point on a demand curve represents a tangency point between an indifference curve and a budget line.

5. Consumers change their purchases of products with changes in prices because of the income and substitution effects. The income effect occurs because a price change has the effect of changing the purchasing power of an individual's income. The substitution effect reflects the consumer's desire to obtain the most for his money by purchasing the "best buys." These two effects constitute the economic explanation for the downward-sloping characteristic of a demand curve.

6. The market demand curve is obtained by adding the demand curves of all the individual consumers in the market. This is done by adding all the quantities demanded by the individuals at each possible price.

7. Price elasticity of demand reflects the responsiveness of consumers to a price change. The elasticity coefficient indicates the percent change in quantity demanded resulting from a 1 percent change in price.

8. Demand is elastic if E_d is greater than 1, indicating that quantity changes by more than 1 percent when price changes 1 percent.

9. Demand is inelastic if E_d is less than 1, indicating that quantity changes by less than 1 percent when price changes 1 percent.

10. The elasticity coefficient can range from zero to minus infinity. Demand is perfectly inelastic if E_d is zero and perfectly elastic if E_d is minus infinity.

11. The elasticity coefficient becomes larger at points high on a downward-sloping, straight-line demand curve and smaller at points further down the curve. This is a mathematical phenomenon explained by changes in the base values that are used to calculate percentage changes.

12. Whether consumers spend more or less on a product after its price changes depends on the product's price elasticity of demand. If demand is elastic, a price rise reduces total revenue or expenditure, whereas total revenue increases with a price rise if demand is inelastic.

13. This relationship between total revenue and elasticity is explained by whether quantity changes by a larger or smaller percentage than price. If price rises 1 percent, total revenue or expenditure on the product will decrease if quantity declines more than 1 percent (elastic demand), whereas total revenue increases if quantity declines less than 1 percent (inelastic demand).

14. The two economic factors affecting price elasticity of demand are the number and acceptability of substitute products available and the importance of the product in the budget. A product with many good substitutes tends to be elastic. Elasticity is increased if it accounts for a sizable portion of consumers' budgets.

15. Income elasticity of demand is defined as the percentage change in quantity demanded resulting from a 1 percent change in income.

Questions for thought and discussion

1. Suppose two of your friends are having an argument. One says that the demand curve shows what quantities people will

buy at various possible prices. The other argues that a demand curve shows the prices people will pay for various possible quantities. Which of your friends is correct? Explain.

2. Distinguish between demand and quantity demanded.

3. The price of a skiing weekend in the mountains is $125. You would like to take six such trips per year. This says that $125 and six represent a point on your demand curve for skiing weekends. True or false? Explain.

4. In chapter 2 we learned that a consumer maximizes his satisfaction by equalizing as much as possible the marginal utility per dollar for all the goods and services he buys. Explain how this concept is related to the downward-sloping nature of a demand curve.

5. Think of two goods or services that are reasonably good (although not perfect) substitutes for each other. Draw in some indifference curves for these two goods that would be realistic for you. Next derive a demand curve for the good represented on the horizontal axis by adding some budget lines assuming three different prices for this good.

6. *a*) Explain what is meant by the income and substitution effects as they relate to the concept of demand.

   b) Illustrate these two effects on an indifference map.

7. Suppose you were to prepare a paper on the effect of changes in ticket prices on the attendance at professional baseball games. You find an economic study that provides the following data for a baseball team:

Ticket price	Season's attendance (thousands)
$6	410
5	415
4	425

   a) Graph a demand curve from these data that conveys the idea that people are not very responsive to changes in ticket prices.

   b) Graph a demand curve from these same data that conveys the idea that people are very responsive to changes in ticket prices.

8. Economists have estimated that the price elasticity of demand for all food, in the aggregate, is −.10. What does this number mean?

9. Suppose everyone in a certain market had a perfectly inelastic demand for coffee within the range of coffee prices where they

buy it. Does this imply that the market demand for coffee in this market also is perfectly inelastic? Explain why or why not.

10. Which would likely be more elastic, the demand for all cars or the demand for Volkswagens? Explain why.

11. Which do you think would be more elastic, the demand for coffee at a local drive-in or at the Waldorf-Astoria? Explain.

12. On many days major league baseball teams play to less than sell-out crowds. If the team owners wished to maximize total revenue from the sale of tickets, do you think they should lower ticket prices on these days? Explain why or why not.

13. Tell whether you would expect the market demand for the following items to be elastic or inelastic. Briefly explain why.
    a) Parking spaces near campus.
    b) Rooms in a campus dormitory.
    c) Food served in the student union.
    d) Tickets to a neighborhood movie theater.

14. Suppose you decided to establish a little theater close to campus. If your objective was to maximize total revenue from ticket sales, how would you go about deciding on what price to charge? To what point on your demand curve would the sales-maximizing price correspond?

4

Producer choice

The concept of production

In turning our attention from the consumer to the producer and product supply, we do not mean to imply that there are two separate groups of people in society, one producing and the other consuming. Almost everyone is both a producer and a consumer. To appreciate this dual role, it is necessary to realize that production is not limited to the factory or farm but characterizes the daily activity of most people.

For many, the word "production" conjures up an image of a factory belching smoke in which people and machines are busily turning out some identifiable product. To others, production might mean the harnessing of nature's resources to produce food, fiber, lumber, metals, and so forth. To be sure, all these activities involve production, but production is more. Indeed, production is any activity that creates present and/or future utility.

When you consider production to be so all-inclusive, many activities that you might not otherwise have classified as production now fall into this category. In filling or pulling a tooth, the dentist may not create present utility, but he certainly creates future utility by preventing a toothache. The artist painting a picture creates present utility for himself and future utility for others who view his work. The symphony orchestra and the vocalist create utility by the production of harmonious sound.

Thus production is not restricted to traditional business firms. Virtually everyone engages in some form of productive activity. The student takes part in a production process by reading books and attending classes. The knowledge and experience that is acquired or produced impart both a present and a future utility. Present utility is created by the satisfaction of learning something new or gaining new experiences. Future utility stems from an increased awareness and understanding of the world, as well as from widened economic opportunities made possible by increased earning power. The activities of housewives in the home also are a form of production. Utility is created or produced by the preparation of meals, the rearing of children, and all the other activities carried out that enhance their own lives and those of their families. So it is that production is found in every aspect of our lives. The fruits or output of production may be exchanged in the market, or they may be enjoyed by the person performing the production. The production of tangible items, from automobiles to pork chops to diamond rings, or intangible outputs ranging from knowledge to personal services may be involved.

In primitive societies of years past (and in developing societies today), production has consisted largely of the traditional activities involving mainly food, clothing, and shelter. As these basic needs are met, a larger share of available resources is devoted to nontraditional production activities—the production of items that provide diversity for daily life, as well as all the services and knowledge which are important in satisfying man's wants.

It would be illogical, therefore, to limit our concept of production to a limited range of products, as was done by early French economists known as the physiocrats. They believed that all true production came from the soil and that all other activities in society, such as teaching and the legal profession, were nonproductive. Occasionally we find some carry-over of this thinking today in references to management as "nonproductive" personnel or to certain people as the "working class." The agricultural fundamentalists who argue that agriculture is the "basic" industry in the economy also reflect this philosophy.

While it is not correct to limit the concept of production only to items we can package, pile up, or count, there are certain activities that could not be classified as production as far as society is concerned. The arsonist, for example, may derive some satisfaction from burning down a building, but such an activity usually reduces the utility of other people. The same is true for the "mugger" or thief. Activities that destroy property or human beings or forcibly transfer wealth from one person to another are better described as destructive rather than productive.

Inputs in production

In any production process there must be inputs that are either transformed or utilized in some way to produce an output. In economics, inputs are also referred to as resources or factors of production. All three names apply to the same thing.

In a modern, economically developed economy, most inputs are themselves the product of some other production activity. For example, the steel input into automobiles is itself an output of the steel industry. Even the human input in virtually all production has been modified or improved by some past training, whether it be formal schooling or informal knowledge gained from family, fellow workers, or experience. Knowledge itself also is the output of a production activity.

Most production utilizes several inputs at the same time or in some time sequence. In fact, it is rather difficult to think of an example where production is carried on with just one input. One that comes close would be the production of sound by a vocalist. But even this would not be strictly correct, since the singer utilizes energy obtained from food, which should also be considered an input.

Economic literature, particularly that dealing with production, classifies or groups inputs in various ways. In years past it was common to classify them into three categories: land, labor, and capital. With the growth of the nonagricultural sector, land has been reduced in importance so that it is now often grouped with capital. An aggregative grouping of inputs in an economy now generally includes only labor and capital. Capital can be thought of as inputs which have been produced by man to facilitate production, such as buildings, machines, and tools. Land, of course, is not man-made, but it is often modified by man in order to be useful in production.

Anyone who has ever cleared trees or rocks from land or has reclaimed it from the sea will appreciate the role that man has played in making land productive.

It will be useful for future discussion to group inputs into two other categories: fixed and variable inputs. In most production processes it is possible to identify certain inputs which contribute to production but which, for the time period under consideration, cannot be increased or decreased in order to change the level of output. These are called fixed inputs. Variable inputs, as the name implies, can be varied according to the desired level of output. For example, in manufacturing, the building would be considered a fixed input because it cannot be readily changed to a different size, and variable inputs would include such things as labor, materials, and fuel. Now, of course, over a long period, the building can be changed in size or a new one constructed, so eventually even a fixed input can become variable. We will emphasize the distinction between fixed and variable inputs as well as the importance of the time dimension to this classification in the discussion that follows, particularly in Chapters 6 and 7.

Production with one variable input

Obviously, for each product or output there are unique inputs and production processes. Moreover, the same output can be produced by different methods and with different inputs. However, there are some general principles of production that hold true for all types of production. It is these general principles that we will consider here.

The best way to begin the study of production is with the simplest possible case. In production, this is the case of one variable input. As we have noted, however, it is quite difficult to imagine a realistic example of production with just one input. But it is not so difficult to visualize production where one or more *fixed* inputs, such as land or some other physical facility, are combined with only one *variable* input, such as labor. In this case, simplicity is maintained without sacrificing realism.

We will find it helpful to consider a specific example in developing the general principles of production, as we did in our study of consumption. Suppose, for example, that there happens to be a ready market in your community for fresh tomatoes. Suppose as well that there is a plot of land in your neighborhood, say one-quarter acre, that is available. You decide that an opportunity exists to earn some extra money during the summer by producing and selling tomatoes. For the present we will assume that only two major inputs are used in your tomato production: land, the fixed input, and your labor, the variable input. Of course you will need some seed and a spade or hoe at the very minimum as additional inputs, but these are relatively minor. If you like, they can be considered fixed inputs along with land. The variable input we will be concerned with is your labor. Specifically, we will be interested in the relationship between the amount of effort you devote to your tomato plants and the resulting output of tomatoes.

A production function

As you begin your tomato-growing endeavor, one of the first decisions you will have to make is how much time you will spend on this activity. Without having any previous experience in tomato culture, it would be difficult to predict how many tomatoes could be produced and harvested with a given input of labor. To obtain some reasonable estimates of what you might expect from your labor, suppose you consult an experienced tomato grower. You tell him some possible amounts of time you might spend in your tomato patch and he tells you how many bushels of tomatoes you could reasonably expect, as shown in columns 1 and 2 of Table 4–1. (You might consider each day as equivalent to eight hours. Each eight-hour day of labor doesn't have to be applied all at one time.) Of course, these numbers would only be estimates, but in actual situations production decisions must often be made on estimates no more accurate than these. The more experience or knowledge a producer has, of course, the more accurate his estimates will be.

In a production process the relationship between input and output is often referred to by economists as a production function. In the example here, the output of tomatoes depends upon, or is a function of, the quantity of labor used. By knowing the production

TABLE 4-1
Hours of labor input and resulting output of tomatoes

(1) *Labor input* *(days)*	(2) *Tomato output* *(bushels)*	(3) *Marginal physical* *product of labor* *(bushels per day)*	(4) *Average physical* *product of labor* *(bushels per day)*
0	0	—	—
1	1	1	1.0
2	8	7	4.0
3	20	12	6.7
4	29	9	7.3
5	36	7	7.2
6	42	6	7.0
7	46	4	6.6
8	48	2	6.0
9	48	0	5.3
10	45	−3	4.5

function, I can tell you how many tomatoes to expect if you tell me how much labor is put in. With zero labor, for example, we would expect zero output. As labor input increases, output increases. Additional labor input enables you to plant and harvest a larger portion of the tomato patch, as well as to do a better job of controlling the weeds, and so forth.

Marginal physical product

Let us examine this relationship, or production function, between labor input and tomato output in more detail. We noted that each additional day of labor brings forth additional bushels of tomatoes. The first day (eight hours) brings forth one bushel. The second day adds seven bushels (eight minus the one produced by the first day's labor). The third day adds 12 bushels over the second, and so on.

The numbers we have been deriving here represent the *additional* output brought forth by an *additional* unit of input. Economists refer to this additional output as the marginal physical product (MPP) of the particular input that is being increased, labor in the example. This is shown in column 3 of Table 4-1. You recall from the discussion in Chapter 2 that the marginal unit is the additional or last unit either added to or subtracted from something. Hence, the marginal product of labor is the additional product obtained by adding one more unit of labor, or the loss of product by reducing labor by one unit.

In the tomato example it is a fairly easy matter to calculate marginal physical product because the labor input increases by only one unit at a time. In many kinds of production, however, it is not always possible to add or subtract just one unit of an input. If General Motors added only one man to its labor force, for example, the growth in output would be too small to measure.

It is useful, therefore, to have a formula that will make it possible to calculate the MPP of an input even if it is not added one unit at a time. The formula is:

$$\text{MPP} = \frac{\text{Change in output}}{\text{Change in input}}$$

This formula will give us the MPP of any input, regardless of whether it is changed (increased or decreased) by one unit or by several units at a time. In the preceding example, increasing labor by one unit, from one to two days, results in an increase in output from one to eight bushels (a seven-unit change). Thus the denominator in the formula is 1 and the numerator is 7. In writing the MPP column you will often see the MPP figures written opposite the input that has been added, for example the 7 is written opposite the second unit of input in Table 4–1. You might try calculating the MPP of labor when it is increased from one to three units at one time. (The answer is 9.5). Economists have estimated the MPP of the inputs employed in producing many products by the same statistical techniques used to estimate price elasticity of demand, as noted in the preceding chapter.

The law of diminishing returns

You probably have noticed the change in size of marginal physical product of labor (column 3, Table 4–1) as we move down the column. At first it increases from 1 to 7 to 12, and then it begins to decline, eventually becoming zero and negative. This simple example depicts fairly well what one might expect in any production process.

At very low levels of use of the variable input, its efficiency is low because it is spread too thinly across the fixed input. For example, an input of only eight hours (one day) might not enable you to adequately prepare the soil, plant, and harvest even a portion of the quarter acre of land. But an additional input of two or three days would make it possible to weed and care for the tomatoes so that output would increase rapidly.

The region where MPP is increasing is known as the region of increasing returns. It extends up to and includes the third unit of the variable input in this example. Increasing returns need not be present in every production process, but at very low levels of variable input use it is reasonable to expect such a region.

The region that is of most interest to us, however, begins at the fourth level of labor input, where MPP of labor starts to decline at each successive increment of labor. This is commonly known as the region of diminishing returns, and the declining characteristic of MPP is referred to as the law of diminishing returns. This principle states that beyond some point the output resulting from each additional unit of a variable input begins to decline.

The economic logic underlying the idea of diminishing returns is fairly simple and reasonable. As more and more of the variable input is added to the fixed input, the productivity of the variable input begins to decline because of crowding and inefficient use of the variable input. Applying more labor to the tomato patch, for example, may increase production because of better preparation of the soil, more careful weeding, and so forth. But there is only so much you can do in a tomato patch. Eventually the added output from more labor becomes negligible. Indeed, if diminishing returns did not materialize, you could continue adding labor until you produced the world's supply of tomatoes on this one small plot of land. In fact, it is not unreasonable to believe that after some point is reached, additional labor input to this fixed land area will have a detrimental effect and will actually reduce output. For example, you may just "tramp down" plants by adding the tenth day of labor.

The law of diminishing returns is also known by two other names: (1) diminishing marginal physical product and (2) the law of variable proportions. The first term is rather self-explanatory. The second stems from the fact that the proportion of total inputs that are variable changes as more and more of the variable input is added.

Average physical product

A second concept stemming from the production function is average physical product (APP). The average physical product of labor, for example, is calculated at each level of labor input by dividing total output by the units of labor employed:

$$APP = \frac{Output}{Input}$$

Notice that this formula is similar to the one used to calculate MPP, except that the absolute amount of output and input is used, rather than changes in output and input.

The APP of labor in the tomato production example is shown by column 4 in Table 4–1. We see that APP increases for a time and then begins to decline, just as we observed for MPP. One difference between the two measures, however, is that APP never becomes negative. It may approach a very small number, but as long as output is positive APP must be positive. It will be helpful to employ a diagram in understanding the relationship between MPP and APP.

Stages of production

Figure 4–1 plots the numbers in columns 3 and 4 of Table 4–1. The diagram is separated into three areas, or stages. Economists refer to these areas as stages of production. Stage I includes the area of increasing returns and extends up to the point where APP reaches a maximum. This stage, however, also includes a portion of the MPP curve that declines. The distinguishing characteristic of stage I is that MPP is greater than APP. As long as the marginal unit is greater than the overall average, the average will always increase.

It is easiest to understand the relationship between the average and marginal unit with a simple example. Suppose your overall

FIGURE 4–1
MPP and APP of labor (tomato production example)

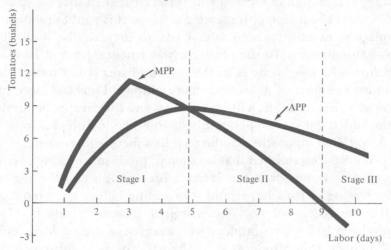

grade point average in college is 3.0 (out of a possible 4.0). Now suppose during the current quarter you work extremely hard and earn a 3.5. When your overall grade point average is recalculated with the current quarter included, you will, of course, observe an increase in your overall average. The current or marginal quarter has pulled it up. Or, if you had earned only a 2.5 for the current quarter, your overall average would have declined.

The distinguishing characteristic of stage II in Figure 4–1 is that MPP is everywhere less than APP. This results in the continual decline of APP. Stage II ends at the point where MPP becomes negative. Stage III begins where the MPP curve crosses the horizontal axis and extends to the right indefinitely as the negative MPP continues to pull APP down lower and lower, approaching zero but never reaching it.

The significance of the three stages of production will become clearer when we relate them to the concept of supply in the next chapter. For now we will have to settle for an intuitive explanation of their importance. It can readily be seen that no producer would ever want to be in stage III. This is evident from the example in Table 4–1. By adding the tenth day of labor, total tomato output actually declines. We would be better off to go fishing or stay in bed than to put in a day of work that brings negative results.

It is also true that no producer would ever want to operate in stage I, although the reason why is less clear than that for stage III. Consider the region of increasing returns. If it paid to produce any quantity at all, it would always pay to increase the level of the variable input until the producer was past the level of increasing returns. As long as he is in the region of increasing returns, each additional unit of input adds more output. Thus the more input he adds, the more efficient he becomes, and the cheaper he produces the added output. Consequently it would be foolish to stop adding the variable input when in the region of increasing returns.

We have established that a rational, profit-maximizing producer would add enough of the variable input to go past the region of increasing returns but would stop adding before he entered stage III, the region of negative marginal physical product. Thus a producer will always produce in the region of diminishing returns. Moreover, if he produces at all, he will always avoid stage I, even though this stage may contain a small region of diminishing returns (as shown in Figure 4–1). For the moment we will just assert this and wait until Chapter 5 to show why it is true.

Production with two variable inputs

Most production processes, of course, utilize a number of variable inputs, along with one or more fixed inputs. More realism can be added to the discussion by considering the case of production with two variable inputs. We can retain the tomato production example by assuming that labor is combined with another variable input. It would be reasonable to assume that even in this small-scale production of tomatoes, the use of some kind of equipment, such as a garden tractor and its various attachments, would be feasible. Suppose we measure the use of a specific size of garden tractor by machine-days.

We will assume as well that it is possible to employ various alternative combinations of labor and machine-hours. For example, if little or no machine-hours are utilized, a relatively large amount of labor would have to be employed to produce a given amount of output, whereas with more machine inputs the same output could be obtained with less labor.

Thus with two or more variable inputs the producer has to decide not only how much to produce but which combination of inputs will be best for him. The remaining part of this chapter will deal with the second question, the optimum combination of inputs, while Chapter 5 will deal with the optimum level of output.

Iso-quants

Economists have found it useful to devise a technique similar to indifference curves to make it possible to summarize the relationship between various combinations of the variable inputs. It is reasonable to believe that a given level of tomato output can be achieved by many different methods using different combinations of labor and machines. We can summarize these combinations by a diagram similar to the indifference curve diagram in Chapter 3.

Figure 4–2 presents what might be some reasonable inputs of labor and machines required to obtain a given level of output. The

FIGURE 4–2
Iso-quants of labor and machines input (tomato production example)

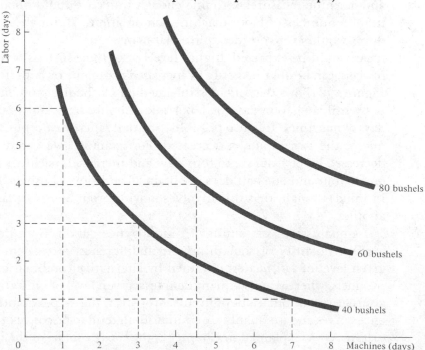

curves drawn in the figure are known as "iso-quants." Since "iso" means "equal," a more literal translation of these curves is "equal quantity." All the points along a given curve represent the same level of output. The lowest curve, for example, represents 40 bushels, the second 60 bushels, and so forth. We could draw in an almost infinite number of such iso-quants, but three will adequately serve as an example.

The figure specifies three alternative combinations of labor and machines required to produce 40 bushels of tomatoes. The combination of six days of labor and one day of machine use illustrates a labor-intensive method of producing tomatoes in which a large part of the work, such as preparing the soil and weeding, is done by hand.

Of course, it is also possible to utilize machines more fully and reduce the amount of hand labor required. This is illustrated by the 1 to 7 labor to machines ratio. (Keep in mind here that we are measuring machines by a certain size, say 12 horsepower.) Something of a middle ground is represented by the three days' labor, three days' machines arrangement. If we wanted to divide the labor and machine measures into fine enough units, we could obtain an infinite number of labor-machine combinations, although no producer would ever consider quite that many.

As would be expected, higher levels of output, such as 60 or 80 bushels, can be obtained only by increased use of one or both inputs. Figure 4–2 shows that one possible method of obtaining 60 bushels is by utilizing four days of labor and roughly four and one-half days of machines. It is also possible to actually increase output when *one* of the two inputs is decreased. For example, we could have decreased labor from six to four days and increased machines from one to four and one-half days to obtain 20 additional bushels. Keep in mind, though, that this involves moving from one iso-quant to another.

Iso-quants are very similar to indifference curves. Both denote a given quantity of something. An indifference curve denotes a given level of *satisfaction* obtained by alternative combinations of products, whereas an iso-quant denotes a given level of *output* from alternative combinations of inputs. Moreover, the shapes of indifference curves and iso-quants are similar. Both tend to be convex to the origin. As we explained in Chapter 2, the convex shape of the indifference curve means that the less you have of a good, the more you will have to receive of a substitute good in order to remain on the same level of satisfaction when giving up successive units of the scarce good.

The convex shape of an iso-quant has a similiar meaning. Essentially it implies that the closer you come to using a zero amount of an input, say labor, the more and more of a substitute input, say machines, you will have to use in order to remain on the same level of output. From an intuitive standpoint, this is a fairly reasonable thing to expect. There are certain jobs in the production process that can best be done by labor, for example, and other jobs done best by machines.

In the tomato production example it may be relatively difficult to substitute machines for labor in, say, harvesting the fruit. Notice as well that the iso-quants do not extend all the way to the two axes. If they did, it would imply that one input had been reduced to zero. It would be difficult to imagine tomato production being carried out with just labor or just machines.

Keep in mind, also, that the concepts of MPP, APP, diminishing returns, and stages of production apply to each of these two variable inputs, just as they did to the single variable input discussed in the preceding sections. We will not derive MPP and APP for each input again, but we could easily do so by varying one of the inputs at a time, holding the other constant.

Substitution possibilities

The shape of the iso-quants also indicates how easily one input can be substituted for another and still remain on the same level of output. The iso-quant drawn in Figure 4–2 illustrates a situation where the inputs are imperfect substitutes for each other. It is possible to substitute, but when you increase one in exchange for the other, it takes more of the abundant input to substitute for the one that is becoming relatively scarce. It is also possible to think of some inputs where it is very *easy* to substitute one for the other; your own labor and hired labor might be one example. Or, we might think of other examples where it becomes extremely difficult to substitute one input for another—seeds and land, for example.

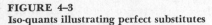

FIGURE 4–3
Iso-quants illustrating perfect substitutes

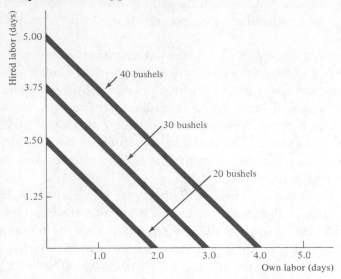

The latter two extreme situations can also be illustrated with iso-quants. Figure 4–3 illustrates a situation where two inputs are perfect substitutes for each other. The iso-quant in this case is a straight, downward-sloping line, indicating that the possibility for substitution remains the same no matter what combination is being considered. In the example, one day of your own labor would substitute for one and one-fourth days of hired labor, at any combination of the two. At the other extreme we have the case of zero substitution possibility, as illustrated by Figure 4–4. In this case the inputs must be used in fixed proportions. Once the "correct" proportion is reached, additional units of one input without more of the other are wasted, since output remains the same.

You may recall that indifference curves also exhibit these two extreme cases. When two goods are perfect substitutes for each other, the indifference curves representing the situation are straight lines, just as are the iso-quants in Figure 4–3. Similarly, when two goods must be used together in a fixed proportion or ratio, the indifference curves are rectangular in shape, similar to the iso-quants in Figure 4–4 (see Figures 2–3 and 2–4).

Economists are interested for the most part in the in-between

FIGURE 4–4
Iso-quants illustrating fixed proportions

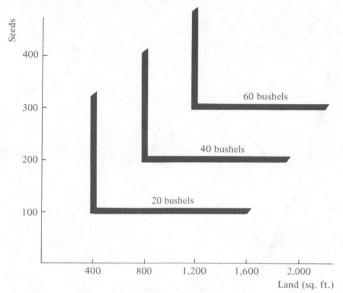

case of imperfect substitutes, where the iso-quants are curved and convex to the origin. However, it is important to keep in mind that different inputs may well exhibit different degrees of substitution for each other. In general, the greater the chance for substitution, the more gentle the curvature of the iso-quant. And the less the chance for substitution, the sharper the curvature of the iso-quant.

Iso-costs

It has been established that in many, and possibly most, production processes there is some chance to substitute one input for another. As long as this possibility exists, the production manager must decide the best combination to use at any given level of output. How shall he decide?

It is reasonable to believe that any manager would prefer to produce a given level of quantity and quality of output at the lowest possible cost. This is true whether we produce for the market or for our own use. By minimizing cost we attain a greater profit if we

FIGURE 4–5
Iso-costs and iso-quant illustrating an optimum input combination

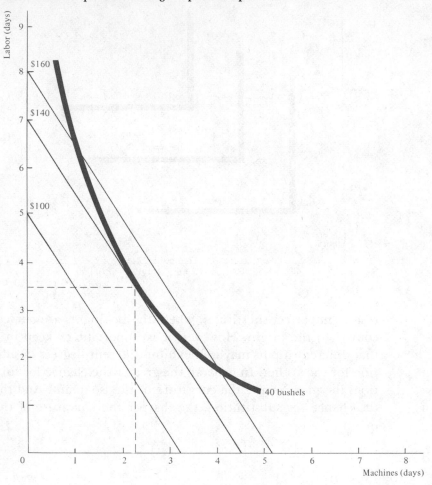

produce for the market or attain more output for a given input if we produce something for ourselves.

It is also reasonable to believe that costs will be minimized if inputs that are relatively inexpensive are utilized as much as possible. We will be able to organize our thinking in this area more easily if we develop what economists call "iso-cost" lines, which are very similar to the idea of budget lines developed above in conjunction with indifference curves.

In order to conceive of an iso-cost line we must know the prices of

the various inputs considered. To continue with the tomato production example, suppose the price of labor is $20 per day and the
rental cost of a given size machine (garden tractor) is $30 a day. It
will make no difference if you provide your own labor or hire it. We
will explain why this is true very shortly, at the beginning of
Chapter 5.

Once we know the prices of the inputs, we can construct an iso-
cost line. The easiest way to begin is to ask how many days of labor
could be obtained for a given expenditure, say $100. Thus at $20,
five days of labor could be hired. Therefore, the $100 iso-cost line
intersects the labor axis of the iso-quant diagram at five days. Secondly, we might ask how many machine days could be obtained
for $100. In this case the iso-cost line would intersect the machine
axis at three and one-third days. To construct an iso-cost line, we
connect these two points with a straight line. Recall that "iso"
means "equal," so all points along this line represent the same total
cost. Figure 4–5 illustrates several iso-cost lines, along with a 40-
bushel iso-quant. The higher the iso-cost, the greater the number of
inputs represented for a given price, hence the higher the total cost.

Optimum input combination

We now have the tools to determine the optimum (least expensive) combination of inputs for a given level of output. Observe in
Figure 4–5 that the $100 iso-cost line does not intersect or touch
any point of the 40-bushel iso-quant. This means that there is no
way you could produce 40 bushels of tomatoes for $100. On the
other hand, the $160 iso-cost line intersects the iso-quant at two
places: at about seven days of labor and slightly less than one
machine day, and at about four and one-half machine days and
just over one day of labor. Thus 40 bushels of tomatoes could be
produced by either of these combinations or any point between
them that is on the iso-cost line.

It would be wasteful to choose one of the combinations on the
$160 iso-cost line, because there is a lower iso-cost line that also
touches the 40-bushel iso-quant, namely, the $140 line. This line is
just tangent to the iso-quant, and the combination of inputs that
corresponds to the point of tangency is about three and one-half

days of labor and two and one-third machine days, which together cost $140. As a general rule the optimum or least-cost combination of inputs is the one that corresponds to the tangency point between the lowest possible iso-cost line and the iso-quant.

Again, notice the similarity between the indifference curve–budget line technique discussed in Chapter 2 and the iso-quant–iso-cost approach just developed. In both cases the tangency point tells you where you get the most for your money. The former tells you how to maximize satisfaction for a given budget or how to minimize the cost of achieving a given level of satisfaction. On the production side the iso-quant–iso-cost technique tells you how to maximize output for a given cost or how to minimize cost for a given output. Both ways of looking at these decisions mean the same thing.

Changing input prices

One of the most important uses of iso-quant–iso-cost technique is to show what happens to the optimum combination of inputs when the price of one of the variable inputs changes. Since the position and slope of a given iso-cost line depend on the price of each input, it can be expected that the slope of the line will change when one of the inputs changes in price. In terms of the previous example, suppose the price of labor increases, say from $20 to $30 per day. Because of this price increase, the iso-cost line will now intersect the labor axis closer to the origin, as illustrated in Figure 4–6. (In this diagram we represent labor on the horizontal axis rather than the vertical one, as in Figure 4–5.)

The increase in the price of labor results in a clockwise rotation of the iso-cost line, indicating two consequences of the increase. First, the total cost of producing these 40 bushels of tomatoes increases. This is illustrated by the fact that the $140 iso-cost line no longer is tangent to the 40-bushel iso-quant, meaning that it is impossible to produce this level of output with $140. The iso-cost line that is now tangent to the 40-bushel iso-quant, denoted by the broken line in Figure 4–6, represents a cost greater than $140.

A second consequence of the labor price increase is that the new

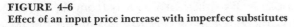

FIGURE 4–6
Effect of an input price increase with imperfect substitutes

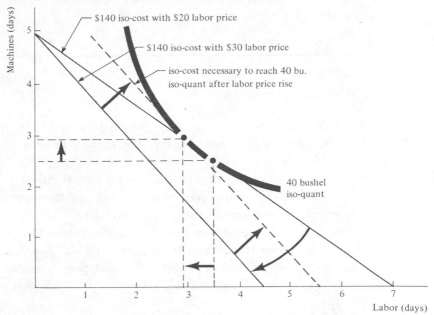

tangency point moves up along the iso-quant, away from the relatively higher priced labor. In economic terms, this means that the producer attempts to substitute the relatively cheaper machines for the higher priced labor.

It is important to recognize also that the amount of substitution that will take place in response to an input price change depends on the substitution possibility that exists between the two inputs. If labor and machines are fairly good substitutes for each other, the iso-quant will not exhibit much curvature and the tangency point will change by a relatively large amount. On the other hand, if the inputs are poor substitutes for each other, the tangency point will not move very much. (You might demonstrate this by drawing a number of diagrams similar to Figure 4–6, keeping the price change the same in each diagram but varying the shape of the iso-quant from nearly fixed proportions to nearly perfect substitutes.)

Regardless of the shape of the iso-quants, however, an increase in the cost of one of the inputs will increase the total cost of producing a given level of output. By substituting away from the more expensive input, the cost increase can be kept to a minimum, but it cannot be escaped entirely.[1]

Main points of Chapter 4

1. To be consistent it is necessary to view production in an all-inclusive context as an activity that creates present and/or future utility.
2. Most kinds of production utilize several inputs either at once or in some time sequence. Many inputs are themselves the product of some former production activity.
3. A useful way of grouping or classifying inputs is by dividing them into two categories: fixed and variable. Fixed inputs cannot be varied with the level of production, whereas variable inputs can be varied according to the desired level of output.
4. A production function is a relationship between inputs and output. The quantity of output depends upon, or is a function of, the amount of inputs employed.
5. Marginal physical product (MPP) of an input is the additional output obtained by adding one more unit of a variable input.
6. According to the law of diminishing returns, the marginal physical product of a variable input will at some point begin to decline as more and more of the variable input is added to one or more fixed inputs.
7. The level of average physical product (APP) of an input will increase as long as MPP is greater than APP. The level of APP declines when MPP is less than APP.
8. Economists have divided production into three stages. During stage I, MPP is greater than APP. In stage II MPP is less than APP, but MPP is positive. In stage III MPP is a negative quantity.

---

[1] An exception may occur if the two inputs are perfect substitutes and the iso-cost and iso-quant exactly coincide before the price increase. After the price increase, the more expensive input would not be used at all. However, this would probably be a relatively rare occurrence.

9. Production should always be carried on somewhere within stage II, which includes the region of diminishing returns.

10. The use of two variable inputs in production is illustrated by iso-quants. An iso-quant, meaning equal quantity, denotes various combinations of the two variable inputs that will result in the same level of output. Iso-quants are analogous to indifference curves on the consumption side.

11. The shape of an iso-quant indicates the extent that one variable input can be substituted for the other. An iso-quant that is convex means that the two inputs are imperfect substitutes. The case of perfect substitution between inputs is illustrated by a straight, downward-sloping line, whereas perfect complements are represented by rectangular-shaped iso-quants.

12. An iso-cost line, meaning equal cost, denotes the various combinations of two variable inputs that cost a specified amount. Iso-cost lines are analogous to budget lines on the consumption side.

13. The point where an iso-quant just barely touches its lowest possible iso-cost line represents the combination of the variable inputs that will minimize the production cost of that level of output.

14. A change in input prices generally leads to a change in the least-cost combination of inputs. The extent of this change depends upon the substitution possibility between inputs, which ranges from perfect substitutes (complete substitution) to fixed proportions (no substitution). In the middle case of imperfect substitutes, the more gentle the curvature of the iso-quant, the larger the change in the optimum combination of inputs that will occur for a given input price change.

Questions for thought and discussion

1. In each of the following activities, identify what is being produced and the major inputs employed:
   a) Baking a cake.   *c)* Cutting a lawn.
   b) Cleaning an apartment   *d)* Providing taxi service.

2. Think of a production activity that you would not have considered as such before you took this class. What is the output of this activity? The major inputs?
3. In what units is the MPP of labor measured in the production of:
   a) Wheat.   *c)* Houses.
   b) Haircuts.   *d)* Dental services.
4. What is a production function? Why might a producer want to know his production function?
5. Increasing a variable input in its region of diminishing returns necessarily leads to a reduction in total output. True or false? Explain why.
6. Think of an activity where you have experienced a diminishing marginal physical product. Try to think of a case where your MPP has been negative.
7. Can you think of a situation where an input might be in stage I? In stage III?
8. What is an iso-quant? In what way is an iso-quant similar to an indifference curve?
9. What is an iso-cost line? In what way is an iso-cost line similar to a budget line?
10. For each of the following pairs of inputs and its respective production activity, draw an iso-quant that you believe describes the degree of substitution that exists between the inputs.
    a) Labor versus machines in mowing an acre of grass.
    b) White-shelled eggs versus brown-shelled eggs in making an omelet.
    c) Cloth versus buttons in making a given type of shirt.
    d) Land versus fertilizer in growing 20 bushels of tomatoes.
11. *a)* Using an iso-cost diagram, explain how an increase in the price of one of the inputs will affect the amount of that input employed.
    b) Does the shape of the iso-quant have any bearing on how much the higher priced input is reduced? Explain.
12. In the less developed nations of the world, where labor is relatively cheap, middle- and high-income families utilize maid service to a much greater extent than families with the same income in the more developed nations, where labor is relatively expensive. Can iso-quants and iso-cost lines be of any help in explaining this difference between nations? Explain.
13. Would you expect there to be any degree of substitution be-

tween expenditures for highway construction and the number of lives lost in automobile accidents per million miles of travel? Explain.

14. Does the answer to question 13 above imply anything about the implicit value of life in the United States? Explain.

5

Product supply

The concept of costs

Product supply is solely derived from or based upon production costs, a fact that will become apparent as we proceed. It is important, therefore, to understand the concept of production costs thoroughly in order to understand product supply.

It will be useful to group production costs into two categories: (1) explicit or cash costs and (2) implicit costs. The first group should be well known. Some examples of explicit costs are wages paid to hired labor, interest paid on borrowed money, rent on buildings, and cost of supplies and raw materials purchased. These are the costs that are paid for purchased inputs, whether they be fixed or variable.

Implicit costs, however, tend to be less obvious. These are the costs that should be charged to inputs that are provided by the firm or whoever is carrying out the production. A good example of implicit costs can be taken from the tomato-growing example in the preceding chapter. In this small-scale enterprise, it is reasonable to believe that you would provide much of the labor yourself. It is necessary to include a charge for your own labor in calculating the total cost of growing a certain output of tomatoes; otherwise you will grossly underestimate the cost of your production. By not including the value of your own labor you could easily make the wrong decision when deciding whether or not to grow tomatoes in the first place or what is the most profitable quantity to produce.

A simple example will help make this clear. Suppose you anticipate that your cash or explicit cost of growing 20 bushels of tomatoes is $20 and that you will be able to sell the tomatoes for $2 per bushel. Thus you anticipate spending $20 and taking in $40. Will it pay you to grow tomatoes? On the surface it seems to be a profitable venture; you are left with $20 after paying your bills. But you still haven't paid yourself. How much is your own labor worth?

The best way to determine the value of your own labor in a self-employed production activity is to determine the wage you could have earned in the best alternative open to you. For example, you might have been able to work part-time at a checkout counter in a grocery store for $2 per hour. If you put in three eight-hour days of labor to grow these 20 bushels of tomatoes, the implicit cost of your labor is $48. In this case we could summarize your total income from and expense for growing 20 bushels of tomatoes as follows:

Total income (20 bushels @ $2)		$40
Explicit costs	$20	
Implicit costs	48	
Total costs		68
Net income		−$28

Including the implicit cost of your own labor reduces the attractiveness of this tomato-growing venture considerably. One way of looking at the outcome is that you paid $28 for the privilege of growing tomatoes. Or, looking at it from another viewpoint, you were able to sell your labor for only $6.67 per day ($20/3) as a tomato grower, whereas you could have sold your labor for $16 per day in the grocery store. Of course, this is only an example; it is not meant to convey the idea that tomato growing is a losing proposition. The main point is that it is necessary to consider all costs, not just explicit costs, when deciding to produce or not to produce.

Thus the total cost (explicit plus implicit) to you of producing something is very dependent on your alternative employment opportunities. If your only alternative to tomato growing is doing nothing, the implicit cost of your labor would be zero. In this case, the tomato venture reaps a $20 net income over costs. You would still have to decide, however, if $20 is enough to compensate you for the three days (24 hours) of leisure you forego.

If the grocery store employment, or any other job, is open to you, it is necessary to decide whether the additional income of this job would be sufficient to compensate you for any disadvantages it may have, compared to tomato growing. For example, you may be the type of person who puts a high value on independence; you like to be your own boss. In this case, you might be willing to sacrifice $9.33 a day for the privilege of doing what you like best. There is nothing irrational or wrong with choosing work that does not maximize your salary. It is important, though, that you realize how much it will cost you to work in more agreeable surroundings.

The concept of profits

We have avoided using the word "profits" so far, not because of any objection to it but because it is another term in economics that can be given different meanings. Economists have divided profits into two categories: (1) normal profits and (2) pure profits.

Normal profits can be defined as the minimum return to inputs owned by the firm or individual that is necessary to keep them in a given production activity. If all production activities were equally agreeable or disagreeable to people, normal profits would be the same thing as implicit costs. In this case, inputs or resources would tend to move to their best-paying alternatives. In the tomato-growing example, the normal profit would have been $48. As it was, however, less than normal profits were earned. If tomato growing and working in the grocery store were equally attractive, it would be foolish to grow tomatoes and forego the extra $28.

As we pointed out, however, there may well be considerations other than earnings that influence the allocation of resources. These considerations probably are not very important for capital, since machines or buildings do not experience psychic pleasure or pain. But people do take nonmonetary factors into consideration. Thus in the tomato example, normal profits might be either less than or greater than $48. They will be less if you like growing tomatoes and are willing to forego earnings to do so; or they may be more if you dislike this activity so much that you would be willing to work for less elsewhere.

Pure profits, on the other hand, are the return to a production activity over and above all costs (explicit and implicit). These profits would not have to be earned in order to hold resources in a given activity. This is not to say, of course, that producers do not care whether they earn pure profits. In fact, it is the possibility of these profits that entices people to take risks and initiate the production of new products or services that just might turn out to be a bonanza and make them rich.

Marginal cost

In deriving the concept of product supply, it will be useful to continue using the tomato production example. And it will be simplest to begin with the case of one variable input—your labor.

The foundation of product supply is marginal cost. Marginal cost is the additional cost of producing and selling one more unit of output. It can also be the reduction in total cost of reducing output by one unit.

In order to determine costs it is first necessary to assign prices to the inputs employed in the production process. You recall that two kinds or categories of inputs were employed: (1) fixed inputs and (2) variable inputs. If we assign prices to these inputs, we have essentially two kinds of costs, (1) fixed costs and (2) variable costs, which apply to these two categories of inputs, respectively. This grouping should not be confused with explicit and implicit costs. A fixed cost can be either implicit, explicit, or both. The same is true for a variable cost. It is important to recognize also that a fixed cost is one that does not vary with different levels of output. Variable costs, as the name implies, vary with the levels of output.

Assume that the fixed cost of the tomato production endeavor is $20. Consider this to be mostly land rent, although it could well include the cost of seeds as well as some small garden tools. Assume also that the implicit cost of your own labor is $2 per hour, or $16 per day. We now have the necessary data to calculate marginal cost (MC) for alternative levels of output.

Columns 1 and 2 in Table 5–1, showing tomato output and labor inputs, respectively, are taken from Table 4–1 in the preceding chapter. Total variable cost (TVC) of the labor input, obtained by multiplying days of labor times $16, is shown in column 3. Total cost (TC), obtained by adding the $20 fixed cost to each level of variable cost, is shown in column 4.

TABLE 5–1
Total and marginal cost

(1) Tomato output (bushels)	(2) Labor input (days)	(3) Total variable cost	(4) Total cost	(5) Marginal cost per unit
0	0	$ 0	$ 20	—
1	1	16	36	$16.00
8	2	32	52	2.29
20	3	48	68	1.33
29	4	64	84	1.78
36	5	80	100	2.29
42	6	96	116	2.67
46	7	112	132	4.00
48	8	128	148	8.00

Marginal cost, shown in the last column, is our main interest at the present. Recall that MC is the additional cost of obtaining one more unit of output. Note that even at zero units of output, total cost is $20. Increasing output to one bushel increases total cost to $36. Thus the MC of this bushel is $16 ($36 − $20).

As is often the case in actual production situations, however, it may not be possible to increase output by just one unit. In this illustration, for example, the second day of labor results in eight bushels of output, or an increase in seven bushels over the output at one day of labor. All we can do in this case is to estimate the "average" marginal cost of the output in the range of one to eight bushels. This is obtained by employing a formula very similar to the one used to calculate marginal physical product (MPP). The formula for MC is:

$$MC = \frac{\Delta \text{ total cost}}{\Delta \text{ output}},$$

in which the Δ symbol is an abbreviation for "change in."

Employing this formula, we see that the change in total cost from one to eight bushels is $16 ($52 − $36), and the change in output is seven (8 − 1), so the "average" marginal cost of an extra bushel in this range of output is $2.29 (16 ÷ 7) per bushel. (You might try to calculate MC at the other levels of output to acquaint yourself with the calculation procedure.)

It is interesting to notice that it is possible to calculate MC using either the TC or TVC figures. Using the TVC figure, the MC of the first bushel is $16 − 0, or $16, just as it was using the total cost figure. Comparable answers are also obtained at the other levels of output. Thus an alternative formula for MC is

$$MC = \frac{\Delta \text{ total variable cost}}{\Delta \text{ output}}.$$

It is not difficult to understand why the use of either TC or TVC results in the same MC when it is recalled that fixed cost remains the same at all levels of output. Thus changing output does not change fixed costs. In other words, the only cost that changes when output changes is TVC. As a consequence, fixed cost does not enter into the MC calculation.

Marginal cost and marginal physical product

As Table 5–1 shows, marginal cost varies considerably over the range of output considered. It begins at a relatively high figure, $16, declines as output increases, and reaches a minimum at 20 bushels of output or three days of labor. After that, MC increases with larger levels of output. The behavior of the MC figures is similar to that of the MPP figures in Chapter 4 (Table 4–1), although with MPP the direction of movement is just opposite; MPP begins as a relatively small number, increases to a maximum, and then declines.

The relationship between MPP and MC is shown more clearly in Figure 5–1. The line representing MPP is the same as shown in Figure 4–1 of the preceding chapter. MPP is graphed against the figures (bushels of tomatoes) on the left-hand vertical axis and the top set of figures (labor inputs) on the horizontal axis. MC is graphed against the cost figures on the right-hand vertical axis and the lower set of numbers (bushels of output) on the horizontal axis. The levels of output shown correspond to their respective labor inputs, as presented in Table 4–1.

The most important characteristic of Figure 5–1 is that MPP reaches its peak just at the exact level of input, or output, where MC reaches its lowest value. This correspondence between MC and

Principles of economics: Micro

FIGURE 5–1
Relationship between marginal physical product and marginal cost

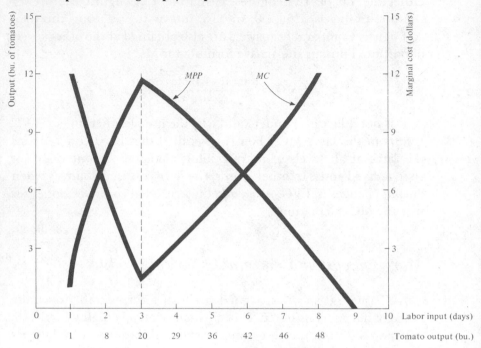

MPP is not a mere coincidence. Both are derived from the variable input—labor, in this example. It is reasonable to expect, therefore, that the more productive labor is, the higher is its MPP, and the less costly it will be to obtain an additional unit of output.

Average costs

In order to derive the concept of product supply it is necessary also to be familiar with the idea of average costs. We shall consider three types of average costs: (1) average fixed costs (AFC), (2) average variable costs (AVC), and (3) average total costs (ATC). As their names imply, each of these average costs is calculated by dividing the corresponding total cost figure by output. Specifically, average fixed cost is found by dividing total fixed cost by the level of output, and average variable cost is obtained by dividing total variable cost by output. Average total cost can be calculated two ways: (1) dividing total cost by output or (2) summing AFC and AVC.

Again it is easier to understand these measures of cost by looking at a specific example. In the tomato production example, recall that total fixed costs (land rent mainly) were $20 and labor costs (variable cost) were $16 per day of labor input. The resulting average cost figures for this example are presented in Table 5–2.

TABLE 5–2
Average fixed, variable, and total cost (tomato production example)

Tomato output (bushels)	Labor input (days)	AFC	AVC	ATC
1	1	$20.00	$16.00	$36.00
8	2	2.50	4.00	6.50
20	3	1.00	2.40	3.40
29	4	0.69	2.21	2.90
36	5	0.56	2.22	2.78
42	6	0.48	2.29	2.77
46	7	0.44	2.44	2.88
48	8	0.42	2.67	3.09

Looking briefly at these average costs, we see first that AFC becomes smaller at larger levels of output. We might expect this, since fixed cost is spread across more units at larger output levels so each unit bears a smaller share of the cost. Perhaps most interesting is the behavior of AVC and ATC. Note first that AVC declines over a range of output, or inputs, reaches a minimum point, and then begins to increase. The same pattern is observed for ATC, only these figures continue to decline until a slightly larger output is reached before they begin to increase.

Average variable cost and average physical product

We will be able to understand the average variable cost figures more thoroughly if we compare them with average physical product (APP), which was developed in Chapter 4. Recall that APP is total output (tomatoes, in the example) divided by the variable input (labor). The relationship between AVC and APP is most easily seen in a diagram.

In Figure 5–2, the line representing APP is again the same as shown in Figure 4–1. APP is graphed against the figures on the left-hand vertical axis (bushels of tomatoes) and the top set of numbers

FIGURE 5–2
Relationship between average physical product and average variable cost

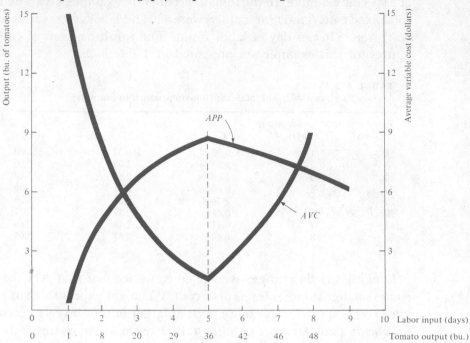

(labor input) on the horizontal axis. AVC is graphed against the cost figures on the right-hand vertical axis and the lower set of numbers (tomato output) on the horizontal axis. The levels of output shown correspond to their respective labor inputs, as shown in Table 4–1.

The most important characteristic of Figure 5–2 is that APP reaches its peak at the exact level of inputs, or output, where AVC reaches its lowest value. Like MC and MPP, the correspondence between APP and AVC is not a coincidence, either. Both are derived from the variable input—labor. The more productive the average unit of labor, the higher its APP, and the lower will be the variable cost of an average unit of output.

A glance back to Figure 4–1 will serve as a reminder that stage II of the production process begins at the point where APP starts to decline. From Figure 5–2 we see that this also corresponds to the point where AVC begins to rise. Thus stage II begins at the minimum point of AVC. Keep this in mind, because it will provide in part the reason why a rational, profit-maximizing producer will choose only to produce somewhere in stage II. It is best to defer the explanation, however, until after the discussion of how to derive product supply.

Marginal and average costs

To fully understand the concept of product supply it is also necessary to understand the relationship between marginal and average costs. As in the previous relationships examined, these are easiest to see when represented by a diagram. In Figure 5–3, the three average costs and marginal cost are superimposed on the same diagram.

Perhaps the most important characteristic to note is that MC

FIGURE 5–3
Relationship between marginal and average costs

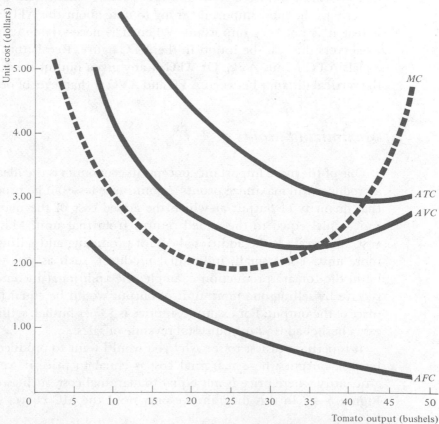

intersects both AVC and ATC at their minimum points. The explanation of this characteristic is essentially the same as that set forth for MPP intersecting APP at its maximum point: If the marginal unit is below the average, it will pull the average down; if above the average, the average will be pulled up. The effect of this quarter's or semester's grade point average on your overall grade average was used as an example. If this quarter's grade average (the marginal quarter) is above the overall average, the overall average will improve, and vice versa.

Exactly the same reasoning applies to marginal and average costs. Marginal costs will continue to pull AVC and ATC lower as long as MC is below the averages. Notice that MC can be increasing during this time, as it is just left of the intersections with AVC and ATC. To the right of the intersections, MC is above the averages and henceforth pulls them up. It follows also from this reasoning that MC must intersect AVC and ATC at their minimum points.

Perhaps the most important thing to note about the AFC curve is that it is not very important. When it is necessary to consider fixed costs they can be found in the ATC figure. Recall that AFC equals ATC minus AVC. Or AFC at any given output is equal to the vertical distance between ATC and AVC at that level of output.

Maximizing profits

One of the more important concepts in economics is the idea that a producer will maximize profits (or minimize losses) if he produces that quantity of output at which the added cost of the marginal unit is just equal to the added returns from that unit. Marginal cost, you recall, is the additional cost of producing and selling one more unit. For a small, individual producer, such as you would be in the tomato production example, the additional income you receive by selling one more unit of output would be equal to the price of the output. For example, if price is $3 per bushel, selling an extra bushel adds $3 to your total revenue or sales.

It is perhaps easiest to see why you would want to produce that level of output where marginal cost is equal to price if we pick a quantity where price is *not* equal to marginal cost, such as Q_0 in Figure 5–4. (In this diagram we only need the MC curve, so we

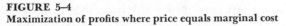

FIGURE 5–4
Maximization of profits where price equals marginal cost

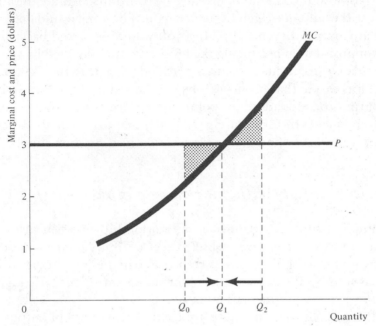

delete the three average-cost curves.) Notice that at Q_0 the additional cost of producing one more bushel is equal to $2. However, if the price of tomatoes happened to be $3, as is assumed here, you could increase your profits by increasing output. By producing the $Q_0 + 1$ unit, you spend roughly $2 but obtain $3 back, leaving a net gain of $1. Anytime you can spend $2 and obtain $3 back, you would be foolish not to produce that extra unit, so you definitely would want to produce $Q_0 + 1$ units. If you ask yourself if $Q_0 + 2$ units should be produced, you would obtain a similar answer, only now the difference between price and marginal cost would be somewhat less than $1. Since you would obtain a net gain, nevertheless, you would not want to stop short of quantity Q_1. If you did stop short you would give up profits equal in value to the area of the shaded triangle to the left of Q_1.

If you produced a quantity greater than Q_1, say Q_2, then MC would be greater than price. Here the marginal unit adds more to total costs, roughly $4, than it does to total revenue, $3, so you would definitely not want to produce the marginal unit at output Q_2. Nor would you want to produce $Q_2 - 1$ units, because the added cost still would outweigh the added gain. The same would hold true for any output beyond Q_1. Thus you would be forced back to Q_1. If you insisted on producing the level of output denoted by Q_2, you would give up profits equal to the shaded triangle to the right of Q_1.

Thus we see that profits will be maximized (or losses minimized) if output corresponds to the point where price of the product equals marginal cost. In formulating this rule, that price equals marginal cost, we will see shortly that we have derived product supply.

Product supply with one variable input

Product supply is defined as a relationship between price and quantity. Intuitively we would expect an individual producer to increase his level of output in response to higher and higher prices. Thus supply, like demand, is not a fixed quantity but rather a relationship between price and quantity.

It is not possible, therefore, to stipulate what level of output will be forthcoming until price is brought into the picture. Given the fact that you decide to produce tomatoes, for example, the number of bushels you produce would likely be different if you could sell each bushel for $10 than if a $2 price prevailed. Quite likely, at the $10 price you would treat your tomato plot with a great deal more tender loving care than at the lower $2 price. But the question remains, how much care?

The derivation of product supply is easily accomplished with a familiar diagram. Figure 5–5 is essentially the same as Figure 5–3, except that AFC has been deleted and some alternative prices, illustrated by the horizontal broken lines, have been added. All we have to do now is apply the rule that price equals marginal cost to find out how much output will be forthcoming at various prices.

At the relatively high $4 price, the broken line intersects the MC curve at 46 bushels of tomato output. Thus, at $4, quantity supplied is 46 bushels. At a lower price, say $3, the intersection of the line representing this price and MC corresponds to a smaller level of output—approximately 43 bushels. As we continue to lower price, the intersection between the price line and MC con-

FIGURE 5–5
Deriving product supply

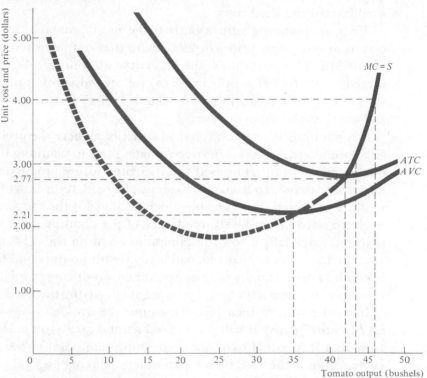

tinues to move downwards and to the left, corresponding to smaller and smaller levels of output. We see, therefore, that our intuitive idea of supply, larger quantities at higher prices, is consistent with the more rigorous concepts of economics.

As we continue to move down along the MC curve with lower prices we soon reach the intersection of MC and ATC. Recall that this intersection corresponds to the lowest point of the ATC curve. As the name implies, average total cost is the average cost per unit of output of all output produced up to that point. For example, at 42 bushels of output the total cost per bushel averages $2.77 for these 42 bushels. Thus if price falls below $2.77, the total income received from the total output will be less than the total cost of producing it, and a loss will be incurred.

It is reasonable to believe, therefore, that in planning future output, no production will take place if price is expected to be below a minimum point on the ATC curve. In the tomato production example, you would decide not to rent the land and, in so doing, would avoid the fixed costs.

Thus, in planning future output, the most profitable level of output at any given price corresponds to that output where price equals MC. In other words, the MC curve above the ATC curve is really the product supply curve *(S)* for an individual producer. All we have to do is label the vertical axis "price" instead of "cost," and we have the supply curve.

It is not unusual, however, to find situations where the producer either underestimates cost or overestimates price in planning future output. In committing himself to anticipated future production he might have to incur a fixed cost that must be paid, regardless of how much is produced. For example, the land rent for the tomato plot might have to be paid well in advance of the planting date. If anticipated price falls below the minimum point on the ATC curve after the fixed cost is incurred, will it pay to still produce and take a loss? The answer might well be yes, for in producing it might be possible to lose less than to not produce at all, paying the fixed costs.

If fixed costs are incurred that cannot be avoided (sometimes called "sunk" costs), it will pay to produce and take a loss as long as price is at least equal to or above the minimum point of the AVC curve. If this is the case, then we are at least making back all of our variable costs plus some of the fixed costs, depending on how much price is above this minimum point. Keep in mind that AFC at any given output level is equal to the vertical distance between ATC and AVC. Thus if price is higher than AVC at the optimum level of output (price equals MC), some of these fixed costs are being made back.

In view of the preceding discussion regarding fixed or "sunk" costs, it is necessary to revise slightly the definition of product supply. If it is impossible to avoid the fixed costs, product supply will consist of the MC curve down to the minimum point on the AVC curve. In Figure 5–5, this is represented by the continuous portion of MC above ATC, as well as the broken-line portion of MC that lies between AVC and ATC.

In no case will the supply curve extend below AVC. If price is below AVC, all the fixed costs are being lost, as well as some of the variable costs. If it is not possible to make the variable costs back, you will lose less by doing nothing.

Stages of production and supply

Chapter 4 defined three stages of production and asserted that production should take place only in stage II. At that time we gave fairly convincing reasons why it would not be rational to produce in the area of increasing returns (the beginning of stage I) or the area of negative MPP (stage III). But it was not possible to explain adequately then why the last part of stage I (MPP decreasing but APP still increasing) was not a rational production area. The reason can now be seen.

Notice in Figure 5–5 that the MC curve turns upward some distance to the left of the point where it intersects AVC. Remember also that the MC curve is a mirror image of the MPP curve, so that MPP turns down at the same point where MC turns up (Figure

FIGURE 5–6
Relationship of stages of production and cost curves

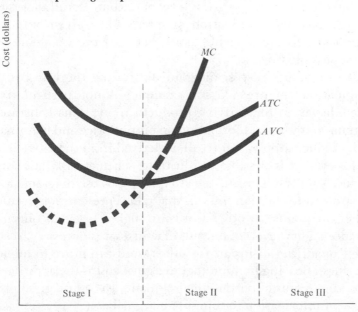

5–1). But it is irrational to produce if price is less than AVC; thus production only takes place somewhere along the upward-sloping portion of AVC, which you recall is comparable to the downward-sloping portion of APP. Thus production is rational only in stage II. Figure 5–6 delineates the three stages of production as they correspond to the ATC, AVC, and MC curves.

Product supply, therefore, is also meaningful only in stage II. Here price intersects MC above the AVC curve. Moreover, unless there are fixed costs that cannot be avoided, production will be forthcoming only above the ATC curve, which in turn means that we are well into the region of diminishing returns before it becomes profitable to produce.

Product supply with two variable inputs

In a preceding section product supply was derived for one variable input. However, as was noted in the latter part of Chapter 4, most production utilizes two or more variable inputs. Chapter 4 also illustrated how relative prices of these inputs would affect the combination used at any given level of output. Recall that the optimum (least-cost) combination of inputs for a given output level corresponds to the tangency point between the iso-quant and its lowest possible iso-cost.

The iso-quant–iso-cost diagram illustrating the least-cost input combination (Figure 4–5 for example) is not particularly well suited, however, for deriving product supply. This is because the diagram contains no information on output price and marginal cost. And, product supply, you recall, is derived from these two items.

However, it is possible to illustrate, schematically at least, how product supply relates to the iso-quant–iso-cost diagram. Moving upward and to the right on this diagram represents a movement to higher iso-quants (in other words, to higher levels of output). To produce higher levels of output, of course, it is necessary to employ larger quantities of inputs (in other words, to move to higher iso-cost lines). Bearing in mind that marginal cost is the additional cost of one more unit of output, the iso-quant–iso-cost diagram provides sufficient information to compute marginal cost.

In Figure 5–7 a few alternative levels of output, as represented by

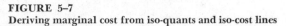

FIGURE 5-7
Deriving marginal cost from iso-quants and iso-cost lines

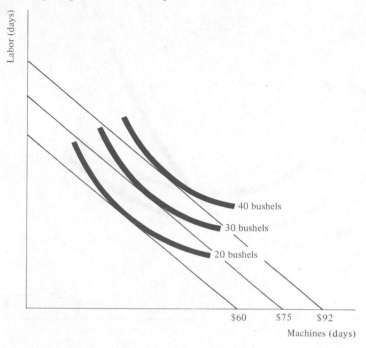

iso-quants together with their corresponding iso-cost lines, are shown. At 20 bushels the lowest possible iso-cost line that is tangent to the 20-bushel iso-quant is $60. At 30 bushels, total cost increases to $75. In this range of output:

$$MC = \frac{\Delta\,TC}{\Delta\,Q} = \frac{15}{10} = \$1.50.$$

Similarly, we could calculate MC for other changes in total cost and output. From 30 to 40 bushels, total cost increases to $92, resulting in a marginal cost of $1.70, and so forth. If we calculate MC for many such changes we could trace out a MC curve such as that shown in Figure 5-8. Keep in mind here that the land input remains fixed. Thus we might expect to run into diminishing returns with regard to the variable inputs—labor and machines. As more and more of these are added, the additional output will at some point become less and less. Again, if this were not so, we could grow the world's supply of tomatoes in this one patch. At any rate, we

FIGURE 5–8
Marginal and average costs derived from Figure 5–7

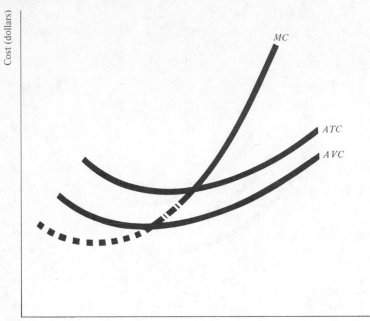

would expect to observe an upward-sloping MC curve, as shown in Figure 5–8. We also could calculate the average costs that correspond to each level of output and plot these as we did with MC. Thus product supply (MC above AVC) can be derived from the two-variable-input case, just as for the simple case of one variable input.

Keep in mind, though, that we have not yet determined which of various possible levels of output will actually be produced. In order to know this we must first know the price that will prevail in the market. We will consider this topic shortly, in Chapter 6.

There is one fairly important characteristic of MC (or the supply curve, if you like) that should be noted at this time. Notice in Figure 5–7 that the total cost figure associated with each level of output presumes that the most efficient combination of resources is used to produce that output. For example, other combinations of inputs could have produced 20 bushels of tomatoes, but they would have all cost more than $60. Thus at all points along an MC or supply curve we assume that the most efficient combination of inputs is used.

Market supply

As was true for demand, supply is most useful when considered in the context of the market. We can visualize the market supply curve as the sum of the supply curves of all individual producers. To obtain the market supply, therefore, we add, at each price, the supply of all individual producers.

Taking a very simple example, suppose there are three producers in a market. The market supply in this case is just the sum of the three quantities supplied at each possible price, as illustrated in

FIGURE 5–9
Deriving market supply
Producer 1

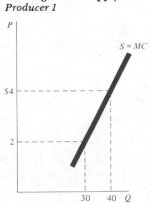

Producer 2

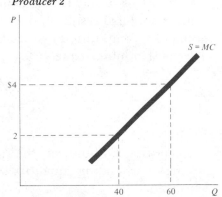

Producer 3

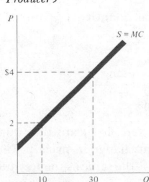

Market supply

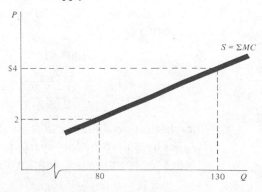

Figure 5–9. Remember that the supply curve of each producer is also his MC curve, so that the market supply is the sum of all individual MC curves.

Elasticity of supply

Thus far we have indicated only that product supply is an upward-sloping line, meaning that producers are willing to produce larger amounts when they expect higher prices. We have not considered how responsive producers are to a price change. Economists employ a concept known as "elasticity of supply" to measure the responsiveness of producers to a price change. We will see that this concept is very similar to price elasticity of demand, studied in Chapter 3.

Elasticity of supply (E_s) is defined as the percentage change in quantity supplied resulting from a 1 percent change in price. The formula for computing E_s is exactly the same as the price elasticity of demand formula, namely:

$$E_s = \frac{\dfrac{Q_0 - Q_1}{Q_0}}{\dfrac{P_0 - P_1}{P_0}}.$$

In computing E_s, however, the quantities Q_0 and Q_1 refer to beginning and ending quantity supplied rather than quantity demanded.

A simple example can be worked out inserting the numbers in Figure 5–10 into the E_s formula. Let \$2.00 be the initial price, P_0; \$2.50 the new price, P_1; 100 the initial quantity, Q_0; and 150 the new quantity, Q_1.

$$E_s = \frac{\dfrac{100 - 150}{100}}{\dfrac{2.00 - 2.50}{2.00}} = \frac{\dfrac{-50}{100}}{\dfrac{-0.50}{2.00}} = \frac{-0.5}{-0.25} = 2.$$

The elasticity coefficient of 2 in this example means that quantity changes by 2 percent for each 1 percent change in price.

Since the formula for computing E_s is the same as the formula for

FIGURE 5–10
Elasticity of supply computation

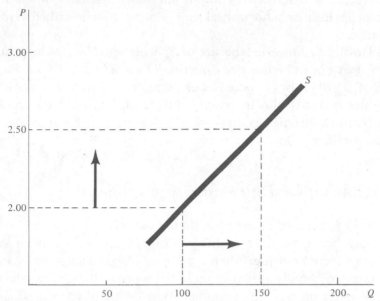

price elasticity of demand, it suffers from some of the same problems. First, it is a "point" elasticity formula, so it should be applied to only very small changes in price and quantity. In measuring E_s for actual products, economists use a statistical technique that measures very small changes. This technique is studied in intermediate-level statistics courses and also in a specialized area of economics known as "econometrics."[1]

Also, E_s varies in size along the supply curve, again because the base values change, although in the case of supply both price and quantity base values (P_0 and Q_0) change in the same direction. As you move up and out along the supply curve, the value of E_s approaches 1. At points low on the supply curve, E_s approaches zero if the curve intersects the quantity axis and approaches infinity if it intersects the price axis. You may want to convince yourself of this by working out a few examples.

Economists also classify E_s similar to E_d. If E_s is less than 1 it is considered inelastic, and a supply elasticity coefficient greater than

---

[1] The "arc elasticity" or "midpoints" formula used to calculate the price elasticity of demand also can be applied to the elasticity-of-supply computation.

1 is said to be elastic. And as E_s approaches zero, a vertical supply curve, E_s is described as highly inelastic. Similarly when it approaches infinity, a horizontal supply curve, E_s is described as highly elastic.

Unlike E_d, however, the size of E_s, whether it be elastic or inelastic, does not influence the direction of movement of total income ($P \times Q$) when price increases or decreases. That is, when price increases quantity also increases, so total income must go up. Similarly, total income declines when price declines because quantity also declines.

Factors influencing elasticity of supply

All products or production do not exhibit the same elasticity of supply. Some products exhibit a highly elastic supply; a slight change in price brings forth a relatively large change in quantity. For others, supply is highly inelastic; a price change has relatively little effect on quantity supplied. Why do we observe these differences in the size of E_s?

There are two major factors influencing the size of the elasticity of supply of a product: (1) the availability of substitute inputs that can be drawn away from other uses and (2) the time allowed for adjustment to take place. Regarding the first factor, if production of a product utilizes inputs that are commonly used to produce other products, it will tend to have a more elastic supply than if it uses specialized inputs suited only for its production. For example, the supply of all agricultural products in the aggregate is found to be relatively inelastic. This is reasonable to expect, since there is only so much agricultural land. If all agricultural prices increase, farmers can increase output somewhat by using land substitutes, such as fertilizer, and more intensive care. But the increase in output would be much larger if additional land could be drawn from other uses into agricultural production.

For an individual agricultural product such as wheat, supply tends to be much more elastic because land and other inputs can be drawn away from other types of agricultural production. In fact, for most individual products or services, it is hard to imagine examples of any input employed that does not exist in some form in an-

other line of work. Even the number of people with highly specialized training, such as economists or heart surgeons, could be increased substantially if prices of their services increased and there
was freedom of entry into the field. This has, of course, happened in
the case of economists, although the number of heart surgeons has
not exhibited as large an increase because of restricted entry into
the medical profession. Surely it is a mistake to underestimate the
latent talents of people or the adaptability of resources to many
different uses. Our experience during national emergencies such as
World War II bears this out.

The second factor, time for adjustment, is important because
most production activities cannot be changed in scale "overnight."
If price should increase, for example, some additional output will
likely be forthcoming from increasing the amount of variable inputs; for instance, more labor can be hired and machines and facilities used more intensely by operating two or three shifts. However,
relatively large changes in output usually cannot be attained until
the level of fixed inputs can be changed, and it takes time to construct facilities and manufacture machines.

It should be recognized that the ability to adjust output is likely
to differ between industries. For example, changes in retail trade
where temporary facilities can be set up are likely to take less time
than changes in the output of heavy industry, where specialized
plants and equipment are required. At any rate, in any given industry, the longer the time that elapses, the greater the change in
output that is physically possible, and the more elastic the supply
is likely to be.

In addition to the purely physical constraints on changing output, particularly increasing it, the economic aspects are very important. Even if it is physically possible to adjust output, it may not
be profitable to do so immediately after a price change. The major
consideration here is the length of time the price change is *expected*
to remain in effect. If the price change is expected to be only temporary, there is little incentive for a rational producer to change his
level of output substantially, because changes in output usually
involve additional expense. To increase output he often must purchase new equipment, buildings, and so forth, or to decrease production he might have to let fixed inputs remain idle but still bear
the fixed cost. Unless producers expect the price change to remain

in effect for a time, it may not pay to incur the expense necessary to adjust output. As an analogy, you generally do not bother to put on a heavy coat to pick up the morning paper on your doorstep on a cold day, but when you expect to be out for an hour the bother of putting on a heavy coat is worth the effort.

Of course, no producer has a crystal ball enabling him to accurately predict whether a price change is going to be temporary or long run in nature. Most producers probably will have an opinion on the duration of a price change based on information about the market, but none can be absolutely sure. The longer the time a price change remains in effect, the more information producers will have, and the more certain they will be as to the duration of the change. As a result, we should not expect to observe much fluctuation in output resulting from short-run, month-to-month fluctuation in output price. Rather we would expect producers to respond mainly to changes in the overall, average level of prices that exist over a period of time. We will illustrate the effect of time for adjustment on the supply curve at the end of the next chapter.

Main points of Chapter 5

1. In measuring the cost of producing an item, both explicit and implicit costs should be included. Explicit costs are the normal cash expenses incurred in production, whereas the implicit cost of an input is the wage that this input could have earned in the best alternative employment available.

2. A rational person may willingly choose not to work at a job that maximizes his salary. It is important, however, to know how much income is sacrificed to work in more agreeable surroundings.

3. Normal profits are defined as the minimum return to inputs owned by the firm necessary to keep them in a given production activity. If all jobs were equally agreeable or disagreeable, implicit costs would equal normal profits.

4. The possibility of pure profits provides the incentive for people to innovate and take risks to provide new products or services.

5.   Marginal cost is the additional cost (explicit plus implicit) of producing and selling one more unit of output.
6.   Variable costs vary with different levels of output, but fixed costs, as the name implies, remain the same, regardless of the level of output.
7.   Marginal costs are derived exclusively from variable costs.
8.   Marginal cost and marginal physical product are mirror images of each other. In other words when MPP reaches its peak, MC bottoms out.
9.   Average variable and average total cost exhibit the same **U**-shaped pattern as marginal costs. Both decline if MC is below them, and both increase if MC is above. MC intersects AVC and ATC at their minimum points.
10.   The same relationship exists between AVC and APP as between MC and MPP. AVC reaches a minimum point at the exact location where APP is at a maximum. Thus stage II begins at the minimum point of AVC.
11.   For a small, individual producer the additional income derived from selling one more unit of output is equal to the price of the unit. Thus if MC is less than price, there is an incentive to produce more because the additional income exceeds the additional cost. On the other hand, if MC exceeds price, there is an incentive to reduce output because the additional expense exceeds the additional income. Thus a producer maximizes profits (the difference between income and expense) at the point where MC equals price.
12.   If a producer is not committed to any fixed costs, the supply curve of a firm is the same as the MC curve above the point where it intersects ATC. If there is a commitment to pay fixed costs, however, the supply curve is the same as the MC curve above the point where it intersects AVC.
13.   Comparing supply with the stages of production, we see that the supply curve lies entirely in stage II, which is characterized at all points by diminishing returns.
14.   The supply curve can also be derived from the iso-quant–iso-cost diagram for two variable inputs. All points along a supply curve represent tangency points between iso-costs and iso-quants.
15.   Market supply is the summation of the supply of all individual producers at given prices.

16. Elasticity of supply is a measure of how responsive producers are to a price change. Its coefficient indicates the percentage change in quantity supplied for each 1 percent change in price.

17. The two major factors influencing elasticity of product supply are the availability of substitute inputs that can be drawn away from other production and time for adjustment. The more substitute inputs that are available and the longer the time for adjustment, the more elastic the supply. There are two dimensions of the time factor. First, there must be sufficient time to change physical facilities which will allow a change in scale of output. Second, it is necessary for the price change to stay in effect long enough so that it is profitable to change the level of output.

Questions for thought and discussion

1. A firm that obtains a greater amount of cash receipts than it pays out in cash expenses is by definition earning a "profit." True or false? Explain.

2. What is the most disagreeable job you can think of? What is the least salary you would take to work at this job? What is the most agreeable job you can think of that requires similar skills as the one above? What is the least salary you would take to work at this job? Is there a difference in the two salaries? Why?

3. "If a teaching job pays $7,000 per year and a sales job pays $10,000 per year, it would be foolish for anyone to take the teaching job." Comment.

4. Using some numbers, develop an example showing that marginal costs are not influenced by different levels of fixed costs.

5. Once a crop such as tomatoes is planted and brought to maturity, would it ever pay not to harvest the crop? Explain.

6. Suppose you owned and operated your own taxicab. How might you estimate the marginal cost of an additional fare? Would it be useful to have this information? Explain.

7. How are the marginal cost and marginal physical product curves related?

8. How are the average variable cost and average physical product curves related?

9. "A firm would not want to increase output to the point where it ran into diminishing returns because this would lead to higher and higher costs." True or false? Explain.

10. Compare and contrast elasticity of supply with price elasticity of demand.

11. Would the elasticity of supply of a product be influenced by how broadly we defined the product? Explain.

12. In recent years many barbers have left their profession because of a lack of business. Can we conclude that now only the best barbers are left in the profession? Why or why not?

13. Economists have estimated that the elasticity of supply of milk is about .20. What does this number mean? Be specific.

14. State in which case you would expect the most response by producers:

    a) The price of a product increases by 10 percent for one year and then returns to its former level.

    b) The price of the product exhibits a permanent 10 percent increase in price. Explain.

6

Demand and supply in the product market

In developing the concepts of demand and supply, we have noted that rational, utility-maximizing behavior by consumers implies a downward-sloping demand curve. Profit-maximizing behavior by producers, on the other hand, is reflected in an upward-sloping supply curve, subject, of course, to an upward-sloping marginal cost curve.[1]

An introduction to price determination by demand and supply was made in Chapter 1. This chapter will begin with a brief review of this process and then consider in more detail the factors responsible for demand and supply shifts and the consequent price changes. We will also discuss how action by government can affect market prices.

Equilibrium in the market

As Chapter 1 noted, we can superimpose the demand and supply curves on one diagram, as in Figure 6–1, to illustrate how the market equilibrium price is established. The process is easiest to under-

---

[1] Recall too that the upward-sloping MC curve is derived ultimately from the downward-sloping MPP curve, which reflects diminishing returns to the variable inputs.

stand if we begin with a market that is not in equilibrium. Consider, first, the price P_1 in Figure 6–1. What would happen in a market for a good or service if this price prevailed? At this rela-

FIGURE 6–1
Demand and supply, showing equilibrium price and quantity

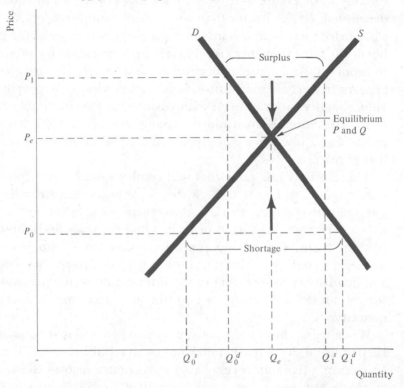

tively high price you will note that a relatively small amount is demanded, Q_0^d in the diagram. On the other hand, a relatively large amount is supplied, Q_1^s in the diagram. Thus at price P_1, the quantity supplied is greater than the quantity demanded. Hence there will be a surplus in the market; more goods or services are offered for sale than are bought. Inventories pile up or people offering services remain underutilized. The inevitable result of this situation is a downward pressure on price. Sellers, in an attempt to dispose of this surplus, are forced to take a lower price.

Equilibrium is defined as a state of stability. Either there is a perfect offsetting of opposing forces, or there are no forces present that can cause movement. It is evident, therefore, that the situation just described is not one of equilibrium. The surplus in the market sets up forces that exert a downward pressure on price.

Let us consider a second situation where the price is relatively low, say P_0 in Figure 6–1. Now we see that at price P_0 the quantity demanded, Q_1^d, is greater than the quantity supplied, Q_0^s. At such a low price there is an incentive for people to buy more of the good, but at the same time there is relatively little incentive for producers to supply it. As a consequence there is a shortage; the product disappears from shelves, inventories are drawn down, or people providing services are swamped with customers. The inevitable result of this situation is an upward pressure on price. Why sell your product at a low price when you can dispose of all you have at a higher price?

There is only one price that will result in neither a surplus nor a shortage–P_e in Figure 6–1. At this price producers are willing to put quantity Q_e on the market, and consumers or buyers are willing to buy this exact quantity at price P_e. Once the price finds this equilibrium point, there is no pressure, either from a surplus or a shortage, to pull price down or push it up. For this reason the price and quantity corresponding to the intersection of the demand and supply curves are known as equilibrium price and equilibrium quantity.

When using the concepts of supply and demand it is necessary to keep in mind that a market may not be in equilibrium at all times. In fact, in a dynamic, ever-changing economy such as the United States or any other free market country, equilibrium situations probably are the exception rather than the rule. The reason is that the equilibrium price is rarely known with certainty by both buyers and sellers. As a result there has to be a continual searching by both buyers and sellers for the price that entices buyers to take off the market the exact quantity that sellers offer.

If, for example, there is an accumulation of unsold goods or services, buyers or sellers, or both parties, know that price is too high and it must come down. Or if shortages are the rule, then one or both parties know that price is too low and upward pressure on price will prevail. Thus there is a continual process of adjustment in most markets which results in small price movements toward the equilibrium. In some cases there may be an overshooting of the equilibrium. If price is above equilibrium and moving down, it may come down too far and result in a shortage. In such cases there will be upward pressure on price which in turn might result in yet another overshooting of the equilibrium. It is this continual process of adjustment to equilibrium that is the distinguishing characteristic of most free markets, rather than an instantaneous change from one equilibrium to another. We will discuss shortly the factors that change equilibrium positions in markets.

The rapidity of adjustment toward equilibrium varies to some extent between different markets. In a market such as the stock exchange where both buyers and sellers are well informed about price and factors affecting the market, the adjustment to a new equilibrium may take only a matter of minutes. With goods that are seldom purchased, and when the exact price for a given quality is difficult to determine, such as in the retail market for eyeglasses, the process of adjustment is slower, and the time to reach equilibrium may run into years.

In spite of the time it takes to reach equilibrium in a market, we might reasonably expect that the markets for all goods or services would, if given enough time, eventually reach it. If this happened, all prices would settle at their equilibrium values and never move again. But we know this does not happen; prices of most goods and services are generally on the move, rarely if ever settling at their equilibrium points. Why? The basic reason is that the equilibrium points are continually changing because of changes, or shifts, in either the demand or the supply curve, or both. The meaning of a demand or supply shift and the factors that cause these shifts to take place will be discussed in the following section.

Change or shift in demand

In Chapters 1 and 3 we saw that demand was a relationship between price and quantity. It was convenient to express this relationship by a demand curve—a downward-sloping line. If the line moves to a different location on the diagram, we have what is termed a change or shift in demand, as shown in Figure 6–2.

Think of D_1 in Figure 6–2 as a demand curve that exists for a

FIGURE 6–2
Shifts in demand

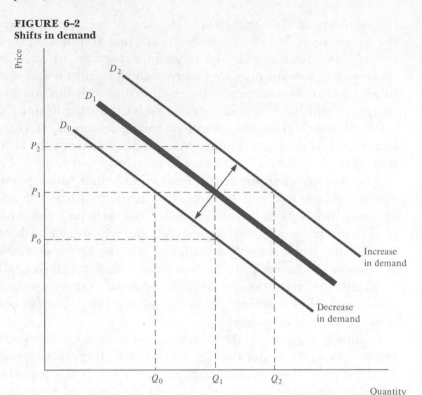

good or service during some time period. Then suppose, for some reason (which we will explain shortly), the demand changes position, say to D_2. This would represent an increase, or an upward shift, in demand. One way of interpreting this shift is that buyers will take more off the market at any given price. For example, with the original demand, D_1, quantity Q_1 is demanded at price P_1. Now with D_2, demanders will buy a larger quantity, Q_2, at price P_1. A second way of looking at an increase in demand is that demanders are willing to pay a higher price for a given quantity. With the increase in demand, buyers will pay price P_2 for quantity Q_1. At the original demand, buyers would only pay P_1 for this quantity.

The meaning of a decrease in demand, as illustrated by D_0, is strictly parallel to an increase. At a given price, say P_1, the quantity demanded declines from Q_1 to Q_0. Or, looking at it the second way, the price buyers will pay for quantity Q_1 declines from P_1 to P_0.

Factors shifting product demand

Whenever a demand curve for a product is conceived of or drawn, it is important to remember that everything that might possibly influence this relationship between price and quantity is held constant. This restriction is necessary because the demand curve deals with only a two-dimensional diagram. In other words, only two items can be considered at a time. With demand, these two items are price and quantity.

The world, of course, is never so kind as to hold everything constant other than the two items we are interested in. Things can and do change, and by doing so they influence the relationship between price and quantity. It is these outside influences that shift the demand, either increasing or decreasing it. There are a number of major factors that economists consider as important product demand shifters. These are:

1. CHANGE IN PRICES OF RELATED PRODUCTS

A. Substitutes. As we saw in the chapter on consumer choice, most products or services have one or more substitutes. We know also that the quantity of substitutes consumed will depend on their price relative to the price of the good or service in question. For example, if the price of margarine declines relative to butter, people will tend to shift their purchases away from the relatively expensive butter to the relatively inexpensive margarine. Therefore, a decrease in the price of a substitute good will decrease or shift downward the demand for the good in question, as illustrated by D_0 in Figure 6–2. Conversely, of course, an increase in the price of a substitute will increase (shift upward) the demand for the good in question, as shown by D_2 in Figure 6–2.

B. Complements. Not all pairs of goods are substitutes for each other. There are certain pairs of products, which we call complementary goods, that are consumed together. Bacon and eggs would be an example. If the price of eggs increases, people tend to have eggs for breakfast less frequently, and as a consequence the quantity of bacon sold decreases. Thus the demand for bacon would decrease, D_0 in Figure 6–2, because of the increase in price of eggs, a complementary product.

2. CHANGE IN CONSUMER INCOMES

An increase in incomes of consumers results in an increase in the demand for many products. Some of the increase can come from using the product more frequently, such as having eggs more times per week, or from additional consumers coming into the market. For example, people tend to enter the Cadillac market as their incomes approach the $35 to $40 thousand per year bracket. The more people there are in this income bracket, the greater the demand for Cadillacs. Economists refer to goods that increase in demand with higher incomes as superior goods. This name does not necessarily imply that such goods are made better or last longer than other goods. It is just a name for the category of goods or services that exhibits an increase in demand as incomes increase.

There are examples of other goods or services that decrease in demand as incomes increase. For example, people tend to buy less of the starchy, high-calorie foods as their incomes grow. With higher incomes they buy more steak, fruit, and fresh vegetables. Thus the demand for starchy foods declines, or shifts to the left, as incomes increase. Economists refer to these goods or services as "inferior" goods, again without any intention to describe the durability or quality of the good.

It is possible to name, as well, goods whose demand does not change at all with an increase in consumer incomes. One example is the aggregate demand for all food in the United States. Because of the relatively high incomes enjoyed by a large part of the U.S. population, food consumption for most people is already at a maximum. For some, food consumption is even too high, causing weight problems. Thus with continued increase in incomes people tend to buy about the same quantity of food, while increasing their purchases of the other amenities of life.

In order to measure the response of consumers to a change in income, economists have developed the concept of "income elasticity." In Chapter 3 we noted briefly that income elasticity is defined as the percentage change in quantity demanded at a given price resulting from a 1 percent change in money income of consumers. This measure can be illustrated by Figure 6–2 above. Suppose demand shifts to D_2 due to an increase in family income, say from \$10,000 to \$11,000 per year. Because of this shift in demand, there is an increase in quantity demanded at any given price. For example, at P_1 quantity increases from Q_1 to Q_2. One can easily calculate the income elasticity coefficient using the formula for computing income elasticity presented in Chapter 3:[2]

$$E_y = \frac{\dfrac{Q_0 - Q_1}{Q_0}}{\dfrac{I_0 - I_1}{I_0}}.$$

(It will be helpful to insert some actual numbers in the formula and compute an income elasticity on your own. Keep in mind that Q_0 and Q_1 represent the initial and the changed quantity demanded, respectively, and I_0 and I_1 represent the initial and the changed level of income.)

Because, with changes in income, demand can increase, decrease, or remain the same, income elasticity can be a positive number, a negative number, or zero. If demand increases, or shifts to the right, with an increase in income, income elasticity is positive. Thus a superior good has a positive income elasticity. The opposite is true for an inferior good. Here demand shifts left with an increase in income, and the resulting income elasticity is negative. If there is no change in quantity with a change in income, E_y is zero.

3. CHANGE IN CONSUMER EXPECTATIONS REGARDING FUTURE PRICES AND INCOMES

Since no one knows the future with certainty, our actions at the present are influenced a great deal by what we expect the future to bring. This is quite important in the case of product demand. If, for example, you expect a product to be scarce and high priced in the future, you will likely increase your purchases (demand) now in order to avoid the higher future price. An expected higher price will likely result in a shift to the right in demand, as illustrated by D_2 in Figure 6–2. Expecting a lower price in the future will, of

[2] Also bear in mind that the arc elasticity, or midpoints, formula also can be applied to the computation of income elasticity.

course, have the opposite effect; present demand will decrease, such as D_0 in Figure 6–2, as buyers wait for more favorable prices.

Anticipated changes in income also tend to affect present demand. If you expected a rich uncle to leave you a million dollars in one or two years, you would likely be a little more liberal in your spending habits even now, well in advance of the date you actually would receive the money. Thus your demand for many products or services would shift to the right, as is shown by D_2 in Figure 6–2. Or, if you expect your present source of income to dry up, you no doubt would become more frugal, meaning that your demand for some items would shift left.

It is important to realize that current demand depends heavily on your long-run expected income. College students illustrate this idea very well. They tend to enjoy a considerably higher standard of living while going to college than people with similar incomes who do not have much hope of substantial raises in the future.

4. CHANGES IN TASTES AND PREFERENCES

There are a few products or services whose demand is influenced by the changing whims or fancies of consumers. Mainly these are the fads or items that often change in fashion or style. For example, there is not much demand nowadays for dresses that extend below the knee, nor is the demand for high-button shoes very large. On the other hand, there seems to be a resurgence in demand for wide neckties and suits with wide lapels. In economic terms, the demand for goods that are no longer "in" shifts to the left, as in D_0, whereas the demand for items that are now "in" shifts to the right, D_2 in Figure 6–2.

5. CHANGES IN POPULATION

Since the market demand for a good or service is made up of the sum of all individual demands, the greater the number of individuals in the market, the greater will be the market demand. Population growth, therefore, is an important factor in shifting the demand to the right, such as D_2 in Figure 6–2. It is about the only factor shifting the demand for all food to the right, for example. In fact, the demand for most goods and services is being shifted steadily to the right because of growth in the size of the population.

Change or shift in product supply

In Chapter 5 we saw that supply is derived from marginal cost
and, like demand, is defined as a relationship between price and
quantity. Supply is conveniently represented by an upward-sloping
line, indicating a larger quantity supplied at higher prices. Just as
is true for demand, representing a supply curve by a two-dimensional diagram makes it necessary to hold constant the other factors
that can affect supply. If these factors do not remain constant, which
is usually the case, there will be a shift in the supply curve from
one position to another. Both an increase and a decrease in supply
are illustrated in Figure 6–3.

An increase in supply, illustrated by a shift from S_1 to S_2 in Figure 6–3, has two meanings. First, at a given price, say P_1, producers
will offer a larger quantity on the market: Q_2 instead of Q_1. A sec-

FIGURE 6–3
Shifts in supply

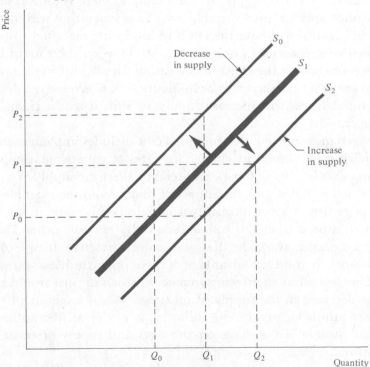

ond way of interpreting an increase in supply is that producers will supply the same quantity, say Q_1, at a lower price. Both ways of looking at an increase in supply have the same meaning.

The meaning of a decrease in supply, as illustrated by S_0 in Figure 6–3, is strictly parallel to an increase. At a given price, say P_1, the quantity supplied declines from Q_1 to Q_0. Or, looking at it the second way, the price suppliers will require for quantity Q_1 increases from P_1 to P_2.

Factors shifting product supply

The major factors that shift product supply are:

1. CHANGE IN PRICES OF INPUTS

As noted in Chapter 5, product supply is really the same thing as marginal cost. Thus anything that changes production costs should eventually change supply. If, for example, there is an increase in the price of labor, total variable cost of a given output will increase, which in turn will have the effect of increasing marginal cost—the added cost of an extra unit of output. Thus an increase in input prices or cost has the effect of decreasing supply, shifting it upward and to the left, as shown by S_0 in Figure 6–3. Conversely, a decrease in input prices will increase supply, or shift it to the right, S_2 in Figure 6–3.

Keep in mind, too, that marginal cost includes implicit as well as explicit costs. Thus any change in wages or employment opportunities in other lines of work will tend to affect the supply of a given product. For example, the supply of tomatoes in the example used in preceding chapters probably would decline if wages in the alternative supermarket job rose substantially or some other kind of work became available that was more attractive than growing tomatoes. If you took advantage of these opportunities, you would devote less effort to growing tomatoes, which in turn would result in a decrease in the supply of tomatoes. When wages or prices of other inputs change in one industry, it is a good idea to inquire what effect will this have on the costs and supply of related industries.

It is interesting to note also that a change in fixed costs will not shift marginal cost or short-run product supply. This is because marginal cost reflects only *changes* in costs between different levels of output, and fixed cost, by definition, does not change as output changes. A change in fixed cost, however, does shift the average total cost curve upward, and as a result the minimum price that will ensure a normal profit rises. Thus after producers are able to relieve themselves of any sunk-cost commitments, the minimum price at which they are willing to produce anything will rise. We will discuss this phenomenon more thoroughly in Chapter 7 when we take up long-run adjustment by a competitive industry.

2. CHANGE IN PRICE OF OTHER PRODUCTS

Most inputs, including labor, can be employed in any one of a number of production activities. If the price of an alternative product that can be produced increases, there is an incentive for producers to shift out of former lines of production into the production of the good that has risen in price. Not to do so would mean that producers deliberately forego higher incomes. For example, in the tomato-growing endeavor, the decision to grow tomatoes would depend upon the price of sweet corn, strawberries, beans, and so forth. If you could sell your labor for $3 per hour growing sweet corn, why should you grow tomatoes when this activity returns only $2 per hour? Thus an increase in prices of other products tends to decrease, or shift to the left, the supply of the product in question. Of course, the converse is also true.

3. CHANGE IN PRODUCER EXPECTATIONS OF FUTURE PRICES

Since producers are human beings and therefore cannot know the future with certainty, many of their present production decisions are based upon what they believe will happen in the future. If producers have a reason to expect changes in future prices, either in the prices of the product they presently produce or in prices of products they could produce, they will likely begin to adjust their production capacity accordingly. However, it is not possible to generalize across all situations the effect of, say, an expected increase in price. Each situation must be analyzed separately. For example, if the product can be stored, an expectation of higher future prices, either for this product or alternative products, may lead to a reduction in the present supply. Of course, the expected price increase must at least compensate for storage costs. For products that cannot be stored, such as tomatoes, the expectation of higher future prices will most likely lead to an increase in present supply as producers begin to expand capacity for the future.

Another important item to keep in mind is the expected duration of a price change. If producers expect only a temporary rise in future prices they will be less willing to make extensive changes in productive capacity than if they expect higher prices to prevail for many years. Thus the magnitude of the supply shift will depend upon the length of time the expected price change is expected to stay in effect. If the expected duration is short, the supply shift will be small, and vice versa.

4. CHANGE IN TECHNOLOGY

In general, new technology has the effect of making presently used inputs more productive or creating new inputs that are more productive than the old ones, which results in higher productivity. Proceeding one step further, we can define higher productivity as decreasing the cost of a given level of output, say Q_1 in Figure 6–3, or increasing the level of output for a given cost, such as P_1 in Figure 6–3. You will recognize that both these changes describe an increase in product supply. Thus new technology has the effect of always increasing supply. We will go into more detail in Chapter 12, where we discuss the economics of science and technology.

5. CHANGE IN NUMBER OF PRODUCERS

As noted in Chapter 5, the market supply of a good or service is the summation of the supplies of all individual producers. Thus the more producers there are of a given size, the greater will be supply. As the population and the economy grow, the growth in number of firms shifts product supply for many goods and services to the right. Of course, if the average size of firm increases substantially, there can be an increase in supply even with a reduction in number of firms. A good example of this phenomenon is agriculture in the United States.

Rising market price

Considering the many factors that can shift demand and supply, it is not surprising that a great deal of price change takes place in product markets. Every time there is a shift in either demand or supply, a new equilibrium price is established which sets in motion forces that tend to either push price up or pull it down toward a new equilibrium. And as price moves, so do the quantities demanded and supplied. We will explore in some detail the factors or combinations of factors that can lead to a rising market price for a good or service.

In a nutshell, any factor that increases demand, decreases supply, or results in some combination of the two can result in a price increase. The simplest cases, an increase in demand or a decrease in supply, are illustrated in Figures 6–4(A) and (B), respectively. The increase in demand can be caused by any one or all of the five factors named above as shifting demand, such as rising consumer incomes, expectation of increased incomes or prices in the future, higher prices of substitute goods, a larger population, or some unexplained shift of preference toward the product. In many situations two or more of these demand shifters can be operating at the same time. Moreover, some of these factors might serve to decrease demand, and in so doing might nullify, or at least mitigate, the upward shift of the other factors.

A decrease, or leftward shift, in supply, as shown in Figure 6–4 (B), can also cause a rise in market price. Again, any one of the supply shifters mentioned earlier, with the exception of technological change, can decrease supply and in so doing create a new, higher equilibrium price. Such factors as higher input prices, higher prices of other products that can be produced, expected higher future prices of storable goods, or an exodus of suppliers all can result in a higher market price of a good or service.

There is no reason, of course, to believe that demand and supply shifters must operate separately. Although a demand shift per se does not cause a supply shift and vice versa, both sets of shifters can and do operate at the same time in the same market.[3] If the demand shifters increase demand and the supply shifters decrease supply, as

---

[3] In fact, the usefulness of the demand and supply concepts depends largely on the requirement that the demand shifters do not operate on supply, and vice versa.

FIGURE 6–4
Factors causing a rising market price
(A) Increase in demand

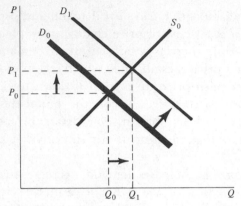

(B) Decrease in supply

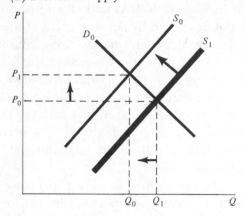

(C) Increase in demand and decrease in supply

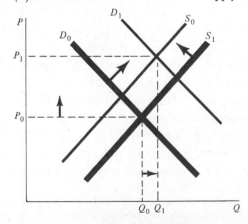

shown in Figure 6–4(C), then both sets of circumstances will lead to an increase in market price. In situations such as these, the price rise is usually substantial.

A rising market price can be associated with either an increase, a decrease, or little if any change in quantity, as illustrated in the three diagrams of Figure 6–4. If there is only an increase in demand, equilibrium quantity will increase; with only a supply decrease, equilibrium quantity will decrease. If both an increase in demand and a decrease in supply take place at the same time, it is impossible to predict what will happen to equilibrium quantity. If the demand increase dominates, quantity will increase, whereas if the supply decrease is most important, quantity will decrease. It is certainly possible that both factors could cancel each other out, and equilibrium quantity would remain the same.

The existence of simultaneous shifts in both demand and supply has caused many people to draw erroneous conclusions about the responsiveness of consumers or producers to a price change. We can observe a price increase, for example, with little or no change in quantity exchanged, as in Figure 6–4(C). As a result, some have argued that demand in many markets is almost perfectly inelastic (price has little or no effect on quantity demanded), while others have said that supply is close to perfectly inelastic (price has little or no effect on quantity supplied). In reality, both are wrong if the situation resembles the one depicted in Figure 6–4(C). In working with demand and supply it is just as important to know of the shifts that can take place as it is to know about the elasticity of demand and supply.

Falling market price

We need not go through the same detail in explaining a falling market price. The same demand and supply shifters, but this time causing demand to decrease, supply to increase, or some combination of the two, can lead to a lower price of a good or service. Moreover, we can observe a decrease, an increase, or no change in quantity with these shifts, as we saw in the previous section. (You might want to prove this to yourself by drawing these demand and supply diagrams.)

Of these ten demand and supply shifters, there is one, a change in technology, which shifts supply only one way—to the right. The reason, as we explained earlier, is because increasing productivity reduces costs and allows suppliers to sell a given quantity for a lower price. Thus technological change always has the effect of reducing market price, or at least making price lower than it would otherwise have been.

The effect of technological change, or the lack of it, is quite noticeable in the U.S. economy in the present. A few products, such as poultry meat, sell for about the same price today as 30 years ago, in spite of the inflation that has taken place. The primary reason is the decrease in production costs, and hence the increase in supply, brought about by new technology. In some areas of production, particularly the service industries, technological change has been slower. This is an important reason for the rapidly increasing costs of schooling; educators have not been very successful in increasing teaching productivity in schools and colleges, while improving or even maintaining quality of instruction.

Government in the market

Society has seen fit to intervene in most markets through the vehicle of direct governmental action or laws. There is a great deal of disagreement between people about the desirability of government in the market. Those with a fairly conservative political outlook argue that markets are capable of running themselves, or at least there is little need for more intervention. Those with a more liberal attitude will in general defend the role of government in the market.

We will not attempt here to argue one point of view over the other. Instead we will attempt to identify and briefly evaluate the effects of some of the major governmental action that has affected markets so that you will be better able to formulate your own opinions on the proper role of government in the market.

ESTABLISHING THE "RULES OF THE GAME"

Although we will not dwell at length on the legal aspects of product markets, it is important to note that in order for any market to function properly, both buyers and sellers must obey certain rules. An important function of the government in any market is to establish basic rules of behavior and enforce them.

Perhaps the most basic rule is the law requiring buyers to pay sellers for goods purchased or services rendered. For many people this rule would not be necessary; payment of one's debts is a matter of personal integrity. But for others, payment would not be forthcoming unless the threat of legal action and punishment existed. A few, of course, still attempt to gain ownership without payment; we call these people thieves. Without reasonable assurance of payment for goods or services, sellers would find it virtually impossible to remain in business. Those that did remain would be required to charge higher prices so that the people who paid would cover the loss of those who did not. Needless to say, a market characterized by gross nonpayment by buyers would soon break down. The honest people would quickly grow tired of paying for the goods and services consumed by their dishonest neighbors.

A second important role of government in the operation of the market is to provide information about products to buyers or to require that this information be made available. As noted in Chapter 2, a consumer maximizes utility by equating marginal utility per dollar for each good purchased. If information about the product or its price is lacking or wrong, it is not possible to compare the marginal utility per dollar of the product against possible alternatives. Most of us have purchased goods or services that we would not have bought had we known their true characteristics or price. The recent truth-in-packaging and truth-in-lending legislation is an attempt to improve buyer information in the market. As a rule it is much easier and more successful to provide buyers with correct information and let competition take its course than it is to attempt to regulate sellers closely.

Government also is active in setting standards and testing products before they are put on the market. This is particularly important for potentially harmful items such as drugs and food. Granted, harmful products would eventually come to the attention of buyers and be forced off the market, but needless injury or death can be avoided if these products are identified beforehand.

CEILING PRICES

There are times, generally during war, when society believes that the prices of certain goods or services are too high. This belief probably stems from the idea that excessive pure profits are being earned in the production or supply of these items. As a consequence the government may enact legislation that establishes maximum prices of certain goods or services, making it illegal for suppliers to sell any of the regulated items for a higher price.

The prices that are established are known as "ceiling prices" because the selling price is not supposed to rise above this maximum. The ceiling price is, of course, below the market equilibrium; otherwise it would not be a ceiling or have any effect in the market.

The consequences of a ceiling price can be most easily illustrated by the use of the traditional demand-supply diagram, as in Figure 6–5, where P_c represents the ceiling price, which is below the market equilibrium price, P_e. You will note at P_c that quantity de-

FIGURE 6–5
Ceiling price in a market

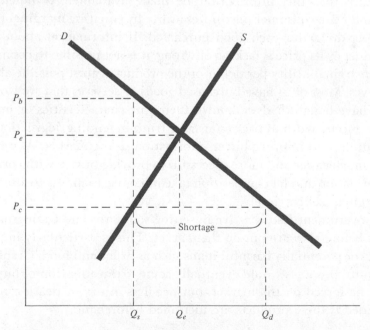

manded, Q_d, is greater than quantity supplied, Q_s. At price P_c, people want to buy more than is being offered for sale. Thus some buyers will have to settle for less than they would like. How should the available supply be allocated?

One option open to the government is to allocate the available quantity on a first-come, first-served basis. The problem with this approach is that it is very wasteful. Countless hours are spent by people standing in line in order to obtain a portion of the scarce item. The total output of goods and services to society could be increased if people devoted their energies to production rather than to standing in line or attempting to bribe the distributors of the product.

An alternative and more efficient method of allocating the available output is to issue ration stamps more or less equally among the population. Although many people cannot buy as much as they like under this scheme, at least there is a little for everyone, and it eliminates a large part of the wasted effort mentioned above. At any rate, it is important to recognize that a ceiling price inevitably creates a shortage in the market and, as a consequence, makes it necessary to impose some sort of rationing scheme.

A second important side effect of a ceiling price is that it reduces the quantity produced of the already scarce commodity. As you can see in Figure 6–5, before the ceiling price, output is at Q_e, whereas after the ceiling is imposed, output declines to Q_s. This happens because the lower price provides an incentive for suppliers to reduce their production of the good or service in question, perhaps increasing their output of nonregulated items.

Because of food shortages and subsequent high food prices, the governments of numerous developing nations have used ceiling prices on food as a device to hold down inflation. However, from our analysis of the effect of ceiling prices, it is quite evident that such a policy only makes the problem worse, because it reduces even more the meager output of food. Low food prices also reduce the incentive for public and private research agencies to provide new technology for agriculture, and as a result there is relatively little increase (shift) in the supply curve of food.

A third effect of a government-imposed ceiling price is the creation of a so-called "black market," where people desiring a larger amount than their quota are willing to pay a very high price in order to obtain it. The exact black market price can be determined from Figure 6–5. At quantity Q_s the demand curve tells us that people are willing to pay the black market price (P_b). However, this price is illegal because it is above the ceiling, which probably explains why it is called the black market price. You might notice, as well, that this price is substantially above the market equilibrium price, P_e. Thus the black market price is not a valid indicator of the price that would prevail without the price ceiling.

SUPPORT PRICES

In other situations society has decided that prices of certain items are too low, and as a result government action is undertaken to keep prices above the market equilibrium. The motivation for this action generally stems from a belief that producers of the supported products suffer from low incomes and that raising the price of the products they sell will in turn raise their incomes.

The effect of a support price in the market can also be seen by use of a demand-supply diagram, Figure 6–6. At the support price, P_s, you will note that the quantity supplied, Q_s, exceeds the quantity demanded, Q_d. As a result there is a surplus in the market, amounting to the difference between Q_s and Q_d. The only way the government can maintain the support price, therefore, is to buy up this surplus and keep it off the market. Otherwise the excess output will exert a downward pressure on price and drive it down toward the equilibrium.

The best example of support prices and their effects can be seen in U.S. agriculture, as well as that of many other developed nations. The clusters of grain bins that used to be observed along the highways of the country were visible evidence of this surplus. In recent years this surplus has become less noticeable, as the government has been paying farmers to store the surplus production on their farms.[4]

The existence of a support price provides an incentive for producers to produce even more of the already overabundant product. At the equilibrium price, P_e, Q_e is supplied, whereas at the higher

---

[4] The large grain sales to China and the Soviet Union during the early 1970s also have drawn down the surpluses to modest amounts.

FIGURE 6–6
Support price in the market

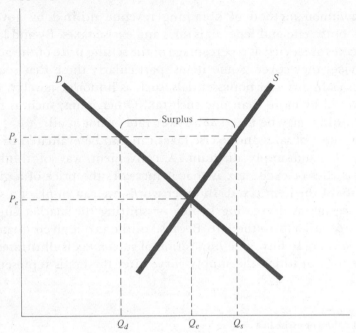

support price, P_s, Q_s is offered for sale. In an attempt to reduce this surplus, the government has restricted the use of land by those producers who wish to sell at the higher support price. Unfortunately, restricting land has not been a very successful means of restricting output because producers have been able to increase output by increasing the use of inputs that substitute for land, particularly fertilizer, herbicides, and improved varieties of crops.

The ability of support price programs to substantially raise the income of producers who really need help is increasingly being questioned. Support price programs in general have not been effective as an income-supporting scheme because the low-income producers tend to be the small producers. Doubling the price of wheat from $1 to $2 per bushel only adds $500 per year to the income of a 500-bushel-per-year producer, but it adds $20,000 per year to a 20,000-bushel producer. Thus price support programs have a tendency to help high-income producers more than their low-income counterparts.

SALES AND EXCISE TAXES

A common method of obtaining revenue utilized by governments, both state and federal, is sales and excise taxes. By and large these taxes are levied as a percentage of the selling price of the goods or services they cover. Some items, particularly those that society regards as luxuries or nonessentials, such as liquor or jewelry, may be covered by more than one such tax. Other items, such as food and clothing, may be taxed at a lower rate or not at all.

The effect of sales and excise taxes can also be evaluated by the simple demand-supply diagram. A convenient way of thinking about a sales or excise tax is that it increases the price of a given quantity of the item taxed. In other words, we can think of a sales or excise tax as decreasing supply or shifting the market supply curve upward and to the left. Because of the tax, a given quantity will cost more to buy. The imposition of such a tax is illustrated in Figure 6–7, in which the supply curve after the tax is represented by S_0.

FIGURE 6–7
Effect of a sales or excise tax

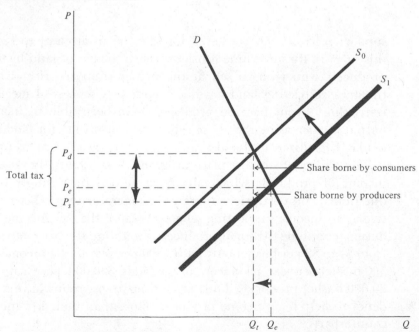

Notice, first, that the market equilibrium price increases from P_e to P_d after the tax is imposed. But it is also important to recognize that with a downward-sloping demand and an upward-sloping supply, the price rise to consumers is less than the amount of the tax. Figure 6–7 shows that the total tax at quantity Q_t is the same as the distance from P_s to P_d on the vertical axis. This is the amount that the supply curve has been shifted up because of the tax.

However, it can also be seen that the price that producers obtain after the tax is reduced by the distance between P_e and P_s. Although the producer (seller) collects price P_d from buyers, he must relinquish an amount equal to the government tax, leaving him with a lower net price than before the tax, as long as the demand curve is downward sloping. As a result producers have an incentive to reduce output of the taxed item and search for something more profitable to produce. We can say, therefore, that the tax in effect "drives a wedge" between the price paid by consumers and the price received by producers.

Because of the increase in price to consumers and the decrease in price realized by producers, it is sometimes said that consumers bear part of the burden of the tax according to how much the price they must pay increases, while producers bear a part of the burden according to how much the net price they receive declines.[5] In the particular example depicted by Figure 6–7, consumers bear a slightly greater share of the burden than producers. This outcome occurs because we have drawn the demand curve steeper (less elastic) than the supply curve. (You may want to illustrate what happens if the supply curve is drawn to be less elastic than the demand curve. Here you should find that the price rises less to consumers than it falls to producers.) Of course, the respective demand and supply elasticities depend on the particular item we happen to be dealing with and the time dimensions involved. Over the long run supply may become very elastic, resulting in most of the tax being borne by consumers. We will consider long-run supply more thoroughly at the end of this chapter and in the following chapter.

---

5 These taxes also are frequently analyzed according to their effect on the earnings of capital and labor. For example, because of the decline in the net price and quantity to producers, are the earnings of labor reduced more or less than the earnings of capital? Again the outcome will depend on the nature of the production process of the commodity in question.

Because of the reduction in the quantity demanded and supplied of a taxed item, the use of selective sales or excise taxes has the effect of distorting the output mix of goods and services produced in an economy. The quantities of nontaxed or less heavily taxed items increase, at the expense of those items taxed at higher rates. This outcome has been of some concern to economists because it causes a reduction in the value of output to society from a given amount of resources employed. An intuitive explanation for this outcome is that resources are pushed into lines of production whose products are valued less highly by society than the taxed item. We will have more to say about the effect of resource allocation on total value of output in the following chapter.

Sales and excise taxes also have been criticized for being "regressive" in nature, that is, for falling most heavily on low-income people. This would occur if low-income people spend a larger share of their income on the taxed items than their higher income counterparts do, over the long run. An attempt is made to mitigate this problem by taxing "nonessentials," such as alcoholic beverages, tobacco, and luxury items, at a relatively high rate and not taxing such "necessities" as food and clothing, or taxing them at a lower rate. This differential in tax rates also is a cause of the distortion in the output mix of goods and services mentioned above.

ILLEGAL GOODS OR SERVICES

Most societies enact laws that forbid the use of certain goods or services. Laws of this kind generally stem from the belief that consumption of the illegal items either harms the individual who consumes them or the people with whom he comes in contact. Examples of illegal goods and services in the United States at the present time include such things as mind-distorting drugs, pornographic literature, prostitution, and certain kinds of gambling. Unfortunately, passing a law against the use of a good or service does not eliminate the demand for it. Indeed, there would be no need for such a law in the first place if the demand for the good or service did not exist.

Just as for any other good or service, we can visualize both a supply and demand for the illegal item. We have no reason to believe that its demand curve will not slope downwards and to the

right, like any other market demand curve. There probably will
not be as many demanders in such a market, because most people
do not buy illegal items. Moreover, as the equilibrium price increases we would expect the number of people who buy in these
markets to decline, as well as the quantity demanded per person.

Regarding market supply of illegal goods, there is no reason to
believe that higher prices would not bring forth additional quantities. As long as there is a demand for the item, there will always
be entrepreneurs ready to supply it for a profit. And as prices increase, so do profits; this provides even more incentive for the illicit
suppliers to do their thing.

Although the market demand and supply of illegal goods and
services can be represented by the traditional downward-sloping
and upward-sloping lines, respectively, there is one important consideration with such goods and services that is not present for their
legal counterparts—the penalty for getting caught. We can think
of the penalty as a demand shifter if it applies only to the person
consuming the good or service. If the penalty only applies to the
supplier, it will primarily be a supply shifter. And if it applies to
both parties, we would expect the penalty to shift both demand
and supply.

In general, the imposition of a penalty or an increase in the harshness of the penalty will decrease (shift to the left) the demand, the
supply, or both. For example, imposing a "slap on the wrist" or a
suspended sentence will not decrease the demand for marijuana
nearly as much as a definite five-year prison term. Thus we can
expect that increasing the harshness of the penalty on buyers will
shift demand to the left, reducing market price and quantity exchanged, as illustrated in Figure 6–8(A).

On the other hand, if there is an increase in the penalty on suppliers, we can expect a decrease in supply. For example, many
"ladies of the evening" likely would find alternative ways of making
a living if the penalty for practicing the trade consisted of a $1,000
fine, compared to a $100 fine. The effect of a penalty on suppliers is
illustrated in Figure 6–8(B).

Although a penalty on either the demander or supplier will decrease the quantity of an illegal good or service, the price change
will depend on who is penalized. Goods or services where only the
supplier is penalized will tend to have a higher price than would

FIGURE 6–8
Effects of penalties in the market for illegal goods and services
(A) Penalty on the consumer

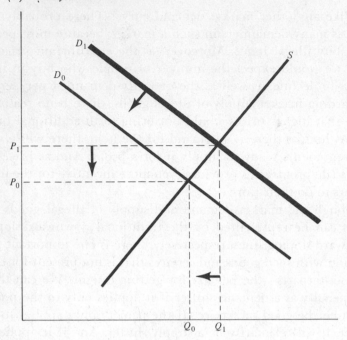

(B) Penalty on the supplier

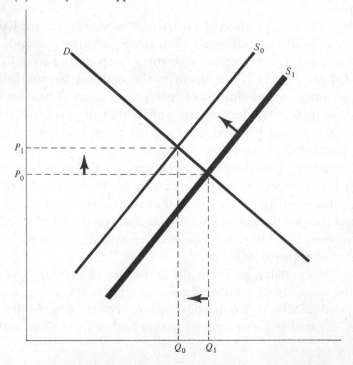

exist in a free market. Most illegal goods or services fit this description. Imposing a penalty on consumers will tend to lower the market price from what it would be in a free market, or from what it would be if only suppliers were penalized.

The rationing function of price

At the beginning of this book we stated that scarcity is the major reason for economics to exist. There is rarely enough of anything to bring everyone to a state of complete contentment. Thus there has to be a scheme for rationing the available output between all who want a piece of the action.

The most successful scheme for rationing output yet devised by man is price. No doubt the key to the success of price as a rationing device is that each individual imposes rationing upon himself rather than having his consumption restricted by a person or agency with power to dole out the available output. Each of us, being mortal, has a limited capacity to produce, and hence we must limit our intake of the goods and services produced in society. Since our income, measured in terms of either money or real output, is limited, we must spend it wisely, trying to get the most for what we have to exchange.

As you recall from the discussion on consumer choice in Chapter 2, each person maximizes his utility or satisfaction if he allocates his purchases so that the marginal utility per dollar is equalized among all the things he purchases. If a good or service becomes scarce, its price will rise. Since marginal utility per dollar is equal to marginal utility divided by price, a rise in price decreases marginal utility per dollar, which in turn provides an incentive to reduce its use and look for other things that will yield more marginal utility per dollar. No one has to tell us or order us to do so; we do it of our own accord. Moreover, there is no incentive for us to cheat by attempting to consume more. Even though we are free to consume a relatively large quantity of a scarce item, it is irrational to do so because it would just reduce our overall satisfaction.

Thus market price is an effective rationing device. It rations available output efficiently and automatically, and scarce resources do not have to be devoted to rationing the available output. This is a serious mistake made by some developing nations which have decided to use too many of their meager resources to ration what little they have. Letting market prices accomplish the rationing task, and freeing resources to produce goods and services, has proven to be a wiser policy. If governmental agencies do the rationing, it can also be very profitable for those obtaining the goods to spend a great deal of time and resources attempting to obtain a larger slice of the pie. Market price, being impersonal, does not respond to favor or bribe.

The fact that price rations the available output automatically and efficiently does not imply, however, that everyone is happy or satisfied with the prevailing price or resulting allocation. Indeed, it is likely that most sellers would like price to be higher and most buyers would like it to be lower. When there is extreme dissatisfaction with price, either by buyers or sellers, the government may step in and establish a ceiling or support price. It is important to remember, though, that establishing a ceiling price takes away the rationing function of price, generally leaving it in the hands of governmental agencies.

The allocating function of price

In addition to rationing the available output, market price also serves to allocate available resources to their most valuable use. For example, if buyers reduce their demand for a product, it has been established that there is a tendency for price to fall as demand shifts left and intersects supply at a lower level. The lower price serves as a signal for producers, telling them that consumers no longer desire as much of a certain product. Producers, seeing their profits decline as price falls, begin to search for other things to produce that consumers might desire more. This action on the part of producers does not have to be motivated by any love or empathy for consumers but rather by a desire to improve their own incomes and purchasing power.

Since market price serves to allocate resources between alternative goods and services, it might be expected that government policies which change market prices, such as ceiling or support prices on selected items, would also change the pattern of resource allocation in the economy. Consider a ceiling price. If price of a good or service is maintained at an artificially low level, producers have an incentive to look for more profitable items to produce, and there is a tendency for resources to leave these areas in search of more profitable opportunities elsewhere.

Unfortunately, this outcome is just the opposite of what we would like to see happen. If the price of an item is relatively high, it is an indication that the item is scarce relative to the demand of consumers. But the imposition of a ceiling price has the effect of driving some resources away from its production, making the item even more scarce than it was before the ceiling. An example of the effect of ceiling prices is provided by rent controls in New York City. Not only has a "shortage" been created for apartments, particularly in the main part of the city, but landlords have had little incentive to maintain their buildings, thus hastening the deterioration of living units in the inner city. Resources that otherwise would have gone to the repair and upkeep of these rent-controlled buildings have gone elsewhere in search of higher returns.

A parallel but opposite problem occurs when price is set artificially high, that is, when there is a support price. In this case the equilibrium price is low because the supply is large relative to the demand of consumers. The existence of a support price that is higher than the equilibrium serves to draw even more resources into the production of an already abundant good. Again the result is just opposite what we would like to see.

Sales and excise taxes also have an impact on the allocation of resources. By "driving a wedge" between the price that consumers pay and what producers receive, a sales or excise tax has the effect of reducing the profitability of producing the taxed item, and thus it has a tendency to drive some resources away from the production of the item to which it is applied. The higher price that consumers pay also tends to discourage its use.

Of course, market prices in general do not allocate resources to the production of public goods and services. Many such products, such as roads, police protection, and the military forces, do not even carry a market price. The allocation of resources to public goods, then, has to be done mainly "by hand." The objective of those in charge of this allocation should be to produce the amount and mix of public goods and services that maximizes the welfare of society, given the wishes of people for private goods and services. This is a very difficult job, not only because no one really knows what such an optimal allocation would look like, but also because it is likely to differ for different people. For example, the more politically conservative members of society tend to prefer a smaller proportion of all output to be public goods, or at least goods and services provided by government, than do their more liberal counterparts. The anticipated benefits from public goods in relation to the amount of taxes one has to pay also can be expected to influence a person's desire for such goods. Few people like to pay for public goods and services that do not appear to be a "good buy" in relation to the private goods and services available. Of course, people who receive public goods without having to pay substantial taxes for them are not as likely to call them a "bad buy."

As we saw earlier, market prices provide the signals that enable producers to decide upon the amount and mix of private goods and services produced in the economy. The signals guiding the action of public decision makers faced with the task of allocating resources to public goods and services are much more varied and complex in nature. Sometimes a "shortage" of such goods can be directly observed, as in the case of crowding in our national parks or congestion on our streets and highways. In other cases the representatives of citizen groups, such as the Sierra Club or Common Cause, may petition public decision makers to reorder their priorities. Professional lobbyists representing special-interest groups are also likely to influence the amount and mix of public goods produced. In recent times we have observed an increase in the use of demonstrations and riots to draw attention to the demands of various groups in society. Most people seem to prefer the use of signals somewhat less violent in nature, however.

In communistic economies, most of the resources employed in the production of both public and private goods are allocated by direct orders of the government. One drawback of allocating resources by political decree as opposed to price signals is that it often forces people to act against their own self-interests, which, to put it mildly, tends to dampen incentives. As an extreme example, you would not likely be very happy if a government official ordered you to quit college or your current job and take a job in the coal mines because of a shortage of fuel. Nor would you likely to be very happy if you were ordered to use coal rather than fuel oil or gas to heat your dwelling. On the other hand, if wages of coal miners rose substantially relative to other occupations, many people would voluntarily enter this occupation in order to increase their own incomes. Similarly, if the price of oil and gas increased relative to coal, there would be a tendency for people to voluntarily increase the use of coal, while conserving on oil and gas.

Time for adjustment

When dealing with prices and markets it is important to realize that change is seldom instantaneous. On the demand side of the market we know from experience that a change in price may not precipitate an immediate response. For example, if the price of our favorite toothpaste increases, it may take us a certain amount of time to even find out about it. The first time we buy another tube the price may seem a bit high, but not having considered another brand we go ahead and buy it. By the time we are ready for the next tube, however, we might well compare prices of the various brands; if our favorite brand is out of line with the others, we might try a lower priced alternative.

The same process can go on in the event of a price decline of a good or service. If we are not already buying it, the lower price will not likely come to our immediate attention. After we have had time to find out about the lower price and something about the good itself, we may give it a try. It is reasonable to believe, therefore, that the longer time consumers have to adjust to a price change, the more responsive they will be.

This idea can be represented by demand curves with differing slopes or elasticities. If only a short time is taken for adjustment to a price change, the demand curve will be relatively steep, or less elastic, than if a long period of time is considered. This is illustrated in Figure 6–9, where D_s represents a demand with only a short time to adjust, whereas D_l represents a demand where adjustment by consumers takes place over a longer period. If supply shifts from S_1 to S_0 (a decrease) and price increases, some consumers begin to decrease their purchases. Quantity sold then begins to decline, approaching Q_{s0} rather quickly. However, as more and more con-

FIGURE 6-9
Effect of time for adjustment on product demand

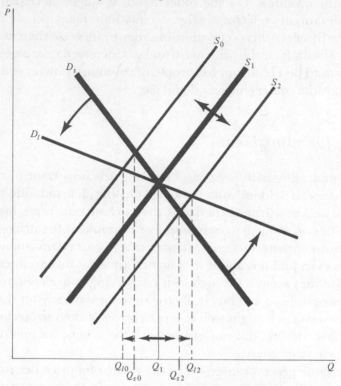

sumers adjust to this price increase, quantity decreases further, eventually reaching Q_{l0}.

The same figure can be used to represent a price decline that might take place following an increase in supply, as illustrated by supply shifting from S_1 to S_2. Here a few consumers increase their purchases soon after the price fall, so that quantity increases to Q_{s2}. Then, as more consumers adjust, quantity continues to increase, eventually approaching Q_{l2}.

It is interesting to note as well the pattern of price changes that take place. With a decrease in supply, price moves upward rather rapidly. Then, as consumers are able to adjust their purchases toward other products, price levels off and even decreases somewhat. With an increase in supply, price falls rather abruptly, but as consumers take note of this and adjust their purchases toward this product, price reaches a minimum and begins to ease upward slightly.

Time for adjustment is perhaps even more important for supply than demand. As noted above, there are two reasons why producers do not adjust immediately to a price change. First, from a technical standpoint, it generally is not physically possible to either acquire fixed inputs rapidly or, because of contractural commitments, to dispose of them quickly. Secondly, from an economic standpoint, changing the level of production to a sizable extent generally requires additional expense. To increase output, new facilities and equipment will have to be bought and additional personnel hired. Thus a producer wants to be sure that a price increase will stay in effect for a fairly long period of time before he undertakes this expense. Similarly, a producer who disposes of a machine or structure before it has been substantially depreciated may have to bear a substantial loss. Thus he may try to ride out a period of low prices, hoping for higher prices in the future.

Because of these factors the elasticity of supply allowing a long period of time to adjust is higher (more elastic) than is elasticity that allows little time to adjust. This is illustrated in Figure 6–10, where price is assumed to change because of shifts in demand. If demand declines, say to D_0, quantity produced will at first decline relatively little, to Q_{s0}. But if price remains low for a time, more adjustment will take place, reducing quantity supplied even more, to Q_{l0}. The same rationale applies to an increase in demand where quantity supplied increases first to Q_{s2} and later to Q_{l2}.

Notice also, as with demand, that the process of moving to a longer time for adjustment affects the price of the good or service. For example, there is a rather abrupt decline in price as demand decreases, but after producers adjust their production downward price eases back up slightly. The same phenomenon can be observed for an increase in demand, only here price rises rather abruptly and then eases back down a little, as producers adjust their production upward.

One very important point that should always be kept in mind when thinking about this process of adjustment either by producers or consumers is that not every producer or consumer need change the quantity produced or consumed when price changes. All

FIGURE 6–10
Effect of time for adjustment on product supply

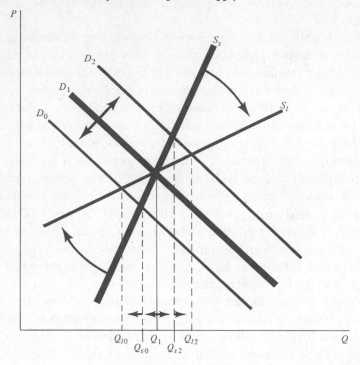

that is required to obtain a market response to a price change is that a few "marginal" people change the quantities they buy or sell. The fact that not everyone changes quantity demanded or supplied with a price change has led many to the erroneous conclusion that price has little effect in the market. Indeed, if everyone reacted to a price change, there would tend to be relatively large changes in quantities exchanged in markets in response to just minor changes in price.

Main points of Chapter 6

1. Equilibrium price and quantity in a market occur when the quantity demanded exactly equals the quantity supplied. This

corresponds to the point where the demand and supply curves intersect.

2. At any point in time there is no reason to expect that a market will be in equilibrium. But if it is not in equilibrium, forces exist which will push or pull price toward the equilibrium.

3. Equilibrium points in markets change because of shifts in demand and supply.

4. A change or shift in demand can be interpreted to mean that buyers change the amount they will buy at a given price or will buy a given amount at a changed price.

5. The major factors shifting demand include *(a)* change in prices of related products (substitutes and complements), *(b)* change in consumer incomes, *(c)* change in consumer expectations regarding future prices and income, *(d)* change in tastes and preferences, and *(e)* change in population.

6. A change or shift in supply can be interpreted to mean that sellers change the amount they will sell at a given price or will sell a given amount at a changed price.

7. The major factors shifting supply include *(a)* change in price of inputs, *(b)* change in price of other products that can be produced, *(c)* change in producer expectations of future prices, *(d)* changes in technology, and *(e)* change in number of firms.

8. A rising market price can be caused by an increase (shift) in demand, a decrease (shift) in supply, or some combination of the two. In the event of an increase in demand and a decrease in supply it is not possible to predict whether equilibrium quantity will increase, decrease, or remain unchanged without knowing the extent of the two shifts.

9. A declining market price can be the result of a decrease in demand, an increase in supply, or some combination of the two.

10. Ceiling prices create a shortage in the market which makes it necessary for the government to impose some kind of rationing scheme. Black-market activities also result from ceiling prices and rationing.

11. Support prices create surpluses in a market, making it necessary for the government to buy up the surplus and keep it off the market in order to hold price up.

12. Sales and excise taxes on products tend to increase the price paid by the consumer and decrease the price received by the producer.

13. Penalties on buyers of illegal goods or services tend to decrease the demand for these items and lower their price. Penalties on sellers tend to decrease supply and increase market price.

14. Price is a relatively efficient rationing device. Individual consumers voluntarily reduce their purchases of a scarce item as its price rises in order to maximize their utility for a given budget.

15. Price also allocates resources to the goods or services most desired by consumers, since a rising price tends to increase profits for producers and thus provides them with an incentive to produce more of the most wanted items. By the same token a decrease in the desirability of a good or service leads to a fall in its price, which tends to lower profits of producers and provides them with an incentive to produce things more appealing to buyers.

16. The process of adjusting to a price change is not instantaneous. Both buyers and sellers require time to adjust their purchases or production after a price change. Thus demand and supply curves that allow for adequate time to adjust are more elastic than those which do not allow sufficient adjustment time.

17. Only a relatively small proportion of buyers or sellers need respond to a price change to obtain a change in the quantity bought and sold in a market.

Questions for thought and discussion

1. Explain the process of adjustment that takes place if the actual price in a market is higher than the equilibrium price. Explain what happens if actual price is lower than equilibrium price.

2. What is the economic meaning of an increase in demand? Similarly, what is the meaning of a decrease in demand? Illustrate each with a diagram.

3. What is the economic meaning of an increase in supply? Similarly, what is the meaning of a decrease in supply? Illustrate each with a diagram.

4. What is the difference between price elasticity of demand and income elasticity of demand? Using a diagram, illustrate what each measures.

5. Suppose in some future year the world's supply of petroleum slowly becomes exhausted so that gasoline prices rise to $1 per gallon. Speculate on the changes that would take place in our means of transportation.

6. Is it possible for the equilibrium price of a good or service to change without observing a change in the equilibrium quantity exchanged in the market? (Assume that neither the demand curve nor the supply curve is perfectly inelastic.) Explain.

7. Is it possible for the equilibrium quantity of a good or service exchanged in a market to change without observing a change in the equilibrium market price? (Assume that neither the demand curve nor the supply curve is perfectly elastic.)

8. The market for many commodities is seasonal in nature. Christmas cards and fresh strawberries are two examples. Christmas cards increase in sales during the holiday season and fresh strawberries are sold mainly during the summer months. However, the price movements of these two products are quite different. Christmas cards increase in price during their peak season, whereas strawberries decrease in price during theirs. Using demand-supply diagrams, explain why we observe this different price behavior between these two items.

9. Do you believe the demand for mind-distorting drugs is elastic or inelastic? In view of your answer, should the drug-pushing industry favor tighter or looser controls over drug traffic? Explain.

10. The price of Volkswagens has increased substantially in the United States over the past 10 to 15 years. However, the number of Volkswagens sold also has increased. Do these facts indicate that the demand curve for Volkswagens is an upward-sloping line, that is, the higher the price, the larger the quantity demanded? Explain.

11. Suppose, because of a decrease in the supply of gasoline coupled with an increase in demand, that the equilibrium price of gasoline increased to about 60 cents per gallon. What would happen if the government placed a ceiling price on

gasoline of 36 cents per gallon? Would you prefer an uncontrolled high price or the problems brought on by a ceiling price? Why?

12. In the United States it has been the policy of the government to place support prices on some agricultural products in order to raise farm incomes. Using supply and demand analysis, what would you expect the effects of the policy to be on the quantity of these farm products demanded and supplied? What must the government do to maintain support prices? Does this policy help large farmers or small farmers the most?

13. It is common to observe the prices of products that are close substitutes fluctuating together in the short run. For example, when the price of beef increases, so does the price of pork and chickens. From what you know about demand and supply, is this behavior of prices to be expected? Explain.

14. Water, one of the basic necessities of life, is in most places very cheap, if not free. Diamonds, on the other hand, a very nonessential item in our lives, are very expensive. Can you explain this rather perverse behavior of price?

15. A sales or excise tax will not affect producers because it is paid by consumers. True or false? Explain.

16. In the event of an increase in demand, the price that would prevail in the long run would be less than the equilibrium price established immediately after the demand shift. True or false? Explain.

17. In the event of an increase in supply, the price that would prevail in the long run would be greater than the equilibrium price established immediately after the supply shift. True or false? Explain.

7

Perfect competition in the product market

Having established the general characteristics of market demand and supply and their interaction in the product market, in this and the next chapter we will consider the individual firms producing and selling goods and services. A great deal of diversity is characteristic of firms doing business in the economy. Some are small, one-person enterprises such as family farms or retail shops. Others are giant corporations employing thousands of people and selling their products throughout the world. To create some order out of this diversity, we will study the characteristics and behavior of different types of firms, beginning in this chapter, with the type of market situation that economists have labeled perfect competition. Agricultural production probably provides the closest example of perfect competition today. Imperfect competition will be the topic of the following chapter.

The perfectly competitive firm: A price taker

A perfectly competitive firm can be defined as one which has no power to alter the price it receives for its product. For this reason, the perfectly competitive firm is sometimes called a "price taker." The firm takes the price of its product as determined in the market. There are two basic reasons why any firm must charge the price determined by the market: (1) it sells a product that is undifferentiated from the product of all the other firms in the market, or (2) it sells a very small proportion of the total market.

The fact that a perfectly competitive firm sells a product indistinguishable from that produced by the other firms in its market means that buyers have no preference for the product of one firm over any other. Thus every firm must sell its product at the price all the other firms are obtaining. Why should buyers pay $2.25 per bushel for wheat from farmer Jones if 10,000 other farmers are selling exactly the same product for $2.00 per bushel? In other words, each producer must conform to the market price.

We know also that because of the downward-sloping nature of market demand curves, market price can only be changed if the quantity sold is changed; quantity must decrease to obtain a higher price, or any increase in quantity demanded must be accompanied by a reduction in price. But because the perfectly competitive firm sells just a minute fraction of the market, each firm cannot alter market price by producing more or less. For example, suppose farmer Jones decides that the market price of wheat is too low. What can he do about it? If he reduces his production by one half (a drastic measure for any firm), the total market supply would remain virtually unchanged, because taking a few hundred bushels or even a few thousand bushels from a market where millions of bushels are traded would have an imperceptible effect; it would be something like taking a handful of sand away from a beach. Thus no matter what quantity the firm decides to produce, within reason, the market price remains the same.

Thus, the characteristic of an undifferentiated product requires each perfectly competitive firm to sell at the same price as all other firms, that is, the market price, and the characteristic of producing just a small fraction of the market means that each perfectly competitive firm has no power to alter market price.

Demand facing a perfectly competitive seller

We can obtain a better understanding of the relationship between a perfectly competitive firm and the market in which it sells by means of diagrams. The traditional market demand and supply curves are depicted in Figure 7–1(A). These are the curves devel-

FIGURE 7–1
Relationship between the market and the perfectly competitive firm
(A) The market   *(B) The individual firm*

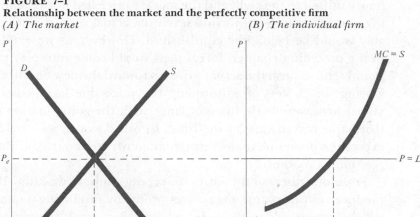

oped in Chapters 1 through 6. The equilibrium price and quantity that will prevail in this market are denoted by P_e and Q_e. The price that each firm will face, therefore, is P_e, if the market is allowed to reach an equilibrium.

The individual perfectly competitive firm operating in this market is represented by Figure 7–1(B). Its supply curve, as we know, is simply the marginal cost (MC) curve above the point where it intersects the average variable cost curve if it is already committed to its fixed costs. The price that the firm can expect to receive for its product is P_e, as determined by market supply and demand. This price, P_e, can be thought of as the demand facing this firm. The price line, P_e in this example, is a demand curve in the sense that it tells the firm what price it will receive for its product. The fact that the demand curve is a perfectly horizontal line (perfectly elastic) means that the firm can produce and sell any output within reason at this price. In other words, the market stands ready to buy any reasonable quantity from this firm at price P_e. Thus the line showing the price is in reality the demand curve facing this firm.

We should bear in mind, of course, that in an actual market situation, the market price that prevails at any point in time need not be the equilibrium price. For example, if market demand had recently shifted to the right and the market price had not yet adjusted to the new higher equilibrium level, the actual market price probably would be below the equilibrium. However, as we explained in the preceding chapter, forces then would come into play which would tend to push the actual price up toward the new equilibrium. During the process of adjustment, the price line facing the individual firm would rise in accordance with the going market price that happened to exist at the time. In other words, we would not expect the price line to shift instantaneously from one equilibrium position to another.

From our discussion relating to product supply we know that a producer of this nature maximizes profits by producing a quantity which corresponds to the point where price equals marginal cost. This quantity is represented by Q_f in Figure 7–1 (B). Notice, of course, that the units of measure on the quantity axis differ greatly between the market and the firm. The market quantity might be measured in terms of millions of units, whereas the firm's quantity might be measured just in number of units. The units of measure on the price axes are, of course, the same for the market and the firm.

We might pause at this point to summarize the different kinds of demand curves we have studied. There are three. The first is the demand of an individual consumer, represented by a downward-sloping line indicating that quantity increases as price decreases, and vice versa. The second demand curve is market demand—the sum of all the individual demanders in the market. This is also represented by a downward-sloping line, as in Figure 7–1 (A). The third is the demand curve facing an individual seller. For the perfectly competitive seller this demand curve is a perfectly horizontal line, indicating that the market will take any reasonable quantity he wishes to produce at the market price.

Price, costs, and profits

The perfectly competitive firm takes the price as determined in the market and decides whether or not it should produce, and if so, how much. Recall from the discussion on product supply in Chapter 5 that pure profits are earned only if price is greater than average total cost at the quantity the firm chooses to produce. We also know that the profit-maximizing quantity will correspond to the point where marginal cost equals price.

The three diagrams in Figure 7–2 illustrate the three possible profit positions for perfectly competitive firms. The price, P_e, that is shown is determined, of course, by market demand and supply, as illustrated in Figure 7–1(A). A firm that is earning pure profits in its business is illustrated in Figure 7–2(A). The resources (in-

FIGURE 7–2
Possible profit or loss positions of perfectly competitive firms
(A) Pure profits earned   *(B) Zero pure profits*   *(C) Loss incurred*

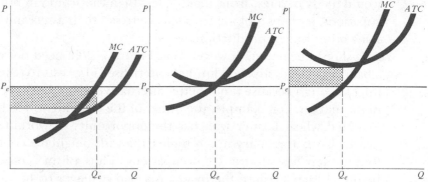

puts) used in this production activity are earning more than they could in other kinds of work. The total pure profits for the firm are represented by the shaded area. Notice that total profits are maximized at a level of output beyond the point where profit per unit is the largest, that is, the point where the distance between price and average total cost (ATC) is the greatest. Such an outcome is reasonable because the firm is interested in maximizing total profits rather than profit per unit.

The situation depicted in Figure 7–2(B), zero pure profits, is one in which the resources employed by this firm are just earning what they could earn in some other alternative occupation. This situation is the only one of the three shown where the firm will produce a quantity corresponding to the minimum point on its ATC curve. The case of a firm that is not covering its costs (implicit plus explicit) is shown in Figure 7–2(C). In this example the resources employed by the firm are not earning what they could in other occupations. This does not necessarily mean, however, that this firm's cash expenses are greater than its total sales because, as noted in Chapter 5, the ATC curve includes a charge for the resources owned by the firm, as well as its cash expenses.

If we were able to measure perfectly the costs of individual firms at any point in time, we would likely observe all three of the above situations existing in a given market or industry. There would be a few well-managed, low-cost firms making pure profits, as illustrated in Figure 7–2 (A). There would be other firms just "breaking even" but doing as well as they could in any other occupation. And there would likely be a few firms making less than they could in other occupations, perhaps looking for a chance to sell their assets and begin some other line of production.

It should be noted, however, that Figure 7–2(C) need not depict a badly managed, slipshod kind of enterprise. The costs for this firm might be high because it has better alternatives than the other firms in the market. For example, the owner of the firm might be a highly educated wheat farmer who has the opportunity of working in a nearby bank at a salary much higher than his neighbors could obtain in their best alternative occupations. Thus a firm's cost might be high either because the owner is a bad manager or because he has superior talents that are in high demand elsewhere. It is not valid to conclude, therefore, that an industry in which firms are decreasing is losing its least productive people. It may well be losing some of these, but at the same time it can be losing its most productive people because they have superior opportunities elsewhere.

Long-run adjustment

Economists have given rather precise definitions to the terms "short run" and "long run" as they apply to production and supply. The short run is defined as the length of time that is too short to change the level of fixed inputs employed or the number of firms in the industry but long enough to change the level of output by means of changing variable inputs. Essentially, the marginal physical product curve, and its mirror image, marginal cost, reflect short-run changes in production.

The long run is defined as a period of time long enough to

change either the level of fixed inputs employed by firms or the number of firms. Unfortunately it is not possible to designate a period of time that constitutes the long run for all different types of firms, or even for different situations. The length of this period differs between types of firms, depending on how difficult or costly it is to change fixed inputs. If production requires extensive fixed inputs, say extensive irrigation or drainage facilities, the length of time to reach a long-run adjustment will be much longer than will be the case for firms carrying on production in small rented facilities, say barber shops.

The length of time to reach a long-run adjustment will depend also on how profitable it is to adjust. If it is very profitable for a firm to expand its fixed inputs or for new firms to enter, the adjustment time will generally be shorter than if it just barely pays to change the level of output or to enter or leave the industry. For example, if it is very profitable to expand facilities, a contractor will in most cases be willing to step up the completion date if he is paid to do so. A higher fee will enable him to pay his employees for overtime work in order to finish the job more quickly.

In looking at this process of long-run adjustment for a perfectly competitive industry in somewhat more detail, we will start where the market is in equilibrium, that is, where price corresponds to the intersection of supply and demand, as shown in Figure 7–3(A). Suppose that the typical firm in the industry is making substantial pure profits, as shown in Figure 7–3(B). Assume as well that each firm is maximizing its profits by producing an output that corresponds to the point where price is equal to marginal cost, Q_f in Figure 7–3 (B). These two conditions—market price is at the point where quantity demanded equals quantity supplied and price equals marginal cost for each firm—constitute a short-run equilibrium for an industry. This situation is illustrated in the two diagrams in Figure 7–3.

If each firm is making pure profits, however, it is reasonable to expect that existing firms will expand their facilities (increase their fixed inputs) and/or additional firms will enter this industry to "get a piece of the action." We need not assume that all firms are making substantial pure profits for this to happen. In fact, some might be characterized by Figures 7–2(B) and (C). All that is necessary is that a sizable portion of existing firms is making pure profits.

Recall from the discussion on product supply that an increase in

FIGURE 7-3
Short-run market equilibrium with pure profits made by the average firm
(A) The market   *(B) The firm*

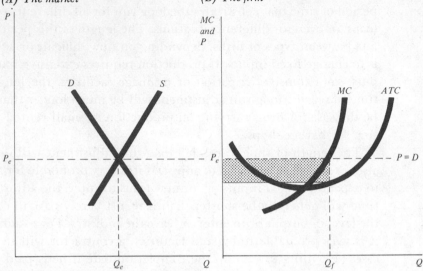

the number of firms or an increase in the size of firms has the effect of shifting the market supply curve to the right, as shown in Figure 7-4 (A). The effect of an increase in supply, of course, is a reduction in market price. As market price falls, so does the price that faces each firm. Thus as supply shifts right and market price falls, the pure profits that each firm is making are competed away. This process is illustrated in Figure 7-4(A) and (B).

This process of new resources coming into an industry to compete away pure profits probably will be most noticeable at levels of pure profits that are relatively high. Then, as price falls closer and closer to the zero profit point (P_0 in Figure 7-4), it is to be expected that entry of additional resources will slow down as the prospects for pure profits diminish, although it is not uncommon to observe situations where firms have built up optimism over a period of time and continue to expand until price falls below the zero pure-profit point. As soon as this happens, of course, some firms find more profitable opportunities elsewhere, move out of this industry, and contribute to a decrease in supply, which eventually pulls price back up toward the zero pure-profit equilibrium.

FIGURE 7–4
Long-run adjustment to pure profits by entry of additional resources or firms
(A) The market   *(B) The firm*

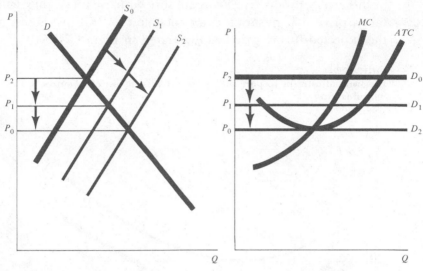

A similar but opposite process of adjustment would take place if a large share of the firms in a market or industry is suffering losses or negative pure profits. Here we would see firms moving out to more profitable opportunities, decreasing market supply, and raising market price. (You may want to illustrate this process with diagrams of your own similar to Figure 7–4(A) and (B)).

Thus the existence of pure profits or losses results in a long-run adjustment characterized by the corresponding entry or exit of resources or firms. It is also possible to observe adjustments on the cost side. In the production of tomatoes, for example, there may be a few firms that enjoy some special advantage, such as very productive soil. The entry of new firms might push price down to the zero profit position for just about every firm in the industry except these privileged few. They might continue to reap pure profits. Eventually these unusually profitable firms will be sold to new owners, and it is reasonable to expect that the price paid for these firms would reflect the pure profits that can be expected in the future; the new owners would be willing to pay more for productive land than for poor land. With an increase in the land price there will be an

increase in the cost of production, mainly because of the increase
in the interest charge (explicit or implicit) and taxes. If the sellers
of these very productive firms are shrewd bargainers, they will obtain a price that pushes average total cost (ATC) just about up to
the expected future price, as illustrated in Figure 7–5.

FIGURE 7–5
**Long-run adjustment to pure profits by increases in cost of resources to the
individual firm**

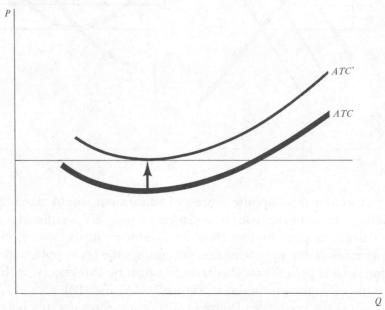

This phenomenon of cost adjusting to price has been particularly
important in U.S. agriculture. As we pointed out in Chapter 6, the
government has attempted to increase incomes by establishing support prices of various products. In this situation price is fixed, but
over the years pure profits have been eroded away because of the
bidding up of land prices. Eventually producers are forced back to
the same zero pure-profit position that existed before the support
prices came into being. Of course, the people who owned the land
during its price rise enjoyed a capital gain. One should also bear in
mind that for this phenomenon to occur a necessary condition is
that product price be maintained at the artificially high level, as is
done by price supports. Without the price support, competitive

forces would tend to drive product price down to the zero pure-profit level, as illustrated by Figure 7–4.

Again we should caution that adjustment is not likely to be instantaneous. Pure profits or losses are likely to exist for different firms at any point in time. But if pure profits or losses exist, we can expect to observe an adjustment to a long-run profit position in a perfectly competitive industry.

The continual search for lower costs

Even though all firms in a perfectly competitive industry face a common market price, there are likely to be substantial differences in *costs* among firms. High costs may be due to low productivity resulting from inept management, or they may be high implicit costs stemming from high-paying opportunities in other lines of work. It has been established that a perfectly competitive firm has no control over the price of its product. It is also true that such a firm cannot alter the opportunities that exist elsewhere. In fact, high implicit costs stemming from superior opportunities elsewhere would be welcomed, because they represent opportunities to increase income.

However, most perfectly competitive firms can do something about the efficiency of their production processes. The more efficient a firm is in transforming inputs into output, the lower will be its production costs and the higher will be its profits. Thus most firms, at least those managed by alert people, are continually searching for new cost-reducing inputs or techniques in order to increase profits. The effect of achieving a cost reduction in production is illustrated by Figure 7–6. Average total costs (ATC) are shifted downward, and marginal cost (MC) is shifted downward and to the right. If price is at P_0, then the firm can move from a zero pure-profit postion to a position of positive pure profits after the cost reduction.

In addition to creating pure profits for the firm in this example, a second very important effect of a cost reduction is the shift downward and to the right of the MC curve. Essentially this tells us that the firms now can produce an additional or marginal unit more cheaply than before. But we must also keep in mind that the MC curve is also the supply curve of the firm. At the original MC, Q_0

FIGURE 7–6
Effects of a cost reduction

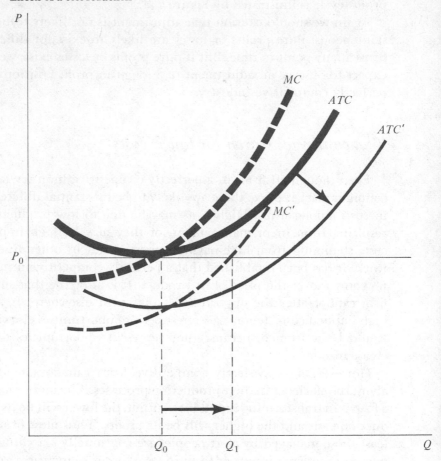

is produced by this firm, whereas at the new, lower MC', Q_1 is produced. Of course, if just one firm finds a way to reduce costs and shift its supply curve, there will be no perceptible effect in the market. Increasing production of wheat by 100 bushels, for example, will not be noticed in a market where millions of bushels are traded.

Although the increased production by a single firm has no appreciable effect on the market, similar action by many such firms will have the effect of shifting the market supply curve to the right, which has the effect of reducing market price. Furthermore, the lowering of market price has the effect of squeezing the newly created pure profits out of the firms that have achieved lower costs.

Once a significant proportion of firms adopts a new cost-reducing input or technique and market price begins to fall, the firms that have not reduced their costs find their profit positions eroding, and consequently they have no choice but to also adopt these inputs or techniques so they will not suffer losses or, eventually, be forced to leave the industry. This process of the early adopters reaping pure profits and the subsequent erosion of these profits to these firms (and losses to the remaining firms) is somewhat like being on a treadmill; each firm must run faster and faster (decrease costs more and more) just to stay even. Although each firm may not appreciate this continuous struggle, consumers and society in general gain from it, because more output is obtained from our scarce resources.

The planning curve

There comes a time in the life of every firm when it must make decisions affecting its long-run future. This might come when it first starts in business or at any point it decides to change the level of its fixed inputs, such as land, buildings, or equipment. A perfectly competitive firm, which by itself cannot affect market price, might reasonably be expected to be interested in finding the level of fixed inputs that will minimize its average total costs, because only by achieving a size that will minimize per-unit cost can it hope to compete in the long run with other firms which are also searching for the most efficient size.

Ideally a firm would like to utilize experts, such as engineers, architects, cost accountants, and economists, to estimate the potential average total costs (ATC) for various levels of output at various levels of fixed inputs. In other words, it would like to know the short-run ATC curves for various sizes of plants or facilities. One possible configuration of short-run ATC curves is represented by Figure 7–7.

In this example the level of ATC is relatively high at relatively small levels of fixed inputs and output, as illustrated by ATC_1. As the size of fixed inputs is increased, the ATC curves shift down and to the right, reaching a minimum at ATC_3. Further increases

FIGURE 7–7
Planning cure or long-run average total cost curve

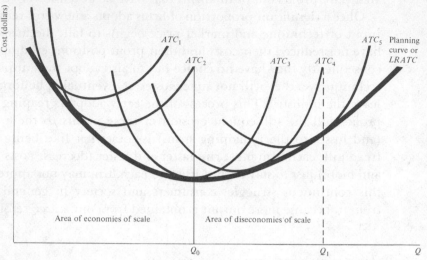

in size of fixed inputs still shift the short-run ATC's to the right, but at the same time they shift them upward, indicating that per-unit costs increase for larger firms.

Although only five alternative sizes are illustrated in Figure 7–7, many more could be estimated and drawn in. The individual firm may not wish to consider an excessive number of alternatives, however, because of the cost of estimating the various ATC's. At any rate, it would be possible with only the number of ATC's shown in Figure 7–7 to estimate what economists call a planning curve or long-run average total cost (LRATC) curve. Such a curve is constructed by tracing out an "envelope" of all the short-run ATC's.

Essentially, the planning curve, or the LRATC, shows the lowest possible cost of obtaining a given output. For example, at output Q_1 the level of fixed inputs represented by ATC_5 would be most efficient. Producing Q_1 by a smaller plant, ATC_4, for example, would result in higher unit costs. The planning curve also shows the level of fixed inputs that would result in the overall lowest possible ATC—represented here by ATC_3. Thus a firm that wanted to minimize ATC in the future would utilize this level of fixed inputs and produce output Q_0. Producing Q_0 by any other level of fixed inputs, say ATC_2 or ATC_4, would result in higher unit costs.

In reality, of course, a firm, especially a small firm, may not wish to incur the expense of estimating in detail many possible short-run ATC's. Instead the firm may simply try to estimate the lowest possible point on a few possible ATC's and, in so doing, attempt to obtain a rough idea of what its planning curve or LRATC might look like. At least, rough information of this kind is helpful in deciding on the size that comes close to minimizing ATC over the long run.

Economies and diseconomies of scale

The planning curve or LRATC brings out a concept long used by economists—economies and diseconomies of scale. As the name implies, the concept of economies of scale means that average total cost declines as the size or scale of the firm increases, as illustrated by the decreasing portion of the planning curve. Perhaps the greatest source of economies of scale is the more efficient utilization of fixed inputs in large compared to small firms. For example, equipment depreciation charge per bushel is likely to be higher on a 100-acre wheat farm than on a 1,000-acre farm. The implicit cost of the farmer's own labor would also have to be covered by fewer bushels on the small farm, unless he is able to obtain a part-time job or produce something else along with the wheat.

Diseconomies of scale implies the opposite, of course, namely that unit costs increase at larger firm sizes, as illustrated by the increasing portion of the planning curve. Management problems appear to be the major factor causing diseconomies of scale. As a firm increases in size, the task of management becomes more and more complex. Managing a firm is something like staging a puppet show. The larger the firm, the greater the number of puppets that must be manipulated at the same time. Men like Henry Ford have a genius for this sort of thing, but others of more normal fabric are not capable of staging such grand productions.

Because people differ a great deal in management ability, it is reasonable to expect that diseconomies of scale set in sooner for some firms than for others. This probably explains why some firms grow larger and larger, continuing to prosper, while others stay about the same size for the life of the owner or manager. Indeed, a relatively poor manager might go bankrupt at the level of production that minimizes costs for a good manager. Thus it is important for the owner or manager to assess his management skills in estimating his firm's LRATC curve.

Although a U-shaped LRATC curve is plausible, economists attempting to obtain an empirical measure of economies and diseconomies of scale rarely find evidence of the upward-sloping portion of the curve, that is, the diseconomies of scale. A more frequent finding is a curve which may reflect some scale economies at small firm sizes but fairly constant costs for a large share of the observed firms. In other words, the observed shape of the LRATC curve is more likely to reflect the shape of a ski-jump, with a long flat portion rather than the traditional U.

One possible explanation for the relative rarity of an upward-sloping portion of the LRATC curve is that firms that find their LRATC increasing as they expand, or those that anticipate costs will increase, may decide to stop growing before they incur significant diseconomies of scale. Or a firm that mistakenly grows to a size that results in high costs may simply cut back in output in order to compete with firms operating in the relatively flat portion of their LRATC curve. A third possibility, of course, is that large high-cost firms are forced out of business and therefore are not observable.

We might expect the relatively small firms operating on the downward-sloping portion of their LRATC to attempt to expand in order to realize the lower unit costs obtainable at larger sizes. In fact, a relatively simple way to detect whether the firms in an industry are able to capture scale economies is to observe changes in their average size over time. If the average size of firm is increasing, we can conclude that large firms are more efficient than small firms in the industry, that is, scale economies exist.[1]

Production costs: The firm versus the industry

Although the preceding discussion of economies and diseconomies of scale focused on the individual firm, it should be kept in

---

[1] This simple test, often called the "survival technique" is presented by George Stigler, in *The Theory of Price,* 3d ed. (New York: Macmillan Co., 1966), pp. 158–60.

mind that a firm's production costs can be affected by what the other firms in the industry do. One way that this can happen is through the price of resources. If just one or a few perfectly competitive firms expand or contract, there is not likely to be any change in the price of resources because they most likely employ a very small part of the industry total. A change in output by all firms in the industry or a substantial change in the number of firms, however, might well change the price of the resources employed in this industry. A substantial contraction by the industry, for example, releases resources that must find alternative employment. To do this they might be required to accept lower prices. On the other hand, if there is interest in attracting a substantial quantity of additional resources, their price might be bid up in order to draw them away from other industries.

From the discussion of product supply, we know that an increase in the price of resources shifts the cost curves for the individual firm upward and to the left. Thus, in the case of industry expansion, two off-setting forces are operating: the increase in size or number of firms shifts product supply to the right, but an increase in resource prices has the opposite effect, so that the net shift is smaller than without the resource price rise.

In addition to resource price increases, expansion by the entire industry can affect the individual firm's cost curves through what economists call "technical or nonpecuniary" diseconomies. The most common example of these is waste disposal. If the industry is small and its firms are scattered, disposing of waste tends to be less costly than if the industry is large and highly concentrated. For example, one or a few small firms may pipe their wastes into a stream or body of water without causing public alarm. But with growth of the industry, each firm may have to construct costly waste disposal facilities, which has the effect of increasing the cost curves of all the individual firms.

Economists refer to industries that experience a rise in costs, either through resource price increases or through technical diseconomies, as increasing-cost industries. As this kind of industry expands, the minimum point on each firm's LRATC curve increases so that the zero pure-profit price rises higher and higher. Thus, as the industry grows larger, the long-run equilibrium price for the industry increases. This situation is illustrated in Figure 7–8

FIGURE 7–8
Long-run average total cost curves for a typical firm in industries in which costs are increasing, constant, and decreasing
(A) Increasing costs

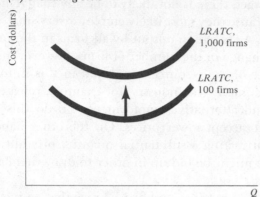

(B) Constant costs

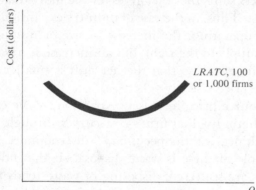

(C) Decreasing costs

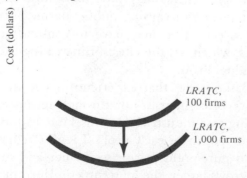

(A), in which it is assumed that the industry expands by adding additional firms.

Although increasing costs can reasonably be expected in many industries, it is not impossible to visualize one that can expand its output without incurring increasing costs. This could happen if the resources employed by the industry make up a small proportion of the total employment of these resources. Tomato production might be a possible example because this industry employs only a small proportion of the total land, labor, and other resources that can be used to produce tomatoes. Also, no technical diseconomies can be present. Economists refer to such an industry as a constant-cost industry because each firm's cost curves and the long-run equilibrium price do not change as the industry expands to large levels of output, as in Figure 7–8 (B).

There is a third possibility, a decreasing-cost industry, in which costs decline as the industry grows. This is less common than the first two cases but still possible. Decreasing costs can occur if the price of the industry's resources decline as the industry grows. This phenomenon would be most likely to occur in new or developing areas. If only a few firms are present, many of the resources it employs will have to be shipped in from distant places or produced locally on a small scale at high costs. If the industry is small and insignificant, there will likely be no public effort to establish institutions to serve it or to train people to work in it should special skills be required. On the other hand, an industry that becomes a significant part of an area's or a nation's economy can expect to enjoy some special advantages. Supporting industries which can supply resources at a minimum cost will emerge, financial institutions will consider it a better risk and will loan money at a lower rate of interest, and public schools might offer special training to young people who want to find employment in the industry. Economists refer to these circumstances as "external economies." The coming of additional firms lowers costs for all firms. It is not totally unexpected, therefore, that industries tend to concentrate in specific areas rather than spreading out excessively. Decreasing costs are illustrated in Figure 7–8(C).

Bear in mind, however, that an industry might exhibit all three situations at different stages of its development. When an industry is young and becoming established, it might enjoy decreasing costs.

Then for a time, when it is moderate in size, it might expand with constant costs. Finally, as it becomes a major industry using a significant proportion of the resources it employs, it may run into increasing costs.

Long-run supply

We know that in a long-run equilibrium, price will tend to adjust to the minimum point of the typical firm's LRATC curve. If each firm's LRATC curve shifts upward as the industry expands or increases output, as illustrated by Figure 7–8(A), then of course this minimum point also will rise. In this situation an increase in output will be forthcoming only with an increase in price. In other words, the long-run supply curve for the industry in this case would slope upward, as illustrated in Figure 7–9(A).

FIGURE 7–9
Long-run supply curves for increasing-cost, constant-cost, and decreasing-cost industries

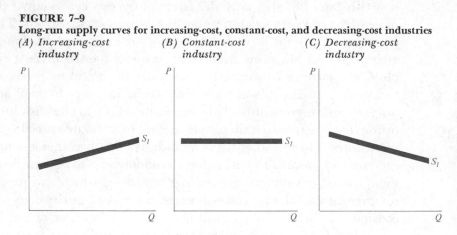

(A) Increasing-cost industry   *(B) Constant-cost industry*   *(C) Decreasing-cost industry*

In the case of a constant-cost industry, output can expand without any change in the level of the firms' LRATC curves. Hence a larger output will be forthcoming at the same price as that for a smaller output. The long-run supply curve in this case will be perfectly elastic, as shown in Figure 7–9(B). The third case, where the minimum-cost point declines as the industry expands, would result in a downward-sloping industry long-run supply curve, as in Figure 7–9(C).

Maximizing value of output

One of the characteristics of perfect competition is that each producer, at least those who attempt to maximize profits, will produce a quantity that corresponds to the point of intersection of the price line and the marginal cost curve (see Figure 7–3(B)). For a perfectly competitive industry, the price of the product will tend to equal its marginal cost. This is a fairly important characteristic because it results in a maximum value of output to society for a given amount of resources. To see why, it is first necessary to understand what price and marginal cost represent.

We can think of the price of a product as the value that society assigns to a marginal unit. For example, if the price of tomatoes is $2 per bushel, we can infer that society values an extra bushel of tomatoes at $2, or it would not choose to buy it for this price.

Marginal cost (MC), on the other hand, represents the cost to society in terms of other products given up for obtaining an extra unit of this product. For example, if the MC of tomatoes is $2, then in order to produce an extra bushel of tomatoes, $2 worth of some other good or service must be given up, assuming that these other things are produced in an industry where price and MC also are equal.

It is perhaps easiest to understand why the equity of price and MC results in a maximum value of output if we first look at situations where price does not equal marginal cost. Suppose that, for some reason, the price of a bushel of tomatoes is $3 and its MC is $2. This means that society values an extra bushel of tomatoes at $3 and values the goods or services given up to produce this extra bushel at $2. Now if one extra bushel of tomatoes is produced, society gains $3 and gives up $2, leaving a net gain of $1. Thus it behooves society to increase the production of tomatoes under these circumstances, because the value of total output is increased using the same amount of resources. In other words, there is a underallocation of resources to the production of a good or service if its price is greater than its MC.

Taking the opposite situation, say price is $1 and MC is $2, we can see that by decreasing the production of tomatoes by one bushel, society gives up $1 worth of tomatoes but gains $2 worth of other goods and services, resulting in a net gain of $1. Thus if price is less than MC, there is an overallocation of resources to the production of this product because by reducing its production, total value of output is increased with a given amount of resources. Now it is possible to see that value of output is maximized only if price equals marginal cost because only when this is the case is it impossible to reallocate resources to increase total value of output. As you recall, perfectly competitive firms attempt to produce at the point where price equals MC. Thus an advantageous characteristic of perfect competition, at least from society's point of view, is that each producer attempting to maximize his own profits by equating price and marginal cost also maximizes the value of output to society.

It should not be concluded from this discussion, however, that perfect competition is the ultimate goal to be striven for in all industries. We will see in the following chapter that the nature of most products precludes perfect competition in their production. However, the further removed an industry becomes from the perfectly competitive model, the greater the chance that society will suffer a significant reduction in the value of output for a given amount of resources.

We ought to mention at this point that the idea of competitive forces working for the good of society was first introduced by 18th-century Scottish economist and philosopher, Adam Smith, in *The Wealth of Nations.* He called this phenomenon the "invisible hand." Each producer attempting to maximize his own profits also maximizes the value of output to society, as though guided by some "invisible hand."

Economics of pollution and other social costs

Society has become very concerned of late with the problem of pollution. When population was smaller and more dispersed and industrial output was considerably smaller, much of our waste material was disposed of by dumping it into water or the atmosphere. Little thought was given to the cost of waste disposal, probably because it was relatively cheap to let nature do the disposing, and relatively few people—at least few with any influence—complained about the effects of waste materials in the environment.

Society is becoming increasingly aware, however, that the cost of disposing of wastes by dumping them into the environment is much greater than that borne solely by the one doing the dumping. For example, the cost of piping waste material into a stream far exceeds the cost of the pipe, at least from society's point of view.

Economists have long been aware that certain production costs are not taken into account by the individual firm but nevertheless represent a cost to society. These are sometimes called "social costs," or "externalities." Pollution represents a rather significant social cost at the present. Accidental destruction of life and property because of alcohol or drugs also is a social cost that has concerned society for some time.

We can obtain a somewhat clearer picture of the economic effects of social costs such as pollution by use of a diagram. Suppose MC in Figure 7–10 represents the traditional implicit and explicit

FIGURE 7–10
Divergence of private and social marginal cost because of pollution

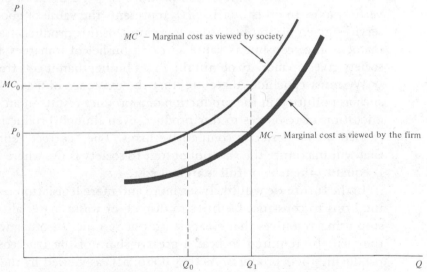

marginal costs of producing a product. Also suppose that the production of this product results in certain waste materials that are disposed of by dumping them into a river. These waste materials, however, represent an additional cost to society, either because they must be taken out downstream in order for the water to be reused, or because people living downstream suffer the cost of viewing unsightly water and are not able to use it for other purposes. For example, if pollution prohibits recreational uses of water, people must bear the cost of traveling to alternative areas where the water is not polluted.

If the firm were required to bear the full cost of disposing of its waste material, then the true or full MC curve would be somewhat higher for a given output, such as MC' in Figure 7–10. If the firm does not have to pay the full cost of waste disposal, it will base its production decisions entirely on MC rather than MC'. In other words, MC is the firm's marginal cost, whereas MC' is society's marginal cost. The latter includes the private marginal cost of the firm plus the social cost of pollution.

Assuming, as is reasonable, that the firm tries to maximize profits, it will produce quantity Q_1 if faced by price P_0. However, you will note that if all costs are taken into account, the additional cost to society of one more unit of the product is given by MC_0 on the vertical axis. In other words, MC_0 represents the value of goods or services given up to obtain one more unit of this product—say tomatoes. Since consumers value an extra bushel of tomatoes at P_0, society gives up more to obtain this extra bushel than it gets from it.

We must conclude, therefore, that the existence of a social cost such as pollution in the production of a product results in an over-allocation of resources to this product, even though production is carried on by perfectly competitive firms. The "correct" amount that will maximize the value of output to society is Q_0, where price is equal to the true or full marginal cost.

In the future we will likely see more and more legislation requiring firms to construct facilities to dispose of waste materials or to stop using resources that create wastes or residue. In other words, they will be required to bear a greater share of the true costs of producing their products. As they do so, MC as viewed by the firm will move up and toward the true marginal cost, MC' in Figure 7–10. We know, however, that an upward shift in the marginal cost for each firm also will have the effect of shifting the market supply curve of the product upward and to the left, as shown in Figure 7–11. And the inevitable consequence of this shift is a rise in the market price of the product.

We should not be surprised, therefore, if our efforts to control

FIGURE 7–11
Effect in the product market of pollution control

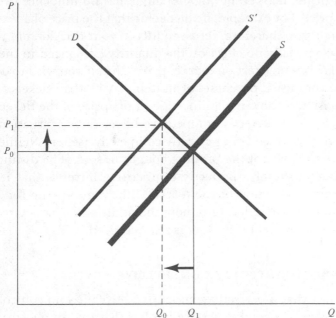

pollution result in higher prices for the products affected. This is not to say that pollution control is undesirable, because we will be buying cleaner air and water along with these products. The main point is that clean air and water are not free goods in an industrialized society.

The perfectly competitive buyer

In discussing perfect competition, we have considered only the selling side of the market. It is necessary, however, to realize that there are two sides to every market: the selling side and the buying side. In the product market, the buying side is made up mainly of ordinary consumers such as yourself. There is only one characteristic that we need consider on the buying side, and that is the amount that each buyer purchases relative to the total market. Economists would classify a market in which each buyer is small and purchases only a small proportion of the item traded as perfectly competitive on the buying side.

Because the perfectly competitive buyer buys only a minute proportion of the market, he (or she) alone has no influence over the market price. For example, if you decide that the price of a textbook is too high and, therefore, refuse to buy it, your decision not to buy will have virtually no effect on the quantity exchanged in the market, and hence no effect on market price. Nor, if you wish to double or triple your usual purchases of an item, say football tickets, would your decision alone cause an increase in the price of the tickets.

In practice, a perfectly competitive buyer faces a situation very similar to that faced by a perfectly competitive seller: Neither can influence the price of the product bought or sold. The distinguishing characteristic of a perfectly competitive buyer is that it buys only a minute fraction of the market. The same is true for a perfectly competitive seller, only here the additional characteristic of selling a homogeneous product is also required.

SUPPLY FACING A PERFECTLY COMPETITIVE BUYER

The fact that a perfectly competitive buyer has no control over market price of a good or service implies that the supply curve facing the individual buyer of this item is represented by a perfectly horizontal line, as in Figure 7–12(B). The meaning of this supply curve is that the individual buyer can purchase any reasonable amount without having to pay a higher price for larger quantities. Essentially, this supply curve reflects the price of the item as determined in the market.

The market supply and demand, which determines price, is illustrated by Figure 7–12(A). If there were no further services involved between the producer and the buyer, Figure 7–12(A) would be exactly the same as Figure 7–1(A). The market price would be P_e, and the total quantity exchanged would be equal to Q_e. Each producer or firm would supply Q_f, as shown in Figure 7–1 (B), and each consumer would buy Q_b, as shown in Figure 7–12(B), on the basis of his own individual demand for the items. Of course, the so-called "going price" facing the individual buyer need not necessarily be the equilibrium price, as shown in Figure 7–12. However, if the actual price is different from the equilibrium, we would again expect market forces to drive price toward the equilibrium.

To summarize, we have studied three different kinds of supply

FIGURE 7–12
Relationship between the market and the perfectly competitive buyer
(A) The market   *(B) The individual buyer*

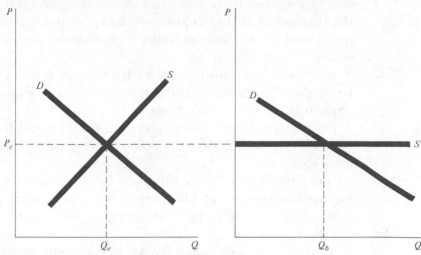

curves: (1) the supply of the individual firm (really his MC curve), (2) the market supply, which is just a summation of the individual firms' supply curves, and (3) the supply curve facing the individual buyer. You might recognize that these three supply curves are strictly analogous to the three different demand curves that were summarized at the beginning of this chapter. With a total of six different demand and supply curves, it is necessary to be careful not to confuse one with another. You should be aware, as well, that a perfectly competitive seller does not have to be a perfectly competitive buyer, and vice versa. In fact, most goods and services are purchased by perfectly competitive buyers but produced by imperfectly competitive sellers, which will be the topic of the following chapter.

Main points of Chapter 7

1. The perfectly competitive firm must take the price as determined in the market because it sells a product that is indis-

tinguishable from other firms in the market, and its sales represent a very small proportion of the total market.

2. We have studied three different kinds of demand curves: (*a*) the demand of an individual consumer, (*b*) the market demand, and (*c*) the demand facing an individual producer or seller.

3. The demand facing a single perfectly competitive firm is perfectly elastic, meaning that the firm can sell any reasonable amount at the going market price.

4. A perfectly competitive firm maximizes profits (or minimizes losses) by producing up to the point where price equals marginal cost.

5. At any point in time, there will likely be some perfectly competitive firms that are making pure profits, others making zero pure profits, and still others incurring negative pure profits (or losses).

6. If a substantial share of the firms is making pure profits, existing firms will likely increase in size and/or new firms will enter, leading to an increase in market supply, a decrease in price, and a competing away of the pure profits.

7. If a substantial share of the firms is incurring negative pure profits (they are earning less than they could in other lines of work), there will be a decrease in size or number of firms leading to a decrease in supply, an increase in price, and a restoration of at least zero pure profits.

8. Long-run adjustment to zero pure profits also can occur because of changes in the price of resources owned by the firm and hence changes in the firm's costs.

9. It is in the interest of each firm to search for cost-reducing techniques or resources in order to increase profits. Firms that do not adopt these eventually incur losses or are forced out of business.

10. The planning curve or long-run average total cost (LRATC) curve represents an envelope of all possible short-run average total cost (ATC) curves. From the planning curve the producer is able to determine the size of fixed inputs that will minimize unit costs of a given output, as well as the size that will minimize unit costs overall.

11. The downward-sloping portion of the planning curve repre-

sents the range of economics of scale. Scale economies generally result from a more efficient utilization of fixed inputs.

12. The upward-sloping portion of the planning curve represents the range of diseconomies of scale. This phenomenon generally results from management problems brought on by increasing firm size.

13. An increasing-cost industry is one in which the production costs of all firms in the industry increase as the industry expands. This takes place because of an increase in the price of resources or because of technical diseconomies which increase production costs for all firms as the industry grows.

14. In a constant-cost industry the expansion of the industry does not affect the cost curves of the individual firms.

15. A decreasing-cost industry is characterized by a reduction in firm costs as the industry grows. This phenomenon is most likely to occur in developing areas.

16. The long-run industry supply curve is upward sloping in an increasing-cost industry, perfectly elastic in a constant-cost industry, and downward-sloping in a decreasing-cost industry.

17. The perfectly competitive industry maximizes value of output to society because each firm attempts to equate output price and marginal cost (MC). Price represents the value to consumers of a marginal unit of this output, and MC represents value of alternative goods or services given up. Thus whenever price does not equal MC it is always possible to reallocate resources to obtain more than is given up, holding constant the quantity of resources employed.

18. The existence of social costs such as pollution results in an underestimation by the firm of the true or full marginal cost of producing a good or service. Since the true MC will be greater than price, there will be an overallocation of resources to goods or services that entail social costs, even though production might be carried on in perfect competition.

19. Laws that require polluting firms to bear a greater share of the cost of pollution likely will shift MC and product supply of their goods or services upward, thus increasing their market price. Pure air and water are not free goods in an industrialized society.

20. On the buying side of the market, perfect competition results

if each individual buyer purchases only a small fraction of the total market. Most individual consumers are perfectly competitive buyers.

21. We have studied three different kinds of supply curves: (*a*) the supply of an individual producer, (*b*) the market supply, and (*c*) the supply facing an individual buyer.

22. The supply curve facing a perfectly competitive buyer is perfectly elastic, meaning that the individual buyer can purchase any reasonable amount at the going market price.

Questions for thought and discussion

1. Christmas-tree production in the United States is carried on by many firms, each of which is selling a product undifferentiated from that of all other firms. Explain, using diagrams, how the price of Christmas trees is determined and how this price relates to the individual firm producing Christmas trees.

2. "Products produced by perfectly competitive firms contradict the theory of demand (people buy more at a lower price and vice versa) because the demand curve for these products is horizontal." Comment.

3. Plant breeders appear to be on the verge of developing new hybrid varieties of wheat that are capable of doubling the yield of old varieties.

   a) Explain, using a diagram, the effect a new variety would have on costs and profits for alert, early-adopting managers.

   b) Explain, using diagrams, the long-run adjustment of the wheat producing industry to this new development.

   c) Explain, using a diagram, what would happen to producers who do not adopt new variety.

4. It has been argued that the major beneficiaries of government price support programs for agriculture are landowners. Comment.

5. "Every perfectly competitive firm is doomed to a life of zero pure profits because competition immediately forces prices down to the zero profit point for each firm." Comment.

6. Farm leaders often talk about a "cost-price" squeeze in regard to unusually low profits in a particular time. From what you

know about a perfectly competitive industry, would you expect a cost-price squeeze to be an abnormal situation? Explain.

7. "Economies of scale contradict the law of diminishing returns because at larger firm sizes unit costs decrease." Comment.   ·

8. Suppose you consider growing tomatoes as a full-time occupation. What major cost factors would you consider, and how would you go about constructing a planning curve for your proposed firm?

9. Do you think expansion or entry of other tomato-producing firms would likely have any effect on the costs in your firm? In view of your conclusions, what would economists call the tomato-producing industry?

10. Suppose you accidentally discovered a tomato plant that yielded twice the number of tomatoes as the best variety now on the market. Illustrate, with a diagram, your production costs and profits as opposed to other producers. What would happen if other tomato producers found out about your discovery?

11. Adam Smith would say that tomato production would proceed as though guided by some "invisible hand." Explain fully what he meant by this phrase.

12. Suppose an insecticide that you used in your tomato patch washed down into a lake, killing off the fish therein. Explain, using a diagram, what effect this phenomenon would have on the allocation of resources in the economy.

13. Suppose the government passed a law forbidding the use of any insecticides you might employ. Illustrate what would happen to the costs for your firm and other tomato producers, as well as the price of tomatoes in the market.

14. Later suppose the government modified this law allowing the use of this insecticide in areas over ten miles from a lake. What would happen to the location of tomato production?

15. In which industry would you expect consumers to bear a greater burden of a sales tax: a constant-cost or an increasing-cost industry? Explain, using a diagram.

16. A student can be referred to as a perfectly competitive buyer of textbooks. What does this statement mean? Illustrate with a diagram.

8

Imperfect competition in the product market

By far the largest proportion of goods and services in the United States is produced or sold in an environment that economists refer to as imperfect competition. In order to understand imperfect competition, however, a full understanding of perfect competition, as developed in the preceding chapter, is necessary. Knowledge of the similarities and differences of these two types of competition will be of help in the study of imperfect competition, the subject of this chapter.

The imperfectly competitive firm: A price maker

As defined in Chapter 7, a perfectly competitive firm has no control over the price it receives for its product; it takes the price that is determined in the market. A perfectly competitive firm, it has been noted, is a "price taker" for two reasons: (1) each firm produces a small share of the market, and (2) each firm produces a product indistinguishable from those of the other firms in the market.

An imperfectly competitive firm can be defined as one which can exercise some control over the price it receives for its product. For this reason an imperfectly competitive firm is sometimes called a price maker. There are two main reasons why a firm might have some control over the price it can charge: (1) each firm produces a sizable share of the market, and (2) each firm sells a product distinguishable from its competitors. Note that these two reasons are the opposite of those given for a perfectly competitive firm. We will see shortly that it is sufficient for a firm to fulfill either of these two requirements to be classified as imperfectly competitive. Some firms, of course, will exhibit both characteristics.

In examining why these two characteristics make it possible for a firm to have some control over the price of its product, we will consider first a firm that sells a relatively large share of the total market, such as U.S. Steel. If U.S. Steel reduced its annual output by 10 to 20 percent, we would likely observe a noticeable decline in total steel output in the United States and a resulting increase in the price of steel, providing the market demand for steel is downward sloping (which is reasonable). As a result of its production cutback, U.S. Steel could then raise the price of its product, at least by a small amount. By the same token a comparable *increase* in output by U.S. Steel would add a noticeable amount to total steel output and result in at least a small decline in the market price of steel. In this case U.S. Steel would likely have to accept a slightly lower price for its product. The main point to note here is that such a firm can manipulate the price it receives for its product by changing its level of output.

A firm which sells a product somewhat different from those of its competitors is also able to exercise some control over the price of its product. In the above example we considered a firm which sells a relatively large share of the market but whose product is virtually the same as its competitors, in order to keep the effect of product differentiation separate from that of share of the market. Now we will consider a firm which sells a small share of the market but whose product is slightly different from those of its competitors —say the local Standard Oil station in your neighborhood. At first glance it might appear that such a firm's main product, gasoline, is the same as that sold by the other stations in the area, or least the same as other Standard stations. However, as we will explain shortly, a retail firm's specific location and the kind of service it renders can result in some difference in its overall product. If some of the firm's customers prefer its product to those of competing stations, the station in question probably could raise its price at least a few cents a gallon over its competitors without having its gasoline sales go to zero. The people who found the station a convenient place to stop or for some reason liked the service probably would continue to patronize it, at least for a time. On the other hand, if the station lowered its price a few cents a gallon below its competitors it would likely attract additional customers. The main point is that a firm which sells a product that is somewhat different from its competitor's products has some leeway in the price it can charge.

Demand facing an imperfectly competitive firm

The imperfectly competitive firm's ability to alter the price of its product is translatable to the demand curve facing such a firm. In the previous chapter it was noted that the perfectly competitive firm faces a perfectly horizontal (perfectly elastic) demand curve, reflecting the fact that it has no control over the price it receives. In the case of an imperfectly competitive firm, its ability to raise price and sell a smaller quantity, or lower price and sell a larger quantity, means in effect that the firm faces a downward-sloping demand curve. This is illustrated in Figure 8–1.

FIGURE 8–1
Demand curve facing an imperfectly competitive firm

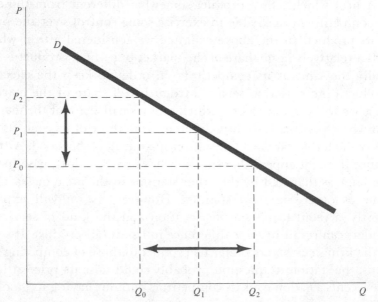

If the firm raises its price, say from P_1 to P_2, it is forced to reduce its sales from Q_1 to Q_0. Or if the firm wishes to increase its sales, say from Q_1 to Q_2, it must lower price from P_1 to P_0. Thus the demand curve of all imperfectly competitive firms is downward sloping. Keep in mind, however, that even though this downward-sloping demand curve facing the individual firm resembles the market demand curve for the product, it is not the same thing as the market demand. (Pure monopoly is an exception, to be discussed later.) As long as there is more than one firm selling in a market, the demand curve facing each firm will be considerably more elastic than the market demand curve.

The concept of marginal revenue

The phenomenon of an individual firm facing a downward-sloping demand curve makes it necessary to introduce a new concept—marginal revenue. Marginal revenue (MR) is defined as the additional revenue obtained by producing and selling one more unit of a good or service, or, conversely, the reduction in revenue caused by a one-unit reduction in sales.

As pointed out in Chapter 4, it is not realistic to believe that a firm can change its production or sales by just one unit. For this reason, economists generally refer to a change in production and sales over a small range of output and compute MR for a unit change of output within this range. The formula for computing marginal revenue is:

$$\text{MR} = \frac{\text{Change in total revenue}}{\text{Change in quantity sold}}$$

This formula will be a bit easier to understand if we apply it to a specific example. Suppose Figure 8–1 depicts a demand curve facing a shoe manufacturer and that the firm charges \$20 per pair for its shoes and sells 1,000 pairs per week. (For the moment we will not be concerned with how the firm arrived at this price.) This price and quantity would correspond to P_1 and Q_1, respectively, in Figure 8–1. Multiplying price times quantity results in a total revenue to the firm of \$20,000 per week.

Now suppose the firm wishes to expand its sales to 1,500 pairs per week and that in order to increase its sales by 500 pairs of shoes per week it must lower their price to $19 per pair. With the new lower price and larger quantity, total revenue becomes $28,500 per week. We now have enough information to compute the marginal revenue of an extra pair of shoes sold in this range of output.

$$MR = \frac{\$28,500 - \$20,000}{1,500 \ - \ 1,000} = \frac{\$8,500}{500} = \$17$$

In this range of output, an extra pair of shoes sold adds $17 to total revenue.

Marginal revenue and price

Because of the downward-sloping demand curve in the above example, the firm had to lower its price from $20 to $19 a pair to sell the additional 500 pairs per week. But we might ask a reasonable question at this point. If an extra pair of shoes sells for $19, why doesn't it add $19 to total revenue?

The reason why marginal revenue is less than price is because the lower $19 price applies to all of the weekly sales, not just to the extra or additional sales that result from the lower $19 price. It would not be reasonable to expect the firm to sell the initial 1,000 pair for $20 per pair and the extra 500 pair for $19. No one would want to buy any of the initial 1,000 pair. Thus when price is reduced to sell more of the product, the lower price must apply to all units sold, not just to the marginal units. As a result, MR is even less than the new lower price because that price reduces the total revenue obtained from the original quantity sold from what it would otherwise be.

Keep in mind, however, that marginal revenue is less than price only if the firm faces a downward-sloping demand curve. If, as in perfect competition, the firm faces a horizontal demand curve, MR will be equal to price. In this situation, the firm does not have to reduce price to sell additional units. So the addition to total revenue (MR) is exactly the same as the price that the marginal unit sells for.

If we were to graph MR at various levels of output, we would obtain for perfect competition a horizontal line that is equal to price, which in turn is equal to the demand curve facing the individual firm, as shown in Figure 8–2(A). For imperfect competition the MR line would be less than price at any given level of output. Thus the MR line would be lower than its corresponding demand curve and slope downward more steeply as in Figure 8–2(B).

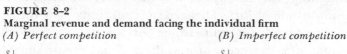

FIGURE 8–2
Marginal revenue and demand facing the individual firm
(A) Perfect competition   *(B) Imperfect competition*

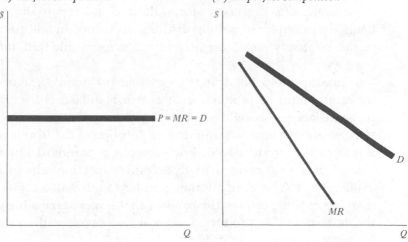

Although imperfectly competitive firms all share one thing in common—they all face downward-sloping demand curves for their good or service—there is a great deal of diversity among them. Economists have attempted to create some order out of this diversity by classifying imperfectly competitive firms into three categories: (1) monopolistic competition, (2) oligopoly, and (3) pure monopoly.

Monopolistic competition

As the name implies, monopolistic competition is similar in some respects to perfect competition. The two distinguishing characteristics of monopolistic competition are (1) there are many firms, each selling a small proportion of the market and (2) each firm sells a product slightly different from those of its competitors.

The characteristic of monopolistic competition that makes it very similar to perfect competition is the fact that there are many firms, each selling a small proportion of the market. However, the fact that each firm sells a product slightly different than those of its competitors results in a downward-sloping demand curve facing each firm. Because its product or service is slightly different from its competitors', the firm has some control over the price it charges.

The multitude of firms engaged in retail trade offer the best examples of monopolistic competition. Service stations, barber shops, department stores, grocery stores, florists, and repair shops of all kinds are examples of monopolistic competition. In addition, most of the relatively small manufacturing firms would fall into this category.

It may appear a bit strange to say that two retail outlets selling the same brand of product, such as two Standard Oil service stations, in fact sell a slightly different product. In the case of retail trade we should bear in mind that the location of the firm is in itself a part of the product sold. For example, a Standard Oil station located on a well-traveled, easily accessible location sells in a sense a different product than another Standard station in a remote location. Other things equal, the product that is more accessible to us is the more desirable product, and most people are willing to pay a bit more for a more desirable product.

Another factor that distinguishes two seemingly identical products is service. Some people prefer to purchase their clothing in intimate little shops where the clerk is very friendly and instantly available for assistance. Others buy their clothes in large department stores with very little assistance and impersonal check-out counters. Even though the physical characteristics of the items sold in these two types of stores may be identical, the customer who wants to consume more service along with the item will buy from the small, intimate shop.

However, providing services involves a cost, so we should expect to pay a higher price where more service is provided. You might have noticed that cut-rate gasoline stations rarely clean windshields or check oil levels. In name-brand stations you generally buy these services along with the gasoline. As an individual consumer we have to decide if the marginal utility per dollar for these services is at least equal to the marginal utility per dollar of other things we buy.

PRICE DETERMINATION IN MONOPOLISTIC COMPETITION

The fact that the goods or services sold by monopolistically competitive firms differ in some respect, either physically or because of location or services, allows a particular firm some flexibility in the price it can charge. This does not mean, of course, that a service station, for example, could charge 50 cents per gallon for regular gas when other stations are charging 42.9 cents. To do so would be foolhardy, because it would soon lose most of its customers. But it might be able to charge somewhere in the range of 40.9 to 44.9 cents per gallon, without either causing a price war or losing most of its sales. If the station manager feels that he can clear more net profit by a narrow-margin, high-volume operation, he will probably charge just a bit less than his competitors. If he thinks he can make more with a wider margin, lower volume business, he will probably charge a bit more than the average price of his competitors.

Thus, in monopolistic competition, the range of price within which the firm can operate is determined largely by the average price of its closest competitors. The individual firm may diverge slightly from the average market price, depending on the kind of business it wishes to operate. It is a mistake, however, to believe that just because a firm selling in monopolistic competition places a price tag on its product it can charge any price it pleases. Most firms in this kind of market are restricted to a rather narrow range of price. They have a bit more freedom, however, than the perfectly competitive firm, which has absolutely no leeway in the price it can charge.

In the case of perfect competition we were a bit more precise in determining price and output for an individual firm. Recall that a perfectly competitive firm maximizes profits if it produces a quantity that corresponds to the point at which marginal cost is equal to market price. We were able to illustrate this point with a diagram. We can utilize a similar technique for monopolistic competition, only in this case we must keep in mind that the firm faces a slightly downward-sloping demand curve. Moreover, the marginal revenue of an additional unit sold is somewhat less than the price of this unit, because the new lower price must apply to all units sold. There is no difference in the way costs are derived between perfect competition and imperfect competition on the selling side, so we can continue to use the average and marginal cost concepts developed in Chapter 7.

As a general rule, an imperfectly competitive firm maximizes profits if it produces or sells a quantity that corresponds to the point at which marginal cost is equal to marginal revenue. Recall that marginal cost (MC) is the cost of producing or selling an additional unit of output, and marginal revenue (MR) is the additional revenue obtained from this extra or marginal unit sold. For example, if it costs a service station 25 cents to sell an extra gallon of gasoline, and the marginal revenue from this extra gallon is 30 cents, the station can increase its profits (or decrease losses) by 5 cents if it sells this extra gallon.

Moreover, it is to the firm's advantage to continue to increase output as long as MR is greater than or at least equal to MC. Why this

FIGURE 8–3
Profit-maximizing price and quantity for a monopolistically competitive firm

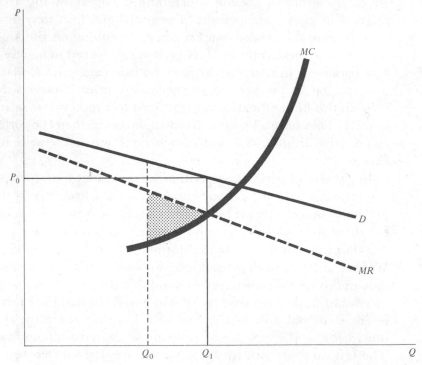

is the case is illustrated in Figure 8–3. Suppose we cut in at a quantity of output just short of the point where MC equals MR, call it Q_0. If we increase output by one additional unit past Q_0 our total costs increase by the distance from the horizontal axis up to the MC curve. However, our total revenue increase is shown by the distance between the horizontal axis and MR. The difference between these two distances represents the additional profit that the firm captures by producing this extra unit.

If we continue to increase output we see that the distance between MC and MR continues to grow smaller, but as long as there is any distance between them at all, total profits can be increased by increasing output. Total profits are maximized (or losses minimized) at the quantity where MR equals MC, Q_1 in Figure 8–3. To stop producing short of this point, say at Q_0, means that the firm needlessly foregoes profits (or incurs unnecessary losses) equal in value to the area of the shaded triangle in Figure 8–3.

We can use Figure 8–3 to illustrate also the profit-maximizing price that a monopolistically competitive firm would charge. If the firm chooses to maximize profits and produce or sell Q_1, the demand curve facing this firm will indicate that the price its customers are willing to pay is equal to P_0. The firm would not want to charge a lower price because in so doing it would just throw away profits. On the other hand, it could not charge a higher price because its customers will only pay price P_0 for quantity Q_1.

In Figure 8–3 there is no indication, however, whether the firm is making a pure profit or incurring a loss. All we can tell from this diagram is that P_0 and Q_1 are the optimum price and quantity, respectively, meaning either that the firm's losses are minimized or its profits are maximized. In order to determine the extent of profit or loss we must know average total cost (ATC). If ATC is below price at the optimum quantity, the firm reaps a pure profit; if ATC is above price, the firm incurs a loss.

Figure 8–4(A) illustrates a situation where the firm is making a pure profit, meaning that the resources employed by the firm are earning more than they could make in some alternative activity or occupation. The total dollar value of the pure profit is illustrated by the shaded area. A firm can find itself in this enviable position for one or both of two reasons: (1) the firm is managed very well so that the firm's costs are low, or (2) the firm sells a desirable product so that the demand curve it faces is high relative to those faced by its competitors.

Figure 8–4(B) depicts a less fortunate firm that is incurring a loss. In this situation the resources employed by the firm are earning less than they could in alternative employment. The total dollar value of the loss is illustrated by the shaded area. A firm can find itself in this circumstance if its costs are high because of either high-paying alternative employment for its resources or poor management. Or the firm can incur losses if the product it sells is not as desirable to consumers as the products sold by its competitors, so that the demand it faces for its goods is relatively low.

To summarize this procedure, we determine the profit-maximizing quantity for an imperfectly competitive firm by the intersection of the MR and MC curves. The profit-maximizing price is then determined by extending the vertical line drawn through the intersection of MR and MC up to the demand curve. The point where this vertical line just touches the demand curve corresponds to the profit-maximizing price on the vertical axis. Notice that the price line is not drawn over from the intersection of MR and MC, because price is determined by the demand curve.

If price as determined by the demand curve is greater than the ATC at the profit-maximizing quantity, then the firm is making a pure profit. The average profit per unit is given by the distance between price and ATC at the profit-maximizing quantity. If we multiply this average profit per unit by the total units sold (the profit-maximizing quantity), we obtain total pure profits. This is illustrated by the shaded rectangle in Figure 8–4(A). By the same token, if price is less than ATC at the profit-maximizing quantity, losses will be incurred. The average loss per unit is equal to the distance between price and ATC, and the total loss is then equal to the shaded rectangle, as illustrated in Figure 8–4(B).

In short, we use MR and MC to determine the quantity to produce, and demand to give us the profit-maximizing price at that quantity. The profit (or loss) is determined by the difference between price and ATC. This procedure holds true for any firm facing a downward-sloping demand curve, that is, any imperfectly competitive firm, including one that is monopolistically competitive.

FIGURE 8–4
Profit and loss situations for a monopolistically competitive firm
(A) Pure profit earned

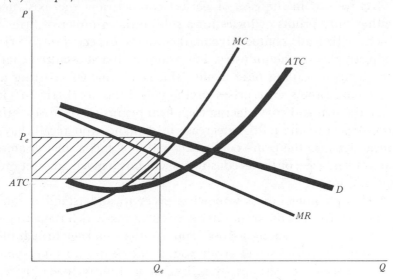

(B) Loss incurred

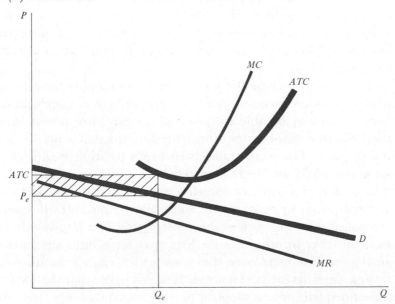

LONG-RUN ADJUSTMENT IN MONOPOLISTIC COMPETITION

As we saw in the case of perfect competition, the existence of either pure profits or losses for a substantial number of firms in a monopolistically competitive market can be expected to give rise to adjustments by the industry. For example, if a substantial share of the firms is reaping pure profits, this is a signal for existing firms to enlarge their enterprises or for new firms to enter. In either case the demand curve facing each firm begins to decrease, shifting downward to the left. A decrease in demand, you recall, has two meanings: (1) the firm's consumers will now buy a smaller amount at a given price, or (2) its consumers will buy a given amount only if price is lower.

This phenomenon is somewhat easier to understand if you visualize yourself as the owner of a service station which is making substantial profits. Seeing a good opportunity, another firm builds a station across the street from yours and begins to take some of your customers, perhaps by selling at a slightly lower price. As some of your customers leave, the demand curve facing your firm begins to decrease. You lower your price somewhat in order to compete with this new firm, and to adjust to new, lower demand and marginal revenue curves. As you lower price, your pure profits decline and you approach a zero pure-profit position, as illustrated in Figure 8–5(A).

There is no reason, of course, why every monopolistically competitive firm has to end up at a zero pure-profit or tangency position. Some firms may be able to continue to reap pure profits because they own or control certain specialized inputs that other firms cannot duplicate. In retail trade, each firm's location is unique, and some are likely to be more accessible to customers than others. The choice of a superior location may be due to the skill of the original owner or manager, to luck, or circumstances beyond the control of the firm, such as the construction of a housing development nearby. In other cases a firm may have built up good will among its customers over the years which cannot be duplicated by new entrants into the market. It is also likely that the owners of some firms will possess superior entrepreneurial ability that cannot be duplicated by competing firms.

Will the owners of such firms continue to reap pure profits? In

FIGURE 8–5
Long-run adjustment by individual firms to pure profits in monopolistic competition
(A) Entry of new firms or resources

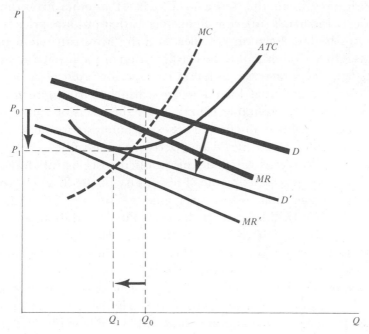

(B) Increase in asset value of profitable firms

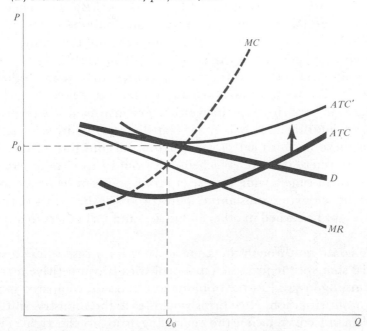

one sense yes, in another sense no. The fact that other firms cannot duplicate the firm's superior inputs means that product price is not likely to be bid down any further, and the firms can retain these profits. On the other hand, the market value of the profitable firm's assets will likely increase, to reflect its superior profit position. We could expect potential buyers to be willing to pay more for the assets of a highly profitable firm than for the assets of a firm earning normal profits or incurring losses. Economists would say that the pure profits would be "capitalized" into the value of the firm. If the owner correctly calculates his implicit costs, mainly foregone interest on the increased value of his equity in the firm, he would find his average total cost has increased, as illustrated by ATC′in Figure 8–5(B). In this sense, the pure profits would disappear into the increased capitalized value of the firm. However the current owner still does not lose these profits because they have contributed to an increase in the value of his assets.

Since owners have finite life spans, it is necessary for profitable firms to eventually change hands. If the original owner or his real estate man is a shrewd bargainer, he should be able to obtain a price that will give the new owner just a normal profit or a normal return on his investment, as illustrated by Figure 8–5(B). The phenomenon is basically the same for corporations, only here the owners (stockholders) may number in the thousands, and the equity value of the firm is reflected in the value of its stock certificates.

It is important to keep in mind, of course, that in any industry circumstances are continually changing. Thus it is not likely there would ever be a situation in which every firm is at a zero profit, long-run equilibrium. It is more realistic to visualize a situation where there is continual movement toward equilibrium but few instances where it is ever reached. We would expect to observe at any point in time a wide variety of profit positions by firms; some might be enjoying substantial pure profits, others just earning what might be earned in other industries, and still others incurring losses.

We could go through the same analysis for a case where a substantial share of the firms in a monopolistically competitive market are running losses. Just the opposite would occur, compared to the pure-profit situation. Now firms would leave the industry, shifting the demand curve facing the remaining firms to the right. (You might find it useful to illustrate this with a diagram of your own similar to Figure 8–5(A).)

Persistent losses also can change the asset value of a firm. As an example, consider a service station or restaurant that is built on a busy two-lane highway which gives way to a new expressway that takes most of the highway traffic. Needless to say, the firm is likely to suffer a major decline in sales and may even go out of business entirely. If the owner sells the structure, it is likely to bring considerably less than it would have in its original use. The new owners may turn the service station into a bicycle repair shop, or the restaurant may be converted to a mortuary. At any rate, if the new owners are shrewd bargainers, they will not pay any more for the structure than assures them a normal profit in the new business.

As an even more prevalent example, firms such as a service station, clothing store, or restaurant that are realizing losses often go out of business. After a few months of remaining vacant, they may open up under new management but in the same kind of business. If the previous owners couldn't make a normal profit, how can the new owners expect to do any better? They may have some ideas on how to improve things, but in addition it is likely that they have been able to purchase the structure at a price that enables them to expect at least a normal profit.

A change in costs due to a revaluation of assets, either up or down, does not affect the price of the product sold or produced. Here we would say that costs are "price determined." In a case where costs are changed because of changes in production technology or input prices, we would expect market price to change because of a change in supply. In the latter case, we would say that costs are "price determining."

Oligopoly

Oligopoly is derived from the Greek word "oligos," meaning few. This meaning provides a hint of the kind of industry in an oligopolistic market situation. Basically an oligopoly is an industry where a few firms, say three or four, produce the major share of the market. Oligopoly is commonly found in heavy industry or in products marketed nationally. Autos, steel, airplanes, drugs, farm equipment, minerals, petroleum, and computers are some examples of products that are produced by oligopolies.

Industries where a few large firms produce the major share of the output come into being mainly because large firms are able to produce the product more efficiently than small firms, that is, because of economies of scale. For example, it is hard to visualize the auto industry consisting of several thousand or even several hundred firms. Each firm would be too small to utilize the most efficient mass production techniques.

Unlike monopolistic competition, the firms in an oligopolistic market do not necessarily produce a differentiated product. In fact, petroleum, steel, and minerals could all be classified as homogeneous products. A ton of steel produced by U.S. Steel is essentially the same product as a ton produced by Bethlehem or Jones and Laughlin. There are, of course, oligopolies that produce differentiated products such as automobiles or appliances. Thus the distinguishing characteristic of an oligopoly is the small number of firms in the market.

PRICE DETERMINATION IN OLIGOPOLY

The fact that each firm sells a substantial share of the market or sells a differentiated product makes it possible for each firm to influence to some degree the price of its product. For example, if one of the large steel companies reduced its output, there would likely be a noticeable decline in the amount of steel on the market. This would, in turn, result in an increase in the price of steel. Thus each firm has some control over the price of the product it sells, which is just another way of saying that each firm in an oligopoly faces a downward-sloping demand curve.

We should note, however, that each firm's ability to influence the price of its product is limited by the substitute products available. Each firm, therefore, must sell its product at a price somewhere in line with the prices of its competitors. It is not likely that Ford would sell many cars if their price were several hundred dollars higher than that for comparable Chevrolet models. For homogeneous products produced in an oligopoly market, there is even less chance for price differentials to exist. Disregarding transportation charges, no one would want to buy steel from U.S. Steel if they charged just slightly more than the other companies.

We should not be surprised, therefore, when we observe all firms in an oligopoly market changing their prices at about the same time. This is an indication that consumers regard the products of the major firms in a oligopoly market as close substitutes. If a firm's price rises out of line with the prices of other firms, its customers soon discover substitute products that give them more for their money.

If the products of firms in an oligopolistic market are close substitutes for one another, as in steel, for example, there will be virtually no difference in price between the products. For products such as luxury automobiles which consumers regard as less perfect substitutes, wider differences in price between firms can be observed.

In dealing with prices of oligopoly products, we ought to distinguish between the list price, the price on the window sticker for automobiles, for example, and the actual price that consumers pay. The difference between these two prices can be substantial for highly differentiated products. The list price of two products might be very similar but the actual price widely divergent, as is shown for Cadillacs and Chryslers in Table 8–1. Although Chrysler's list

TABLE 8–1
List price versus actual price for selected makes of 1973 automobiles*

	List price	Actual price
Cadillac Coupe deVille $7,089		$6,199
Chrysler Imperial two-door 7,147		5,905
Chevrolet Impala two-door hardtop 4,535		3,706
Ford Galaxie 500 two-door hardtop 4,560		3,700

* All models comparably equipped with air conditioning, automatic transmission, electric clock, AM-FM radio, tinted glass, and vinyl roof.
Source: *1973 Best Buys and Discount Prices*, published by Consumer's Guide.

price is above the Cadillac list, its actual price is nearly $300 lower. This implies that consumers do not regard these two automobiles as close substitutes. On the other hand, the difference between list price and actual price is about the same for Fords and Chevrolets, implying that these two makes are very close substitutes in the minds of consumers.

The figures in Table 8–1 also help make it clear that oligopolies are not able to charge any price they would like. No doubt all of these firms would like to charge the list price, but none of them can. If these firms did hold to the list price, they would find themselves with a substantial stock of unsold automobiles at the end of the model year. The actual price is the price that makes consumers willing to buy the number of cars that are manufactured.

Like monopolistic competition, oligopoly price determination can also be illustrated with a diagram (Figure 8–6). As a matter of fact, the exact same diagram used for illustrating optimum price and quantity for a monopolistically competitive firm might also be used for an oligopoly. We might expect, however, that an oligopoly would face a slightly less elastic demand curve, because by definition it sells a larger share of the market. It is risky to generalize about this because of differences in the degree of product differentiation between the two types of firms and because of possible differences in the elasticity of the market demand for the general category of product, such as steel versus women's clothing. Also we would expect the demand facing an oligopolist selling a homogeneous product to be somewhat more elastic than would be the case for one selling a product different from its competitors'.

At any rate, the two types of firms (monopolistic competitors and

FIGURE 8–6
Profit-maximizing price and quantity for an oligopoly

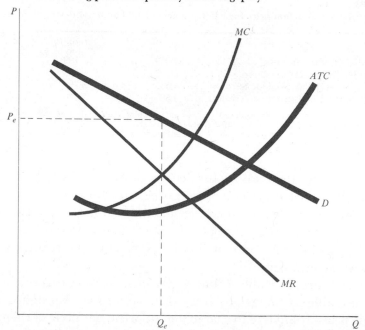

oligopoly) are similar in that the oligopoly attempts also to equate
MC with MR to determine the most profitable output. The price
charged by the firm is determined by the demand that faces the firm
at this output. The profit-maximizing price shown in Figure 8–6
is actual price, not list price.

In this particular example, price is greater than average total
costs, so the firm would be earning a pure profit. Of course, this is
only an example. If the ATC curve was everywhere above the firm's
demand curve, the firm would have no choice but to take a loss or
shut down. (You might illustrate this situation by drawing a similar
diagram.)

INTERDEPENDENCE OF FIRMS IN OLIGOPOLY

An inevitable result of the small number of firms in an oligopoly
market is that the action of any one of the major firms will have a
significant effect on thé sales and/or price of the other firms in the
market. For example, suppose General Motors grants a wage increase to its employees, which in turn leads to an increase in the cost
of production, as shown in Figure 8–7(A). We can see from Figure
8–7(A) that it would be in GM's interest to raise the price of its
cars from P_0 to P_1 and reduce quantity sold from Q_1 to Q_0 in order
to again equate MC and MR. If they continued to charge P_0 and
sell Q_1, MC would be greater than MR, so they would be losing
money on the marginal units produced.

Recall from our discussion of consumer demand that when the
price of a good increases there is an increase in demand for substitute goods. We can predict, therefore, that an increase in the price
of GM cars will lead to an increase in demand for the other makes,
as shown in Figure 8–7(B). Consumers will try to avoid the higher
prices of GM cars by purchasing more of other makes. But an
increase in the demand for other makes will in turn lead to an
increase in both price and quantity of these cars, as the other firms
attempt to equate MC with MR, as shown in Figure 8–7(B). We see,
therefore, that an increase in costs and price of just one of the
major firms in an oligopoly market leads to an increase in price of
the other firms as well. (You might also want to prove to yourself
that a decrease in costs and price by one firm will also lead to a
decrease in price of other firms by constructing diagrams of your
own.)

FIGURE 8–7
Effects of an increase in manufacturing costs of General Motors automobiles
(A) General Motors

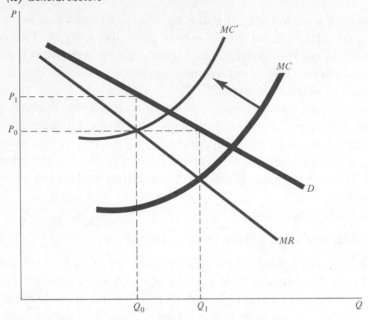

(B) Other auto manufacturers

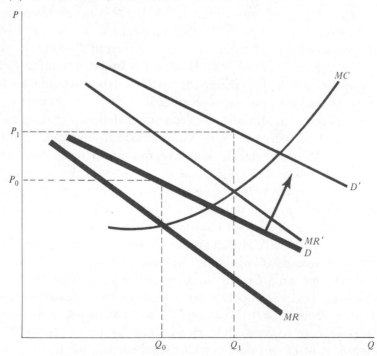

It should also be pointed out that the increase in demand and price shown in Figure 8–7(B) will in turn lead to a slight increase in demand for GM cars, resulting in a slightly greater increase in price for these cars than was originally specified in Figure 8–7(A). In fact, we could trace this process of cause and effect back and forth indefinitely. As a rule, however, the largest and most interesting changes come on the first round, so economists have not been greatly concerned with the second- or third-order effects.

THE KINKED DEMAND CURVE

Another apparent characterictic of an oligopolistic market is the relative "stickyness" of product price. Compared to perfectly competitive and monopolistically competitive firms, oligopolies tend to change the price of their products infrequently. For example, once an auto manufacturer announces the list prices of its new cars, it tends to stick with them, often for the entire model year. We should bear in mind, however, that these are list prices, not actual prices.

In an effort to formulate a theory that takes these characteristics specifically into account, economists have developed the idea of the "kinked" demand curve facing the firm. The basic assumption of this theory is that each firm attempts to retain its present customers or attract new ones. Let us see how the kinked demand curve is derived. Suppose General Motors raises its price. It is assumed in this case that the other auto manufacturers will hold to their original price in order to take GM's customers. Thus GM experiences a substantial reduction in sales, as shown in Figure 8–8, where price increases from P_1 to P_2 and quantity declines from Q_1 to Q_0. On the other hand, if GM reduces prices from P_1 to P_0, it is assumed that other firms will also reduce their prices. Thus GM is able to obtain only a modest increase in sales, say from Q_1 to Q_2, and we have a kink in the demand curve facing the firm.

Notice also that the kinked demand curve results in a discontinuous MR curve. The more elastic portion of the MR curve is derived from the more elastic segment of the demand curve, and the less elastic portion of MR is derived from the lower, less elastic portion of the total demand curve. The resulting two segments of the MR curve are joined by a vertical line. Now if MC should intersect MR at some point within this vertical section, a shift in MC, as shown in Figure 8–8, would not change the optimum price and quantity for the firm. That is, the profit-maximizing price and quantity would remain at P_1 and Q_1, respectively, for either MC or MC'. As a result, the kinked demand curve is sometimes used to explain why oligopoly prices do not exhibit a large amount of fluctuation.

FIGURE 8–8
Kinked demand curve

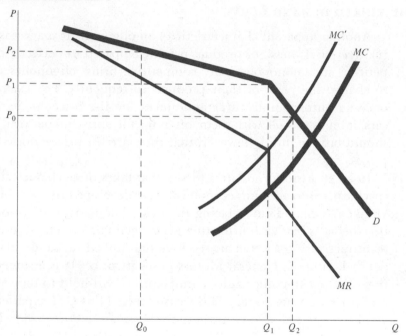

The theory of the kinked demand curve has been criticized by some economists. For one thing, it is argued that it is not possible to derive from the kinked demand curve how the going price and quantity come to be what they are. These magnitudes have to be assumed as given. Secondly, doubt has been expressed as to whether oligopoly prices are as inflexible as generally assumed. Even though list prices might remain unchanged over a long period, actual prices may vary considerably. For example, the actual price of a new car tends to fall from the beginning to the end of the model year, even though the list price stays the same. The same is true for appliances. Or if an oligopolistic firm mistakenly produces more of an item than it thought would sell at the list price, price cuts are in evidence in order to get rid of the excess inventory.

PRICE SEARCHING

Although the diagrams developed in the previous sections are helpful in providing a framework for thinking about the operation of an oligopolistic firm and market, we should not lose sight of the complexities involved, particularly in reference to price determination by the individual firm. It is one thing to equate marginal cost with marginal revenue, follow the line up to the demand curve, and determine price and quantity. It is quite another thing to find out what these magnitudes actually are.

To be sure, each large oligopolistic firm is likely to have a staff of economists, cost accountants, market researchers, and the like to assess costs and market demand. But there is still a good deal of trial and error involved in price determination. This is particularly true for a new product or an entirely new firm. If there are similar products already on the market, the firm, of course, would want to set a price somewhere in line with that for the established items. The firm also would want to compare such a price with its unit production costs. It is likely to have a fairly good idea of average costs and may even have some idea of marginal costs.

Once a particular price is set and a production decision has been made, the firm will begin to receive information not only from the market but also from its own cost and profit figures. If the product is not selling and inventories are piling up, it may be an indication that it is overpriced. When breaking in with a new product, it usually is necessary to offer consumers a bit more for their money than they receive from established items, else they have little incentive to change. As time goes by and sales pick up, (i.e., demand facing the firms increases or shifts to the right), the firm may want to adjust price upward slightly, especially if production cannot keep up with sales. Of course, in times of inflation, with increased wages and prices of raw materials, product price will have to be increased, or the firm is likely to find its average total costs exceeding product price.

Naturally each firm must keep its eye on its major competitors. Indeed, if the firm is relatively small or new in the business, it might decide to play follow the leader. If the large, dominant firm increases price, the small firm follows suit. Or if the large firm lowers price, so does the small one. This kind of behavior, quite common in oligopolistic markets, is referred to as "price leadership." In addition to relieving the small firm of the task of periodically deciding on its product price, this practice reduces the likelihood that the small firm will provoke the large one into a price war, possibly wiping out the small firm.

Even under price leadership, at least one firm in an oligopolistic market must bear the responsibility of setting a price. One possible procedure for such a firm is to engage in what is sometimes called "average cost pricing." Here the firm determines the average total cost of an item, adds a certain percent of that figure for profit, and uses this figure for its price. Of course, this does not guarantee the firm a profit regardless of its costs. If the firm becomes inefficient, other firms may decide that they can sell at a lower price and still cover their costs, plus an "acceptable" profit. Thus even a so-called dominant firm has no guarantee of remaining dominant. In addition to contending with the up and coming firms on the home scene, it may have to contend with foreign competition. Competitive forces from foreign firms are especially evident in such industries as autos, steel, ship building, shoes, radios, and textiles.

We should also point out that the potential competition of each firm is not limited to existing firms in its own industry. If excessive pure profits are evident in an industry, usually there is nothing to stop established firms in other industries from moving in to get a piece of the action. For example, if bicycle manufacturing should become very profitable, there is nothing to stop General Motors or Ford from getting into the bicycle business. Indeed many of the so-called conglomerates of today are involved in several industries simultaneously.

MERGERS AND CONGLOMERATES

Many firms find themselves in a situation where they must become larger in order to become more efficient (i.e., attain economies of scale) and remain competitive in their field. Since internal growth is often a relatively slow and difficult process, the merging of two or more firms has proven a popular vehicle for growth. A better appreciation for its popularity can be gained by looking at some of the advantages of a merger. Two or more firms that become one may be able to gain some advantages of specialization by devoting entire plants to the production of one or two components of their overall product. In the case of an auto firm, one plant might manufacture engines, another bodies, and so on. It may also be possible to gain some scale economies by sharing a common management and administrative structure. Instead of having two or three main offices and staffs, the merged firm may be able to get by with one. A larger firm may be able to take advantage of a more efficient advertising media, such as nationwide television, to borrow at a lower rate of interest, or to sell stock more easily.

In addition to pure scale economies, some firms have found it possible to obtain tax savings through merger. For example, if a firm that is incurring losses merges with one reaping pure profits, their overall tax bill may be reduced by writing off the one's losses against the other's profits. Another advantage is the possibility of easing the competitive pressure faced by each firm. It is evident that the merger of two intense rivals would likely make life considerably more pleasant for all involved. However, where the merger of two competing firms would result in a virtual monopoly, the Justice Department is likely to step in and forbid the merger.

Merger, of course, is not limited to firms in the same industry. When two or more firms in separate industries merge to become one, they form what is known as a "conglomerate." A well-known conglomerate is International Telephone and Telegraph (ITT), which has holdings in numerous industries. Large firms such as this often have sufficient assets to simply acquire control of other firms and take over their management, as opposed to working out a mutual agreement, as in a merger. As a result some people have expressed concern over the large amount of "economic power" wielded by conglomerates and have called for tighter control over their actions.

COLLUSION AND ANTITRUST LEGISLATION

The small number of firms in an oligopolistic market opens up the possibility for two or more rival firms to agree not to compete. Agreements of this nature can be informal in nature, with rivals agreeing to maintain a certain price or to divide up the market. There is the possibility also that participating firms will enter into formal, written agreements whereby they agree to a specified price that will be charged and the quantity of the product each will produce. This arrangement is commonly referred to as a "cartel." In essence, a cartel, or even a binding informal agreement, results in a market situation resembling that of a monopoly. It is as though there were only one firm in the market. As a consequence we would expect a higher price than would exist if there were many firms competing in the market.

The two main legal tools that the government uses to fight nonsanctioned monopolies or cartels are the Sherman Antitrust Act of 1890 and the Clayton Antitrust Act of 1914. The Sherman Act makes "restraint of trade" or any attempt to monopolize trade a misdemeanor, that is, a criminal offense against the federal government. This means going to jail if convicted of the crime. The Clayton Act essentially duplicates the Sherman Act but does spell out in a bit more detail the various illegal activities that might eventually lead to monopoly or cartel. The intention of this act was to curb monopoly before it came into existence, rather than to just punish it after the fact. The Federal Trade Commission (FTC), also set up in 1914, was given power to investigate "unfair" business practices and to take legal action if required.

In addition to government action against monopolies, or cartels, there is a market force acting as a continual deterrent. This is the temptation by colluding firms to cheat on one another. As shown in Figure 8–9, an industry that becomes a monopoly or cartel must reduce its output in order to raise price. Thus each individual firm that agrees to collude must agree to reduce its output in order for the scheme to work. But if each firm is maximizing profits by equating MR with MC before the collusion takes place, as is reasonable to expect, then after they agree to reduce quantity and raise price, MR for each firm will be greater than MC, as shown in Figure 8–9. Before collusion each firm maximizes profits by producing Q_1—that quantity that corresponds to the intersection of the MC and MR curves. During collusion each firm reduces output to Q_0. We cannot, however, illustrate the new higher price that will result from collusion on the diagrams in Figure 8–9 because these are demand curves facing each firm, not the market demand. We

FIGURE 8–9
Effect on individual firms of colluding to reduce
quantity and raise price
Firm A

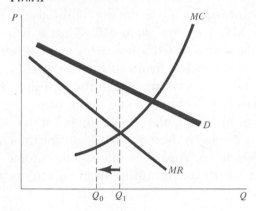

Firm B

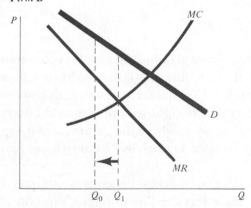

Firm C

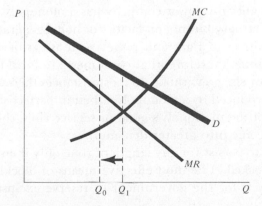

can only assume that the new higher price will result in higher net profits for each firm, else it would not pay to collude in the first place.

But the important point to note is that during collusion each firm is in a situation where MR is greater than MC. Thus it is in the interest of each individual firm to sell a few extra units of output "under the table." By doing so the firm can increase profits even more. But when all or most firms taking part in the collusion cheat in this manner, the market price must come down, otherwise the additional output cannot be sold. Unless the group of colluders can impose a penalty on the cheaters, there is a tendency for the collusive agreement to break down. And it is difficult to enforce any kind of penalty against a firm for refraining from an activity that is itself illegal.

Pure monopoly

At the other end of the spectrum of industry types is pure monopoly, which exists where there is just one firm providing a good or service in a market. This kind of market tends to exist only when the government has the exclusive right to supply a good or service, such as the post office used to be, or where the government has given exclusive right for a firm to operate, such as a local light and power company.

The existence of a pure monopoly depends also upon how broadly we define a good or service. For example, the post office has a monopoly on official mail service but not upon all communications. Or the local light and power company has a monopoly on centrally generated electricity but not on factory or home-generated electricity, or other sources of light and power such as gas or oil. It is not correct to assume, therefore, that consumers are forced to buy from a monopoly or else go without. In most instances there are substitutes for goods produced by a monopoly, albeit imperfect substitutes. As the price of the monopoly's good or service rises, these imperfect substitutes come into greater demand.

A monopoly is able to persist for any length of time only if entry into the industry is blocked. The most effective means of blocking entry into an industry is for the government to reserve exclusive right of production to itself or to firms that it designates by means of a license. Sometimes a firm can gain a temporary monopoly by discovering a new product or input and patenting it. Monopolies such as this, however, tend to be shortlived, or at least very narrowly defined, because patents can usually be circumvented by producing something just slightly different.[1]

The reason usually given for creating and nurturing government-sanctioned monopolies is to capture economies of scale, mainly by avoiding unnecessary duplication of facilities. For example, if there were several telephone companies in your area, there would have to be as many sets of lines and switchboards. Moreover it would be inconvenient for people on one company's lines to attempt to call people buying telephone service from a different company, unless there were some sort of central clearinghouse for calls.

In recent years an increasing amount of criticism has been directed at government-sanctioned monopolies. It is becoming less clear that the benefits of avoiding all duplication exceed the costs of such a policy. As long as a firm or an institution enjoys exclusive right to operate free from competitors, there is little incentive for it to search for cost-reducing techniques or to provide better goods or services. There is nothing like a little competition, even one competitor, to keep the supplier of a good or service on his toes. Complaints of bad service, protests, and the like tend to be not nearly so effective as the possibility of losing one's job to a competitor.

In the field of education, also, it can be questioned whether the monopoly held by the public school system is necessary or in the best interests of society. At the elementary and secondary levels of education, and to some extent at the college level, everyone must pay for public schools regardless of whether their children attend them or not. This tends to place the private and parochial schools at a competitive disadvantage in providing an educational service. Under the present system, public schools can become very bad before it pays parents to send their children to private schools. It has been suggested that a system of providing educational vouchers to students which they could "spend" at the school of their choice is one means of promoting more competition in the education "in-

---

1 There are, of course, exceptions, such as the Polaroid Land camera.

dustry." It has been argued also that the general public would gain if public schools were allowed to compete with one another. Under the present setup a child is forced to attend a designated public school or no public school at all. Hence it is argued that improvements would be made in the poorer public schools if the children attending these schools were allowed to take their business elsewhere. By and large, public school officials have not greeted the voucher idea with a great deal of enthusiasm. However, one should bear in mind that people who happen to enjoy monopoly privileges usually are against change and generally have an ample supply of reasons for keeping things as they are.

MONOPOLY PRICE DETERMINATION

Since government has created or at least sanctioned most present-day monopolies and therefore controls their prices, there is relatively little chance for a private monopoly to set a profit-maximizing price. We might, however, determine what this price might be and then determine the "socially optimum" price of a monopoly-supplied good or service.

The diagram for illustrating price and output for a monopoly is essentially the same as those employed to illustrate price and output for monopolistic competition and an oligopoly. The only difference for a monopoly is that the demand curve facing the firm is the same as the market demand curve for the good or service sold by the monopoly. Thus for a given good or service the demand facing a monopoly should be somewhat steeper (or more inelastic) than the demand facing an oligopoly firm, given the product sold.

As shown in Figure 8–10, the profit-maximizing price and quantity are P_m and Q_m, respectively. We should not take this to mean, however, that a monopoly is always assured of a pure profit. If the average total cost (ATC) curve is everywhere above the demand curve, the monopoly either takes a loss or shuts down. In fact, cases of monopoly losses are not uncommon in the public utilities. (You might illustrate a monopoly loss situation with a diagram of your own.)

Since present-day monopoly is generally regulated by the government, and since the government is supposed to represent the general public, at least in a democracy, we would expect it to set a

FIGURE 8-10
Monopoly price and quantity

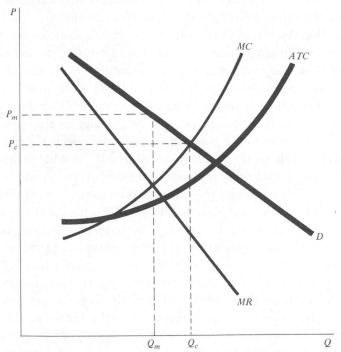

price and quantity that would somehow maximize the general welfare of the people (i.e., consumers). To understand what this price and quantity might be, it is necessary to go back to what we said about perfect competition.

Recall that the value of output to society is maximized if each firm produces up to the point where the price of the marginal unit produced is equal to its marginal cost. Recall also that the price of the marginal unit is its measure of value to society, and its marginal cost (MC) is the value of goods given up to produce this extra unit. You will note in Figure 8–9, however, that price is greater than MC at the profit-maximizing price and quantity. This means, as we pointed out in Chapter 7, that there is an underallocation of resources to the production of this good or service.

It is fairly evident, then, that if the government wishes to maximize the total value of output to society for a given amount of resources, it should set a price that corresponds to the intersection of the MC curve and the demand curve—P_c in Figure 8–10. At this point, price is equal to MC, so that value of the marginal unit is just equal to the value of goods given up to produce it.

Notice that the socially optimum price, P_c, is somewhat less than the profit-maximizing price, P_m, and the optimum quantity, Q_c, is greater than the profit-maximizing quantity, Q_m. It can also be seen that the monopoly firm is still making a pure profit at the regulated price and quantity, because price is still greater than ATC. Because of this pure profit, you might suggest that price be lowered still further to the point where ATC intersects the demand curve. But if this were done, we see that MC would be greater than price, indicating an overallocation of resources to this production activity. If competing firms were allowed to enter this industry, there would be a decrease in demand facing this firm and a gradual competing away of these pure profits. The government, however, in order to maintain the monopoly, prohibits entry of other firms.

Does the monopoly, then, continue to reap pure profits? Probably not indefinitely. The likely outcome of this situation would be an eventual bidding up of the value of the firm's assets, pushing the ATC curve upward. For example, over the years the value of New York City taxicab medallions, which represent an exclusive right to operate taxis in New York City, has increased substantially. The original or past owners enjoyed a capital gain, while new or future owners probably earn or will earn just a normal return on their labor and investment, taking into account the increased cost of operating a cab because of the interest charge (explicit or implicit) on the medallion.

In the case of government-regulated monopolies, there are some people who argue that the "regulator" soon becomes the "regulatee." They argue that monopolies develop powerful lobbies to influence the decisions of the governmental agencies that are supposed to regulate them. We see some evidence of this when the government either raises or lowers prices in response to pressure from regulated firms or industries. It is possible to argue, therefore, that a regulated price is not greatly different from a profit-maximizing price.

Moreover, we cannot be certain that a regulated price is always lower than the profit-maximizing price. If new technology comes on the scene, lowering MC, downward adjustments in the regulated price probably lag behind the adjustments that would automatically take place if the monopoly purposely tried to maximize profits. Remember that higher prices do not necessarily mean higher profits.

WHY MINIMIZE MONOPOLY?

We have seen that in some industries, mainly the public utilities, the government creates and maintains monopolies. However, in other industries the government attempts to discourage monopoly power and to maintain an atmosphere of competition. There are probably several reasons why this is so.

First, as discussed in the preceding section, any situation where price is greater than marginal cost results in a misallocation of resources, resulting in a smaller total value of output for society, given the resources available. Of course, the same criticism can be levied against any firm that faces a downward-sloping demand curve (i.e., is imperfectly competitive). But economists have found that the loss of output in the U.S. economy because of a misallocation of resources stemming from monopoly power of firms is relatively small.[2] It is also true that politicians and the general public have not become very concerned about a misallocation of resources, probably because they are not able to envision the total value of output without the misallocation.

The general public does, however, have an idea of what is a reasonable or "just" level of profit. And it is assumed, probably correctly, that a firm which is able to monopolize an industry will reap excessive profits, resulting in an unjustifiable transfer of income from consumers to the owners of the monopoly. An atmosphere of competition is maintained, therefore, to keep profits down to what people consider a reasonable level.

A third reason for attempting to maintain competition is to encourage the adoption of cost-reducing technology or the development of new and better products. Again, if a firm has no competition there is little incentive to risk or develop anything new.

---

2 See Arnold C. Harberger, "Monopoly and Resource Allocation," *American Economic Review*, May 1954, pp. 77–87.

Advertising

Advertising includes a wide range of activities. The homemade "for sale" sign on an automobile, the want ads in the newspaper, roadside signs, and radio and TV commercials are all examples of advertising. Some advertising is done by buyers, such as help-wanted ads, although the majority probably is done by sellers.

Essentially advertising can be divided into two major types: informational and persuasive. Informational advertising, as the name implies, is intended to inform prospective customers about what is for sale, its characteristics, and its price. Some examples of informational advertising are the grocery store advertisements in the newspaper telling the prices of various items that can be bought at a particular store. Persuasive advertising, on the other hand, attempts to persuade people to buy one product over another. Most of the advertising we see on television or hear on radio is of the persuasive variety.

All advertising attempts to accomplish one objective: to increase the demand for the good or service being advertised. Of course, it must be realized that advertising costs money. Thus when a firm or group of firms decides to advertise, we can only assume that the marginal revenue obtained by advertising is at least as great as the marginal cost (including advertising expense) of the extra units sold. The economic effects of advertising are illustrated in Figure 8–11; demand shifts upward and to the right, but ATC and MC also shift upward.

A great deal of disagreement exists over the merits of advertising. Most people, including economists, probably would agree, however, that informational advertising is beneficial. In order for consumers to maximize utility they must know what is for sale, something about the good or service being sold, and the selling price.

Much less agreement exists, though, about persuasive advertising. The advertising industry argues that advertising stimulates the economy by enticing people to spend. Others, particularly those who have recently experienced a rather nauseating commercial, argue that persuasive advertising is pure waste because the effect of one firm's advertising is just to cancel out the advertising of other firms.

FIGURE 8–11
Effects of advertising

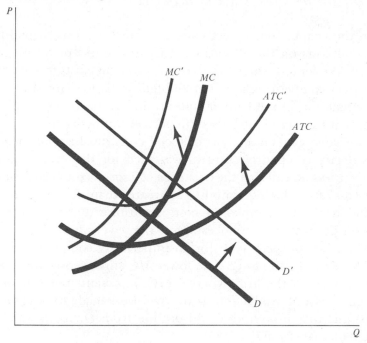

A truly objective appraisal of advertising, if such is possible, would likely rate it somewhere between these two extreme views. No doubt advertising stimulates spending on the item being advertised, or it would not pay to advertise. But it is less clear if advertising really makes people spend a larger share of their income. Expenditures on advertising have increased greatly during the past three or four decades, but on the average people spend about the same proportion of their income today as they did 30 or 40 years ago. Nor is it clear that it is even desirable that people spend a larger share of their present income on consumer goods.

It has been suggested that the government ban advertising of the persuasive variety and allow only informational advertising. The problem, however, is to separate the two. One could argue, for example, that telling people that product A is superior to all competitive products is really informational advertising. It is likely that a ban on persuasive advertising also would result in much waste in the form of lawyers' fees and court costs.

Pollution by imperfect competition

In the chapter on perfect competition, the effects of pollution or social costs on the allocation of resources and prices were discussed. We should emphasize that this problem exists in the area of imperfect competition also. Undoubtedly a large share of the total waste material in the United States results from the production of firms that fall in the category of imperfect competition.

The same general analysis of social costs can be applied to the imperfectly competitive firm as was used for the firm in perfect competition. Recall that the existence of a social cost means that the true cost of producing a product is greater than the cost perceived by the firm. For example, the cost of getting rid of waste material exceeds the cost of the smokestack or the sewer pipe.

The effect of social costs for an imperfectly competitive firm is illustrated in Figure 8–12. The lower MC curve represents the cost as perceived by the firm, whereas MC' represents the true or full marginal cost of production. If the firm were made to bear the full costs, quantity produced would decline from Q_1 to Q_0 and price would increase from P_0 to P_1.[3]

Again, if the firm is made to bear a larger share of the costs of eliminating waste materials, there will be an inevitable increase in the price of the product produced. This is not to say that pollution control is undesirable, but that a clean environment is not a free good. It appears that society is becoming more willing than in years past to pay the price of pollution control, especially people in the upper income brackets.

Marginal cost and supply

Throughout the discussion on imperfect competition we have deliberately avoided the use of the word "supply." This is because an imperfectly competitive firm does not have a supply curve as such. Recall in the case of perfect competition that the firm's

---

3 It is interesting to note that the existence of imperfect competition can result in a more optimum allocation of resources if pollution is occurring than if the market were perfectly competitive and polluting the same amount.

FIGURE 8–12
Effect of pollution control on the firm in imperfect competition

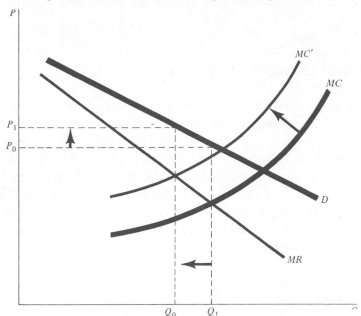

marginal cost (MC) curve is essentially its supply curve. The firm, faced with a given price, maximizes profits by producing up to the point where price equals MC. The MC curve, therefore, is the supply curve, because it denotes the quantity that will be produced at a given price, or vice versa.

The MC curve of an imperfectly competitive firm, however, is not its supply curve, because for a given quantity the price charged will depend upon the demand curve facing the firm. Thus we cannot determine both price and quantity from the MC curve alone. We have to know both MC and demand in order to determine price and quantity for a firm operating in imperfect competition, as we have shown in this chapter's diagrams.

However, the same factors that shift the MC or supply curve of a perfectly competitive firm also shift the MC curve of a firm in imperfect competition. Moreover the result of a shift in MC is the same as a shift in supply. For example, a shift to the left, or an increase in MC, reduces quantity and increases price in imperfect competition, which is the same as a decrease in supply in perfect competition. Remember from our discussion of product supply that an increase in costs results in a decrease in supply, and vice versa.

Demand facing the firm: A summary

It will be useful at this point to summarize and compare the demand curve facing each of the four types of firms we have studied. We began in Chapter 7 with the perfectly competitive firm, which faces a perfectly elastic demand. In this chapter we looked at three types of imperfectly competitive firms: monopolistic competition, oligopoly, and pure monopoly. Each of these types of firms faces a downward-sloping demand. In general, the smaller the number of firms and the more differentiated the product of each firm, the steeper or more inelastic the demand facing each firm. The demand curve facing the firm in each of the four market situations is illustrated in Figure 8–13.

It is best to think of these four types of firms as a continuous distribution, from perfect competition to pure monopoly, rather than four hard and fast categories. These categories are useful to the extent that they identify where in the distribution a given firm would be located. Most firms in the U.S. economy would fall somewhere within the two extremes of perfect competition and pure monopoly. As a result, economists will often describe a firm by the degree of monopoly power it wields, instead of trying to decide if it is a monopolistically competitive firm or an oligopoly.

A measure of a firm's monopoly power can be expressed as the ratio of its selling price to marginal cost. For a perfectly competitive firm, this ratio is 1. As the firm moves closer to pure monopoly, the ratio tends to become progressively larger than 1.

The imperfectly competitive buyer

In this chapter we have been concerned exclusively with the selling side of the market. It is possible, although less common, to observe firms that would be classified as imperfectly competitive buyers. Imperfect competition on the buying side of the market

FIGURE 8–13
Summary of demand curves facing the firms in the four major types of market situations

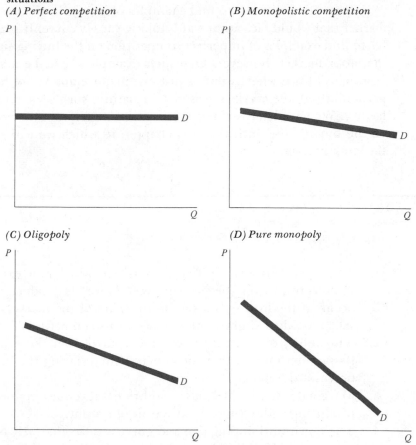

(A) Perfect competition

(B) Monopolistic competition

(C) Oligopoly

(D) Pure monopoly

results if there is a relatively small number of buyers, each purchasing a significant share of the market.

An imperfectly competitive buyer is one that has some control over the price it pays for whatever it buys. If it reduces its purchases, there is a noticeable decline in the total market purchases, so the price that sellers can obtain tends to decline. Or if this buyer increases its purchases, a noticeable amount is taken off the market, and the price that sellers can obtain will rise. The implication of this behavior is that the supply curve facing the individual imperfectly competitive buyer is an upward-sloping line. If it buys less, it can pay less; if it buys a larger amount, it has to pay a higher price per unit.

It is rather difficult to find examples of buyers in the product market that would face an upward-sloping supply curve. It is possible to find examples of imperfect competition on the buying side in the labor market, however. One such example might be a small "company" town where there is just one major employer of labor, particularly if the work is seasonal in nature, such as a canning factory. We will defer further discussion of imperfect competition on the buying side until the next chapter, in which we will study the labor market.

Main points of Chapter 8

1. An imperfectly competitive firm is one which can exercise some control over the price it receives for its product. This occurs if the firm sells a significant share of the market or it sells a product slightly different from its competitors'.
2. The ability of a firm to have some control over the price of its product implies that the demand curve facing the firm is downward sloping.
3. Marginal revenue (MR) is the additional revenue obtained by producing and selling an extra unit of output.
4. The downward-sloping demand curve implies that MR is less than price. MR is less than price for the firm in imperfect competition because additional units can be sold only if price is lowered, and the lower price must apply to all units sold, not just to the marginal units.
5. Monopolistic competition is characterized by a market in which there are many firms, each selling a small proportion of the market and a slightly differentiated product. Retail trade is an example of monopolistic competition.
6. The firm in monopolistic competition is restricted to a price that is relatively close to its competitors.' However, each firm attempting to maximize profits produces up to the point where MC is equal to MR.

7. If a substantial share of the firms in monopolistic competition is reaping pure profits, there is a tendency for additional firms or resources to enter the industry, with a resulting decrease in the demand facing each firm. If a firm is able to reap pure profits over an extended time because of the ownership or control of some specialized resource, there is a tendency for the pure profits to be capitalized into the value of the firm's assets, thereby shifting the firm's ATC curve upward. Similarly, there is a tendency for assets of a firm making persistent losses to be revalued downward.

8. An oligopoly is a market where there are a few firms, each selling a substantial share of the market. An oligopoly may or may not sell a differentiated product. Oligopoly is common in heavy industry or nationally marketed products.

9. Products produced by oligopolies that have close substitutes must sell for about the same price as the substitutes. However, each oligopoly attempting to maximize profits produces up to the point where MC is equal to MR.

10. Because of the small number of firms, the action of each firm in an oligopoly has a direct effect on its competitors. For example, an increase in costs and price for one firm results in an increase in demand and price charged by other firms.

11. The kinked demand curve is an attempt to describe the interaction of firms in an oligopoly market and to explain the apparent inflexibility of prices charged by oligopolies. It is derived under the assumption that each firm tries to hold present customers or attract new ones.

12. Actual price determination by an oligopoly is likely to include considerable trial and error, in which price is adjusted up or down in response to new information that the firm receives. Price leadership and average cost pricing are two phenomena characteristic of an oligopoly market.

13. Growth obtained through merger can make it possible for firms to reduce costs by gaining some economies of scale. Merging can also result in tax savings and the easing of competitive forces. Conglomerates are firms that have resulted from the merger of firms in different industries.

14. The Clayton and Sherman antitrust acts provide the government with legislation to fight monopoly or restraint of trade.

The temptation of colluding firms to cheat on one another also provides a check on cartels or collusion.

15. Pure monopoly exists when there is just one firm providing a good or service, although relatively imperfect substitutes generally are available for monopoly produced products.

16. In order for a monopoly to persist for any length of time, entry into the market must be blocked. The most effective method of blocking entry is by government-issued licenses.

17. The U.S. postal service and the public utilities provide the best examples of pure monopoly. The reason for creating monopoly is to avoid costly duplication of facilities.

18. The socially optimum price and quantity for a public monopoly corresponds to the point where the MC curve intersects the demand curve. At this point MC will equal price. The profit-maximizing output for a monopoly corresponds to the point where MC equals MR, the same as is true for monopolistic competition and oligopoly.

19. The existence of private monopoly or monopoly power results in a misallocation of resources because profit-maximizing price is greater than marginal cost. Public condemnation of private monopoly, however, probably stems from fear of excessive monopoly profits, which would mean a transfer of income from consumers to the owners of the monopoly.

20. The objective of advertising is to shift product demand to the right. However, advertising also increases costs, so the additional sales from advertising must outweigh the additional expense, or it will not be undertaken.

21. The existence of pollution by firms in imperfect competition means the cost as viewed by the firm is less than the true or full costs of production. Pollution control by firms will have the inevitable result of increasing costs and prices of products.

22. The MC curve of an imperfectly competitive firm is not its supply curve, as is true for the perfectly competitive firm. In order for the MC curve to be a supply curve it must show the quantity produced for a given price, or vice versa. For imperfect competition demand and MR combine with MC to determine price and quantity.

23. Moving from perfect competition to pure monopoly, the demand curve facing each firm becomes more inelastic.

24. The imperfectly competitive buyer faces a supply curve that is upward sloping. This is a relatively rare situation, most likely to occur in the labor market.

Questions for thought and discussion

1. A common characteristic shared by all imperfectly competitive firms is that they all face a downward-sloping demand curve. What does this mean in economic terms?

2. Imperfectly competitive firms tend to place price tags on their products. Does this mean they are free to charge any price they please? Explain.

3. Suppose by lowering its price from 34.9 to 33.9 cents per gallon a service station can sell 1,500 gallons of gasoline per week, as opposed to 1,000. Can we infer from these figures that the marginal revenue of an extra gallon sold in this range of output is 33.9 cents? Why or why not? What is MR in this case?

4. Explain why an imperfectly competitive firm will maximize profits or minimize losses if it produces the level of output that corresponds to the point where MR equals MC.

5. Using a diagram, explain the long-run process of adjustment that would likely take place if a grocery store in an expanding resort area is making pure profits.

6. Frequently we observe gasoline stations going out of business because of insufficient profits, only to be opened up again a month or two later by another owner. Can you explain why this should happen? If the original owner couldn't make a profit, how can the second owner expect to do any better?

7. In a market characterized by monopolistic competition, we would expect to observe all firms making zero pure profits. True or false? Explain.

8. Under what assumptions is the kinked demand curve derived? How can it be used to explain "sticky" prices in an oligopolistic market situation?

9. Explain what would likely occur if the actual prices of comparable models of Chevrolets and Fords were not just about the same.

10. Why do you suppose Cadillacs sell for substantially more

than comparable models of Chryslers even though both have about the same list prices?

11. Explain why a private monopoly results in a misallocation of resources.

12. "A monopoly is guaranteed a pure profit because it can set any price it pleases." True or false? Explain.

13. The socially optimum price for a public monopoly corresponds to the point where its ATC curve intersects its demand curve, so no pure profits are being made. True or false? Explain.

14. Suppose you and two other people owned the only three service stations in a small town. Do you think the three of you could get together and collude to set gas prices higher than if you competed with one another? Explain.

15. Why do individual firms advertise? Do you think society would be better or worse off if all advertising were banned? Explain.

16. The distinguishing characteristic of imperfectly competitive firms is that the demand curve facing the firm is the same as the industry or market demand curve. True or false? Explain.

9

The labor market

To this point we have been concerned with the market for consumer goods and services and the activities of individual firms within that market. In this and the next chapter we will study two other markets: those for the two primary factors of production, labor and capital. It is true, of course, that most production utilizes inputs in addition to labor and capital, such as fuel, light and power, and raw materials of all kinds. But these latter elements, often referred to as intermediate inputs, are themselves a product of some production activity. If we trace through the manufacture of these intermediate inputs we find that all are derived ultimately from labor and capital. In years past, when agriculture was the predominant industry, economists generally included land as a separate primary input, but in most cases land is now also thought of as capital.

Labor as a factor of production

Economists at times have been accused of being callous or insensitive to the feelings of human beings by treating labor as an input or factor of production. It is argued that such treatment dehumanizes labor, making people equivalent to inanimate objects that are bought or sold.

In fact, economists are probably no more or less callous than any other group in society, with the possible exception of the clergy. Economists recognize that people are not bought and sold but their labor or services are (professional athletes may be an exception). And economists have found that economic principles can be brought to bear in analyzing past behavior of the market for human services (labor) and predicting future behavior. Moreover, as we shall see, the special attributes of labor, such as the feelings of individuals, are reflected in the labor market.

We should also note that there is a certain amount of capital embodied (no pun intended) in labor, because of the education and training that people receive. As we will see in Chapter 11, education or training of any kind can be thought of as an investment that results in the creation of human capital. In a modern society there is relatively little demand for a person who does not possess some human capital and has only labor to sell. In this sense, workers have become capitalists.

The labor market, like the product market, is made up of demanders and suppliers. We will see that the price of labor (wages or salaries) is determined by the interaction of demand and supply. Society, or at least certain groups in society, may not like the wage that the market determines and as a result may attempt to change the wage. But let us first see how the market functions before we study attempts to modify it.

Input demand with perfect competition in the product market

Our study of the labor market will begin by deriving the demand for labor by a firm selling its product in a perfectly competitive market. As we saw in Chapter 7, this is the type of firm that faces a perfectly elastic demand curve for its product.

You might be surprised to learn that we have already constructed (in Chapter 4) the basic foundation of the demand for labor: the marginal physical product (MPP) of labor. Recall that the MPP of labor is the additional output obtained from adding one more unit of labor, holding other inputs constant. Remember also that after some point the MPP of labor begins to decline. We referred to this phenomenon as the law of diminishing returns. In our discussion of labor demand we will only be concerned with the area of diminishing returns, that is, the downward-sloping portion of the curve representing MPP.

In order to derive the demand for labor we need only to assign a value to MPP. Keep in mind that MPP is given in physical units of the product. We used bushels of tomatoes in the example in Chapter 4. In order to determine the value of MPP we simply multiply the price of the product times MPP. For example, if the MPP for a certain input of labor is 7 bushels of tomatoes and the price of tomatoes is $3 per bushel, then the value of the marginal product (VMP) of this labor is $21.

The relationship between MPP and VMP is illustrated in Figure 9–1(A) and (B). Both curves look exactly the same, except the measure on the vertical axis is bushels for MPP and dollars for VMP. The line or curve depicting VMP is downward sloping, meaning that successive increments of the input, labor in this example, add less and less to the total value of output. The downward-sloping characteristic of the line is due entirely to the law of diminishing returns.

FIGURE 9–1
Relationship between marginal physical product and value of marginal product
(A) Marginal physical product   *(B) Value of marginal product*

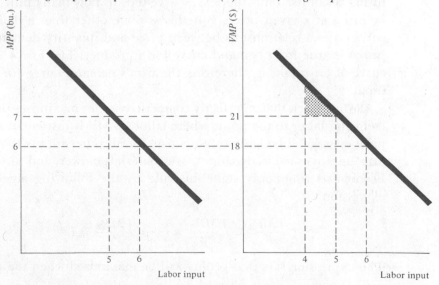

Once VMP has been derived, it is possible to determine how many units of labor the firm will hire, given the price of labor. Suppose for example that the price of labor is $21 per day, regardless of how many units the firm hires. To choose a number from Figure 9–1(B), suppose the firm hires four units. At four units of labor, the VMP of the last or fourth unit hired is somewhat greater than $21. In other words, if the firm spends $21 for an extra unit of labor, this labor will earn somewhat more than $21 for the firm. Anytime you can spend a dollar and receive more than one dollar in return, do it. Thus the firm would definitely want to hire the fourth unit.

But would the firm want to stop hiring at four units of labor? To answer this question, assume that the firm can hire some fraction of a unit, say an hour. We can see from Figure 9–1(B) that adding an extra hour over the fourth unit also adds more to total revenue than to total cost, that is, profits are increased. Thus as long as VMP is greater than the price of the input, the firm can add to total profits by hiring more of the input. And it will continue to add more of the input until its VMP comes down to the price of the input, at five units in Figure 9–1(B). If the firm had stopped at four units it would have foregone profits equal in value to the shaded triangle in Figure 9–1(B).

At another price (or wage), say $18, the firm maximizes profits by hiring six units. Thus the VMP curve tells us how many units will be hired at a given price. But this is none other than a demand curve. It is a relationship between price and quantity demanded, just as is true for a demand curve for a product. The firm's VMP curve of an input, is, therefore, the firm's demand curve for that input.

We have seen that a perfectly competitive seller maximizes profits by hiring labor to the point where labor's VMP is just equal to its price or wage. The same thing is true for all other inputs that the firm employs such as machines, raw materials, power, and so forth. Economists commonly state this rule by the following algebraic expression

$$\frac{VMP_A}{P_A} = \frac{VMP_B}{P_B} = \cdots = \frac{VMP_Z}{P_Z} = 1$$

This expression says that profits will be maximized when the price of each input employed is equal to its VMP, that is, when the ratio of VMP to price is equal to one.

MARKET DEMAND

We can obtain the market demand for an input by summing all the individual firms' demand curves. The technique for summing input demand is much the same as that used for summing product demand back in Figure 3–5. At each input price, all the individual quantities are summed to obtain the total quantity demanded in the market at that price.[1]

When deriving market demand for an input by summing all firms' VMP curves, we should bear in mind that this procedure implies that all other inputs used in the production process are being held constant. (Recall the definition of MPP.) Although this is a perfectly legitimate way to define market demand for an input, it is generally a bit more useful and realistic to hold the *price* of other inputs constant but allow the *quantity* of each to vary, according to its most profitable level of use. In such a situation, the firm can substitute more of a relatively cheaper input for one that has risen in price. For example, when the price of labor increases relative to that of capital, producers in many cases can substitute capital for labor.[2] (We presented the rationale underlying this phenomenon back in Chapter 4.)

If we allow the quantities of related inputs to vary, then the quantity demanded of an input will increase when its price decreases, for two reasons. First, a decline in the price of an input lowers production costs and as a result output is increased because of the increase in product supply. (Recall the factors that shift product supply.) And as firms find it profitable to increase output, they of course increase the employment of the input that has declined in price. Second, a decline in input price provides an incentive to substitute it for other inputs, as mentioned in the previous paragraph.

---

[1] We are assuming here that product price remains constant at all levels of input use. If we allowed product price to decline with increased employment of the input, the market demand would be somewhat less elastic.

[2] It might also be noted that the demand for an input will be more elastic when prices of related inputs are held constant than when their quantities remain fixed.

Both factors contribute to the increased use of a relatively cheaper input.

Input demand with imperfect competition in the product market

Once deriving the demand for labor under perfect competition is understood, it is a relatively easy task to derive labor demand under imperfect competition. Because the imperfectly competitive firm faces a downward-sloping demand curve for its product, the marginal revenue of an extra unit produced or sold is less than the price of this unit. Since MR is less than price, in this case we are not able to determine the value of the marginal product of an input by multiplying MPP by product price. The reason is that the price of the product must fall in order for the firm to sell any extra units produced, and this price reduction must apply to all units produced, not just the marginal unit. In this case, therefore, the value of the additional output obtained by adding an extra unit of labor is equal to MR times MPP. Economists refer to the product of MR times MPP as the marginal revenue product (MRP). Thus, where the demand curve for an input of a perfectly competitive firm is commonly denoted by VMP, input demand of a firm in imperfect competition is known as MRP.

Since price equals marginal revenue for a perfectly competitive seller, there is really no difference in the method of calculating input demand for each of the four types of firms. The abbreviations VMP and MRP are useful, however, in identifying the type of market we are dealing with.

Since MR is less than price, it is reasonable to expect that for a given level of input use, MRP would be less than VMP. This is illustrated in Figure 9–2, where MRP declines at a faster rate than VMP. It is a bit easier to understand this if it is realized that VMP declines only because of the law of diminishing returns. On the other hand, MRP declines for two reasons: (1) the law of diminishing returns, which is reflected in a declining MPP, and (2) the decline in marginal revenue as larger quantities of the product are sold.

FIGURE 9–2
Comparing value of marginal product and marginal revenue product

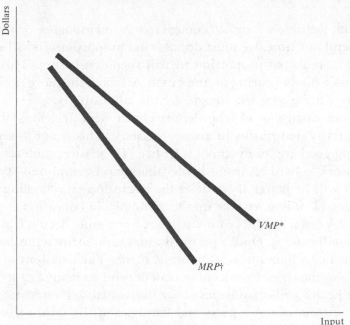

VMP*

MRP†

Dollars

Input

* Denotes a perfectly competitive seller.
† Denotes an imperfectly competitive seller.

The rule for employing the optimum amount of inputs by an imperfectly competitive seller on the product market basically is the same as the rule we presented earlier for a perfectly competitive seller. The only difference is that we now use MRP rather than VMP. Thus the algebraic expression for maximizing profits becomes

$$\frac{MRP_A}{P_A} = \frac{MRP_B}{P_B} = \cdots = \frac{MRP_Z}{P_Z} = 1$$

Although our interest in this chapter is primarily with labor, we have seen that much of the material on the demand side of the market can be applied to the employment of inputs in general. Let us now turn our attention to the supply side of the labor market. Here we will see that labor possesses some unique characteristics. We begin with the labor-leisure choice.

The labor-leisure choice

From the time we are old enough to have an influence on the way we spend our time, we must decide what proportion we will spend working and what proportion we will spend on leisure. This decision has a direct bearing on the supply of labor; the more time people are willing to work, the greater the labor supply.

In our discussion of labor-leisure choice we will define labor as any activity that results in a wage or salary. This is not to say that earning good grades in school is leisure. To be sure, students probably work as hard as, if not harder than, most "employed" people. But it will be better if we defer the discussion on schooling until Chapter 11, where we take up the economics of education.

Each person available for the labor force must decide first if he or she will enter it. Once a person decides to do so, then the decision of how many hours to work must be made. The decisions to go to work and the type of work chosen can depend on many factors, such as the health and capabilities of the individual; self-esteem, as well as the esteem of one's peers and family; and the satisfaction that results from mastering a difficult task. However, the economic factor is almost always present. Most of us have to earn a living. Moreover, the wage or salary we obtain can be expected to influence our choice of work and how much we will work.

The effect of wages and salaries on our work decisions can be made a bit clearer if we think of leisure as a good. Like any other good, a certain amount of it brings us satisfaction. Since few of us are paid for our leisure time, the decision to spend some of our time at leisure means that we must forego a certain amount of income. In reality then, the price of an extra hour of leisure is the income we forego by not working this hour.

As is true for everything else we buy, price has an important bearing on the quantity we consume. Recall from the discussion of Chapter 3 on product demand that consumers change their purchases of products with a change in prices because of the substitution and income effects. For example, if your wage increases, the price of your leisure increases. The substitution effect says that you will substitute other goods and services for leisure—you will work more. On the other hand, a higher wage also gives you a higher income, which you may use in part to "buy" more leisure.

We can illustrate the income and substitution effects between income and leisure on an indifference curve–budget line diagram similar to the one developed in Chapter 3, only now we will let the indifference curves represent the choice between money (or income) and leisure. Presumably we can visualize ourselves being equally well off between various possible combinations of money and leisure. By working a long workweek we have more money and less leisure; if we work relatively few hours per week, we have less money but more leisure or freedom to enjoy it. It is not unreasonable to suppose that two or more of such combinations could make us equally well off or satisfied. Each indifference curve drawn in Figure 9–3 therefore denotes various possible combinations of money and leisure that could make us equally well off.

The budget line in Figure 9–3 denotes the money income earned at various levels of leisure for a given wage rate. If we consider an entire week as the unit of analysis, the budget line will intersect the leisure axis at 168 hours (7 days times 24 hours). In this case we

FIGURE 9–3
Labor-leisure choice illustrated by an indifference curve–budget line diagram

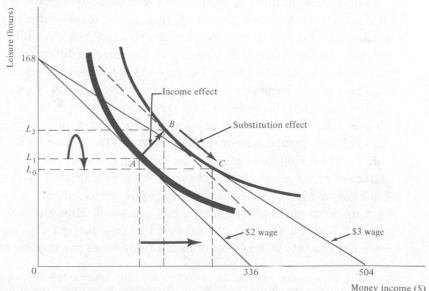

would have zero income but 168 hours of leisure per week. We can find the point where the budget line intersects the income axis by multiplying 168 times the hourly wage rate. For example if the wage rate is $2 an hour, the point of intersection will be $336. In this case we would have zero leisure but $336 income.

Of course it is not reasonable to believe that we would choose either all leisure or all money income (zero leisure). At the very least we need to sleep, and most of us are willing to give up some income for the opportunity to engage in other "nonwork" activities. Assuming that we are free to choose that combination of income and leisure that provides the maximum satisfaction for a given wage rate, we could identify that combination which corresponds to the tangency point between the budget line and the highest possible indifference curve. At the $2 wage rate, this is represented by point A on Figure 9–3.

Now suppose the wage increases to $3 per hour. The maximum income we could earn per week at this wage increases to $504 ($3 × 168), so the budget line rotates in a counterclockwise fashion. As a result, the optimum money-leisure mix changes to point C. Notice, however, that C corresponds to slightly less leisure (more hours of work) than A.

The process of moving from A to C can demonstrate the income and substitution effects. The magnitude of the income effect can be measured by drawing in a hypothetical budget line parallel to the original budget line but tangent to the new indifference curve (shown by the broken line in Figure 9–3). This line tells us that the increase in our income stemming from a higher wage allows us to "buy" more leisure, as shown by the movement from L_1 to L_2 on the vertical axis. However, because leisure is now more expensive, we in effect attempt to substitute other goods for leisure by working more and earning more income. In this particular example the substitution effect more than offsets the income effect by pulling us back toward less leisure than we originally "purchased." Thus we end up working slightly more hours per week after the wage increase.[3] (Of course, it would be possible to construct an example where the substitution effect does not fully offset the income effect,

[3] It is also possible and equally correct to show the substitution effect along the original indifference curve by drawing the hypothetical budget line tangent to it but parallel to the new budget line.

thus leaving us with slightly more leisure. You might try this with a diagram of your own.)

In summary, the income effect pulls us toward more leisure, while the substitution effect offsets this and pulls us back toward less leisure, or more work. Which effect prevails depends on the individual. At low levels of income a raise in wages probably increases work and decreases leisure. At relatively high levels of income, a person can "afford" more leisure, so he might work less or at least not increase hours worked as the wage rate increases.

You might reasonably ask at this point whether an individual really has much choice regarding the amount of leisure he can "purchase." After all, most jobs require the standard 40-hour workweek. However, there probably is more flexibility in this choice than one might first suppose. First, everyone has a chance to work more hours by "moonlighting" or holding two jobs. By the same token a person usually can work slightly less hours by increasing his rate of absenteeism or finding a job that requires a shorter work week. If enough people wanted to work only 30 hours per week, for example, we would likely see some employers offering jobs with this option. The fact that the workweek for most occupations has averaged just a bit over 40 hours since the end of World War II is strong evidence that most people prefer to work about this many hours per week. In other words, as wages have increased, the substitution effect has just about offset the income effect during the past 25 years.

Labor supply

The supply of labor, like the supply of a product, denotes a relationship between price and quantity. As indicated by the substitution and income effects on the labor-leisure choice, we can reasonably expect hours worked to increase as wages increase, at least at relatively low wage levels. At higher wage levels, however, people can afford more leisure, so we might expect a smaller degree of response to wage increases.

The changing response to wage increases is illustrated in Figure 9–4. The first three diagrams represent the supply of labor by three individuals. At $2 per hour, individual 1 is willing to supply 40

FIGURE 9–4
Wage response and market supply of labor

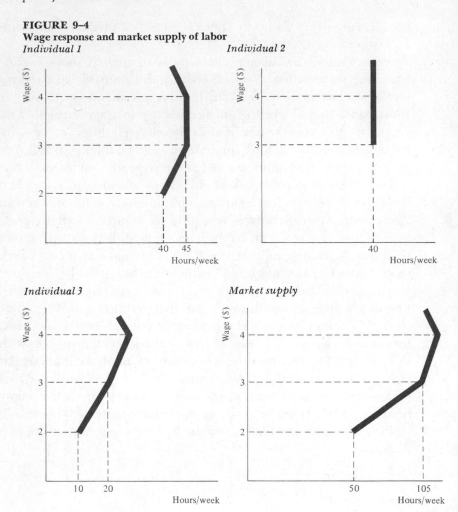

Individual 1

Individual 2

Individual 3

Market supply

hours a week of labor. As the wage increases to $3 per hour, he in-
creases his workweek to 45 hours. At $4 per hour he works the same
amount, 45 hours, and at wages exceeding $4 he reduces the length
of his workweek. In other words, at the $4 and over wage the sub-
stitution effect does not override the income effect. Individual 2, on
the other hand, does not enter the labor force until wages rise to $3
per hour. In the range of wages considered, the workweek remains
at 40 hours. Individual 3 will work 20 hours per week at the $3 wage

but does not increase his hours worked very much as wages rise. These, of course, are just examples of what we might expect from different individuals. The first person might be the main "breadwinner" of a family, the second a housewife who decides to enter the labor market at a $3 wage, and the third a college student holding a part-time job.

If it is assumed, to keep the example simple, that these three individuals comprise the available supply of labor, the market supply can be derived by adding together the quantity supplied at each price. At $2 per hour, individuals 1 and 3 supply 40 and 10 hours, respectively, making a total of 50 hours. At the $3-per-hour wage level, individual 2 is included in the labor force. Thus, along with the slight increase in labor offered by individuals 1 and 3, raising the wage to $3 obtains a total of 105 hours supplied.

We should take note that the market supply of labor is likely to be more elastic than the supply of individuals currently working in the market. This occurs because of the entrance of people into the labor market as wages rise. The result may be greater response to wage increases for the market than is true for any given individual in the market.

We should also note, of course, that in any given area there are likely to be a number of labor markets: for unskilled or semiskilled labor, for the skilled trades, and for professional and managerial personnel. In general, the more highly skilled the labor involved, the wider the market area. For example, the market for economists is considered to be nationwide or perhaps even international in scope.

Wage determination with perfect competition in the labor market

Preceding chapters have developed the concept that the prices of goods and services are determined by the forces of demand and supply. We can apply these same principles to the market for labor. The market demand for labor can be expected to be represented by a downward-sloping line similar to the market demand for a good or service. On the supply side, total amount of labor forthcoming in any given labor market can be expected to increase with an increase in wage rates, as illustrated by the market supply curve in Figure 9–4 above. The wage that is determined in the market is a result of the interaction of the demand and supply of labor. The process of wage determination is illustrated in Figure 9–5(A).

FIGURE 9–5
Wage determination: Perfect competition in the labor market
(A) The market   *(B) The individual employer*

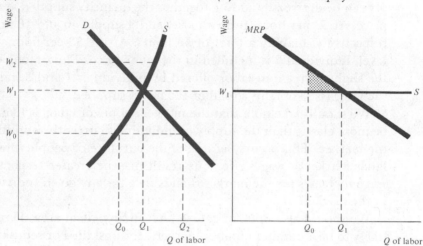

If the wage happened to be above the equilibrium, say W_2, more people would be willing to work than are demanded by prospective employers. As a result there would be a number of unemployed people willing to work at a wage lower than W_2. Knowing this, employers will reduce wages down to W_1, because they would not want to pay more than what people are willing to work for. Of course, as wages come down to W_1, the quantity of labor supplied decreases and the quantity demanded increases. At W_1 these two quantities coincide so that everyone who is willing to work at this wage has employment.

If wages are lower than the equilibrium, say at W_0, employers would like to hire more labor than what people will supply. At this low wage and relatively small employment, the marginal revenue product of labor for employers in the market is greater than the wage. Thus employers can increase profits by increasing wages to induce a larger quantity of labor to be offered in the market. As wages rise, the quantity of labor offered increases and the quantity demanded decreases. The increase will continue until it reaches W_1. At this point the incentive for employers to pay higher wages to obtain more labor disappears.

If we assume that the market is in equilibrium, with wage W_1 prevailing, the perfectly competitive employer of labor faces a supply curve of labor such as that shown by S in Figure 9–5(B). Such a supply curve implies that the individual employer cannot influence the wage he pays; he takes the wage as determined in the market. This situation exists if the firm hires a small share of the labor force in his community or area.

Even though the firm depicted in Figure 9–5(B) is a perfectly competitive buyer of labor, it can be either a perfectly competitive or imperfectly competitive seller in the product market. If perfectly competitive, the downward-sloping line in Figure 9–5(B) could be referred to as the firm's value of marginal product (VMP) curve, whereas according to our previous notation it would be marginal revenue product (MRP) if imperfectly competitive on the selling side. In order to minimize confusion over notation, we refer to the curve in Figure 9–5(B) as MRP, keeping in mind that the same reasoning would apply if we called it the VMP curve. Similarly, whenever we mention MRP in the discussion that follows or denote an MRP curve on a diagram, bear in mind that VMP could be inserted in its place.[4]

If the firm wishes to maximize profits it will hire labor up to the point where the wage W_1 is equal to the firm's MRP. If it stopped short of this point, say Q_0, then the contributions of a marginal worker would be greater than the wage of this worker. Suppose that MRP is $3 at Q_0 and the wage is $2.50. By adding an extra hour of labor, the firm pays out $2.50 but receives $3.00 in return. These two figures come closer and closer together as the firm continues to add labor but total profits continue to increase. If the firm stopped hiring at Q_0, it would forego profits equal in value to the shaded triangle shown in Figure 9–5(B).

---

4 Since MR equals price for a perfectly competitive seller, it is still correct to refer to VMP as MRP, even if we are dealing with a perfectly competitive seller.

The implication of a horizontal supply curve of labor facing a firm is that the firm has no control over the wage it pays, and if it lowers the wage slightly the quantity of labor available to it will fall to zero. But because labor is not strictly homogeneous, like bushels of wheat or corn, the firm probably can get by with paying a slightly lower wage than the average of other employers in its vicinity. Firms that pay a slightly lower wage, however, usually attract employees who are slightly less qualified or less productive than the average. Low-wage firms also tend to have a higher turnover of personnel, which adds to the cost of training or "breaking in" employees. Thus it is not always in the interest of the employer to pay a lower than average wage. Firms that pay relatively high wages can be more selective in whom they hire and can avoid a high turnover of personnel.

At any rate, the perfectly elastic supply curve of labor facing such a firm is more accurately interpreted as a range of wages around the average. For example, if the average wage is $2.75 per hour for a given type of labor, an individual employer might pay anywhere from $2.50 to $3 per hour.

Wage determination with imperfect competition in the labor market

Although imperfect competition on the buying side of the labor market is less frequent than perfect competition, it is possible to observe cases where employers hire a fairly large share of the labor in an area. Some examples might be a "company" mining town in the West or a canning factory in a farming community.

A common characteristic of all imperfectly competitive employers is that they face an upward-sloping supply curve of labor, which implies that the employer must pay a higher wage if he wishes to increase his labor force. Or, if he wishes to reduce the number of people he employs, he can reduce the wage he pays.

An inevitable result of an upward-sloping curve facing a firm is that the additional or marginal cost of adding more labor exceeds the wage of the extra workers. The reason for this phenomenon is that the firm must pay a higher wage to attract additional employees, and this higher wage must then be paid to all employees.

Economists refer to the cost of adding additional labor as the marginal resource cost (MRC) of labor. At any level of labor hired, the MRC of labor is greater than the wage paid. Thus if we wish to represent this relationship on a diagram, the MRC curve would lie above the supply curve and would rise at a faster rate, as shown in Figure 9–6.

You will note that marginal resource cost on the buying side of the labor market is strictly analogous to marginal revenue (MR) on the selling side of the product market. Marginal revenue is less than price because to sell more the price reduction must apply to all units sold; MRC is greater than the wage because to hire more the higher wage must apply to all labor employed, not just the marginal workers. In other words, the MRC of an additional worker is the wage paid to this worker plus the small increase in total wages that must be paid to each of the firm's other employees.

If the firm wishes to maximize profits it will attempt to equate the MRC of its labor with labor's MRP and hire Q_1 of labor. If it stopped short of this point, say at Q_0, the contribution of a marginal unit of labor would exceed its cost. And as we saw in the preceding section, increasing the labor hired from Q_0 to Q_1 results in an addition to total profits equal in value to the shaded triangle in Figure 9–6.

We should take note also in Figure 9–6 that the wage paid by the imperfectly competitive employer of labor is equal to W_0, the point on the supply curve corresponding to Q_1, the quantity of labor hired. At this quantity of labor, people are willing to work for W_0. Unlike the situation for a perfectly competitive employer, MRP is greater than the wage. This is not to say that the imperfectly competitive firm "exploits" labor. By attempting to maximize profits, this type of firm is behaving in exactly the same manner as a perfectly competitive employer. It is hiring labor up to the point where the additional cost of adding another unit of labor (MRC) is just equal to the contribution of that worker to value of output (MRP).

We should point out also that wages paid by a perfectly competitive buyer of labor should not be any different from wages paid by an imperfectly competitive buyer of comparable labor in the

FIGURE 9–6
Wage determination: Imperfect competition in the labor market

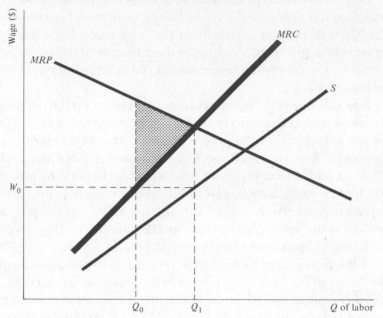

same labor market. If wages were not about equal, employees would have a strong incentive to quit the low-paying employer and switch to the higher paying one.[5]

It is important to recognize as well that it is not necessary for all employees to be mobile in order to prevent long-run wage differences between individual employers or markets. When wages paid by an employer get out of line with wages elsewhere, a movement of a relatively small percentage of all employees from the low- to the high-wage employers usually is enough to force wages up in the low-wage markets and bring them down in the high-wage jobs. Also an inequality of wages between areas or regions usually results in some employers moving to the low-wage areas, as illustrated by the movement of northern industry to the South since the end of

---

[5] We are assuming in this situation that the labor market consists of one or more imperfectly competitive buyers of labor and several smaller employers.

World War II. This has the effect of increasing labor demand in the low-wage areas and decreasing demand in the high-wage areas. As a result, any wage differences tend to narrow or disappear completely.

In order to differentiate imperfect competition on the buying side of the market from the selling side, economists have labeled a market where there are few buyers as an "oligopsony." This is comparable to oligopoly, which characterizes a situation of few sellers in a market. If there is only one buyer of labor, the firm would be referred to as a "monopsony," comparable to monopoly on the selling side.

This does not mean, however, that an oligopoly on the selling side results in oligopsony on the buying side, or vice versa. The same is true of monopsony. For example, a local light and power company might have a virtual monopoly on the sale of electricity, but in all likelihood it is a perfectly competitive buyer of labor.

Shifts in demand for labor

So far in this chapter we have studied how wages are determined in the two kinds of labor markets. Now we will attempt to explain changes in wages and levels of employment. We have noted, in Chapter 6, that if a product market is in equilibrium, the only way a change in price can occur is by a change or shift in either demand or supply of the product, or both. The same is true for labor. Wages change in response to a change in market demand, supply, or both.

Let us look first at changes or shifts in the demand for labor. Most of what we have said about shifts in demand for labor can be applied to the demand for any other input as well. Recall from our discussion of the product market that an increase in demand occurs when it shifts upward and to the right, as shown by D_2 in Figure 9–7(A), or MRP_1 in Figure 9–7(B). You will notice in this case that the equilibrium or profit-maximizing wage will also increase, and, as you might expect, a decrease in labor demand will result in a decrease in wages, as illustrated by D_0 or MRP_0 in the diagrams in Figure 9–7.

Because value of marginal product (VMP) for a perfectly competitive buyer of labor is derived by multiplying marginal physical product (MPP) times product price, we would expect either a change in product price or a change in MPP of labor to shift the demand for labor. The same would be true for an imperfectly competitive buyer of labor because a change in price also results in a change in marginal revenue. We can conclude, therefore, that the demand for labor will shift in response to a change in product price or a change in the productivity of labor. The same would hold true for any input. The following is a summary of these changes.

1. *Change in product price.* A rise in product price, of course, results in a higher VMP or marginal revenue product for a given level of input use. The opposite would be true for a decline in product price.

2. *Change in marginal physical product.* There are three major factors that can change or shift an input's MPP. These are:

   a) *Change in quantity or quality of complementary inputs.* Economists define a complementary input as one that increases the MPP of a given input when the use of the complement is increased. Consider, for example, a man digging a hole with a spade. Give him a power shovel, and his productivity or MPP will increase. Thus the power shovel would be considered a complement to labor, as would raw materials of all kinds. Without bricks, mortar, or lumber, for example, a construction worker would not be productive.

   An increase in the quality of a complementary input has the same effect as an increase in its quantity, that is, it increases, or shifts to the right, the MPP curve of the input in question. For example, a secretary with a new electric typewriter is likely to be more productive than she would be with a slower, manual model.

   b) *Changes in quantity or quality of substitute inputs.* Economists define a substitute input as one that decreases the MPP of a given input when the use of the substitute is increased. For example, the use of a second man on one spade would reduce the MPP of the first man, because he could use it only part of the time.

   It is not obvious in a given production activity whether two inputs are complements or substitutes. Furthermore, this relationship can change at different levels or mixes of

FIGURE 9–7
Shifts in the demand for labor
(A) Perfectly competitive market

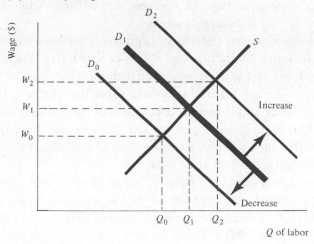

(B) Imperfectly competitive employer

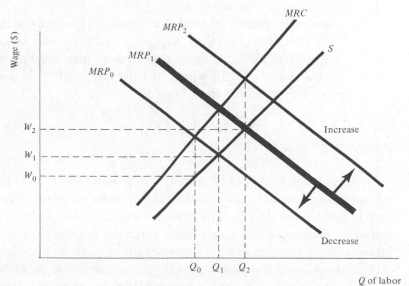

input use. For example, giving the power shovel to the two men with the spade will increase the MPP of the man who operates the machine but decrease the MPP of the second man if he just stands and watches.

For some labor, therefore, capital or machines serve as complements, by increasing labor's productivity. For other labor, however, usually those with the lowest skills or seniority on the job, capital may be a substitute, forcing them to find other employment. It is this latter situation that we hear about most in regard to automation and unemployment. But let us defer our discussion of the effects of automation until later in the chapter.

An increase in the quality of a substitute input also has an effect similar to an increase in the quantity of such an input. In this case, quality improvement decreases, or shifts to the left, the MPP curve of the input in question. For example, an increase in the speed and capacity of a computer will decrease the MPP of a bookkeeper if it leaves him (or her) with nothing to do.

c) *Changes in quality of the input itself.* This factor is especially important for labor. Through education and training people have become more productive, that is, they have increased their MPP, which in turn has resulted in an increased demand for their labor.

Shifts in the supply of labor

In general the supply of labor tends to be more stable than labor demand. The overall supply of labor to the entire economy depends largely on the population. The more people there are, the more labor will be supplied at a given wage. Thus the aggregate supply of labor in the United States has increased along with its population. The proportion of the population participating in the labor force also affects the labor supply. During recent years in the United States an increasing proportion of women have joined the labor force, thus increasing the nation's overall supply of labor. And a greater proportion of college students are working part time, which also adds to the nation's labor force.

In a sense we can also think of the increase in education and skills of the labor force as contributing to the supply of labor. If we measure labor in homogeneous "efficiency units," then a given number of highly skilled people is equivalent to more labor than an equal number of less skilled people. In the previous section, we mentioned that an increase in skills of people tends to increase their productivity, hence their MPP and demand. An increase in the wages from increased skills requires, therefore, that the demand for skills increases more than the supply of skills.

The supply of labor facing a given industry or area would, of course, depend also on the population of the area, although in this case the supply of labor can shift also in response to a change in wages in some other industry or area. Suppose, for example, there is a sudden increase in the demand for labor, as occurred in the recent oil discoveries in northern Alaska. The increase in wages for people to man the oil rigs attracts more labor to this occupation. But this in turn tends to reduce (shifts to the left) the supply of labor to other nearby industries such as mining, trapping, or the service trades. It might be useful to illustrate this situation with two supply-demand diagrams of your own, one for oil drilling, the second for the other industries that employ similar types of labor.)

Wages and employment changes

We know there has been a long-run upward trend in both wages and employment in the United States. We also know that because of our population growth and the increased participation of women in the labor force, the supply of labor has been increasing or shifting to the right. From this information we would have to conclude that the demand for labor has been shifting to the right more rapidly than the labor supply. Otherwise, there could not have been an increase in both wages and employment.

The two main factors shifting labor demand to the right, thus raising wages, have been (1) an increase in the use of complementary inputs, mainly capital, and (2) an increase in the quality of the labor force through education. Recall from the preceding section that these two factors increase the productivity or MPP of labor and thereby increase labor demand.

For individual geographic areas, industries, or firms, however, there are instances where we can observe a decrease in demand for labor. This can occur if there is a decrease in demand for the good or service produced. As a result the firms involved reduce the quantity of inputs used that are complementary to labor, mainly capital and raw materials. There is a corresponding decline in labor's MPP and consequently a decline in labor demand, as shown in D_0 in Figure 9–7(A) above, for example.

The logical thing to expect in this situation is a decline in wages and employment. If we were dealing with a nonhuman input, no doubt this would occur. But in the case of labor, it is rather unwise for a firm to immediately reduce wages of its employees in response to a decrease in its marginal revenue product (MRP) of labor. An across-the-board wage cut affects all of a firm's employees and, to say the least, leaves employees unhappy. Disgruntled employees generally are not conducive to high labor productivity and profits. Moreover, if labor is represented by a union, the wage contract may forbid any decrease in wages.

Rather than reduce wages when there is a decline in demand for labor, most firms will choose to lay off more people, at least in the short run. A layoff affects only a relatively few of the firm's "marginal" employees, leaving the remainder virtually untouched. The people who are laid off may be disgruntled, but they are not around to affect the firm's productivity anyway. Of course, in the event of a severe and prolonged decline in the demand for labor in an area or by an industry, we would likely see some downward adjustment in money wages, such as occurred during the Great Depression. A more common occurrence, nowadays, however, is for the wages in a depressed area or industry to remain relatively stable or to rise less than wages in the overall economy. As a result these wages tend to decline relative to wages in other areas or occupations, and some employees leave voluntarily. This kind of adjustment is a bit easier to take than an absolute reduction in money wages.

As individuals in the labor market, it is important for us to realize that we must contribute at least as much to the output of our employer as we are paid. For example, if we are paid $7,000 per year and produce only $6,000 per year of goods or services, the firm loses $1,000 per year on us. A firm that loses $1,000 per year on an employee is better off without the employee, so we could look forward to losing our job. This does not mean that employers are inhuman or heartless. A firm that pays more out than it takes in soon goes out of business.

The situation does not change if we work for a public agency, even though the agency is not "profit minded." Here if we produce less than our wage taxpayers obtain less than what they pay for. Unless taxpayers or our fellow citizens wish to make a gift to us equal to the difference between our MRP and our wages, we will find our job in jeopardy. We might bemoan the fact that the world is so cruel, but it is a situation no one can change, regardless of the economic system.

It is, of course, possible for a person's wages to be somewhat greater than his MRP during the period he is learning or getting used to a new job. In this case, the employer might anticipate that the employee's MRP would exceed his wage sometime in the future when he is no longer a new and therefore marginal employee. It is reasonable to expect also, that in many occupations an individual's wage may not be exactly equal to his contribution to output. Hardworking, productive employees may be paid less than their MRP, while lazy, unproductive individuals might be paid more than they are worth. In many instances it is not possible for employers to distinguish between employees on the basis of their MRP. The union contract may not allow it, or it may not be economically feasible for a large firm to even attempt to make such a distinction. A common method of attempting to approximate MRP differences is to pay according to a seniority scale. This presumes that older, more experienced employees are more productive than younger, less experienced ones.

Wage differences

The large differences that exist between the wages or salaries of different people or groups sometimes seem unjustified. The movie star or professional athlete may earn $100,000 per year, working possibly six months, while the poor but honest laborer has to toil from dawn to dusk for a meager $4,000 per year.

Wage differences can largely be explained by demand and supply. A person lucky enough to possess some scarce talent that is in relatively high demand, such as being able to throw a baseball or football exceedingly well, tends to enjoy a relatively high wage. Other talents, such as being able to push or pull a lever on a machine all day, that are in abundant supply relative to their demand will be less well paid.

Some occupations require lengthy training periods, which has the effect of reducing the supply. The doctor, lawyer, or college professor who spends eight to ten years preparing for his profession must be compensated for the investment he has made in himself, or it would not pay him to enter the profession. Of course, substantial wage differences exist within and between professions even though the educational requirement is similar. For example, the internationally known heart surgeon or Nobel prize winner is likely to enjoy a salary (or income) several times larger than his relatively unknown colleagues. In large part, these salary or income differences reflect differences in ability and productivity. One does not enjoy an international reputation without some special accomplishment.

Some professions enjoy a higher average level of income than others with similar educational requirements because of a relatively strong union. Medical doctors, for example, tend to earn substantially more than college professors with a Ph.D. The former are represented by a strong "union," the American Medical Association (AMA), while college professors are not, for the most part, "unionized." We will discuss how unions such as the AMA are able to influence the income of their members in a following section.

Wages or salaries also tend to reflect differences in working conditions. An occupation that requires exposure to the elements or involves some special hazard tends to pay a higher salary than those that provide comfortable, safe working conditions. Construction workers, for example, tend to earn substantially more per year than bank clerks or shoe salesmen. Similarly, steel workers who put together the superstructure of today's "skyscrapers" are well paid for the physically demanding work they do and the risks they take. In general, jobs that present special risks or other disadvantages, such as working in remote areas, have to offer higher salaries in order to attract people. We might say that the supply of people to these jobs is small relative to the demand, so their wages are high. The relatively high wages of construction workers also can be attributed at least in part to a relatively strong union, which we will discuss shortly, and to the seasonality of their work. The wages lost during days when work is not possible because of bad weather conditions have to be made up during days when they can work.

On the other hand, occupations that allow one to work in air-conditioned comfort tend to offer somewhat lower salaries, given the educational requirements that usually accompany such jobs. We might say that people who work in these jobs take part of their salaries in attractive working conditions. For these jobs, the supply of people is large relative to the demand, so wages tend to be lower than in less attractive jobs.

Automation

While automation, the substitution of machines for human effort in a production activity, has become popular in recent years, it is not by any means new. In fact it probably began at the dawn of history when man discovered that by using the wheel one individual could pull as much as two or three could carry. As we think of it today, automation probably began with the Industrial Revolution over 100 years ago, although in recent years the computer has opened up more possibilities for automated production.

Is automation good or bad? Ask this question of wage earners and chances are many will say bad, especially if it is a threat to their jobs. But we must ask what life would be like if there had never been any automation. Most of us would be living in caves or tents, scratching a meager living from the soil with a few crude tools. Without the aid of machines, man is a relatively unproductive creature. Obviously we who are living in the 20th century benefit a great deal from past automation or mechanization of production.

As we noted in the section on labor demand, machines or capital serve as a complement to some labor, shifting its MPP curve upward and to the right. As man's real output increases, so do his wage and income. But machines or capital can at the same time be a substitute for other people, reducing their MPP and eliminating their jobs. It is this latter group of people who fear automation, and with good reason, for relatively few people like to see their jobs disappear. But the picture may not be quite so dark as might first appear. Because automation represents a more productive or cheaper method of production, the supply of the final product will be shifted to the right.

As consumers respond to the lower price of the product by purchasing more of it, the firm or industry will, of course, purchase more raw materials, which in turn will shift the MPP of the marginal workers to the right also. If the increase in output is sufficient to absorb the jobs eliminated by the automation, labor can end up in the happy situation of higher pay with a greater number of jobs.

We should note also that because of population growth and the expanding economy in the United States today, most industries are increasing their output. The effect of automation in this case is for employers not to take on additional labor as they increase output, a situation which is not nearly so unpleasant to labor as losing jobs that were already in existence. A good illustration of this phenomenon exists in the growth in the service trades relative to manufacturing, where automation has been more prevalent.

A prevalent fear is that because of automation jobs will become more and more scarce. Some go as far as to say that people will have to reduce their workweek to 20 to 30 hours in order for everyone to be employed. But this fear will remain unfounded until everyone has reached a state of complete satisfaction. As long as some people desire to consume more goods or services than they now do, there is no reason why everyone who wants a job cannot be working. Knowing human nature, we should not expect to see the day soon when everyone is satiated. Contrary to popular opinion, it is not jobs that are scarce but people and resources to do the jobs that produce the goods and services we all desire.

Discrimination

It is very difficult, if not impossible, to assess the full effect of discrimination in the labor market unless we ourselves have been denied a job because of our race, creed, or color. The full effect goes much deeper than the loss of income. The feeling of frustration, hopelessness, and low self-esteem can only be known by those discriminated against. Since this is a book on economics, however, we can only recognize that discrimination results in more than just economic harm.

In instances of discrimination there is a tendency to place the major blame on employers. Obviously, it is argued, employers who deny employment because of race, creed, or color are guilty of discrimination. But the problem usually goes a bit deeper than this. If the hiring of people from a minority group creates bitterness, strife, and the loss of productivity among workers already employed, no employer is going to be very eager to hire these people. In this situation the blame for discrimination must be shared by employees, as well as the employer.

In addition, there can well be discrimination against the output of a firm that hires from a minority group. This situation can easily prevail in the services or retail trades. For example, if consumers discriminate against stores that employ minority sales persons, employers may be reluctant to hire them. In this case the blame must fall also on the consumers.

This is not intended, of course, to furnish an excuse to the employer who discriminates against certain groups or offers only token integration. The main point is that equality of opportunity is not likely to become a reality until everyone starts accepting everyone else as individuals rather than as members of a particular race or group. The entertainment profession and the academic community must be given high marks in this regard.

Discrimination occurs also at the elementary and secondary levels of school. Since minority groups tend to live in poor neighborhoods and because schools obtain a large share of their financing from local taxes, the quality of instruction tends to be much lower among minority-group children than among the children of high- or middle-income parents. The result, of course, is poor preparation for the labor market or for further training. If minority people possess only minimum skills, hence a low marginal physical productivity, they can only qualify for low-paying jobs. Thus discrimination and poverty tend to perpetuate themselves; poor schooling leads to low income, and low income results in poor schooling.

In addition to the low quality of schooling, young people from minority groups often terminate their schooling much sooner than young people from middle-class neighborhoods. Since schooling is such an important prerequisite for a decent job in modern society, at first glance it appears that dropping out of high school or deciding not to attend a college or technical school is not very rational. A closer look, however, reveals that because of discrimination in the job market, it may indeed be rational not to invest in schooling. If the jobs that can be obtained with further schooling are not open to certain people, there is little incentive to train for them.

Women's liberation

In recent years the "women's lib" movement has drawn our attention to existing inequalities in women's salaries and opportunities, in comparison to those available to men. Over a long period of time certain occupations, such as nurse, secretarial worker, and airline stewardess, have traditionally become associated with women, while other occupations, such as construction worker, truck driver, and stevedore have been generally considered to be in the domain of men. Many people, especially women, are now questioning whether these traditional roles of men and women are justified.

It might be argued, of course, that some jobs require certain characteristics that are more likely to be inherent in women than in men, or vice versa. For example, women on the average probably have greater manual dexterity than men, but they do not possess as great physical strength. This may at least partly explain why typists tend to be women and construction and dock workers tend to be men. To the extent that physical differences between men and women do exist and these differences are important to certain jobs, the mix of men and women can be expected to be different. If the occupations that require staffing by men exhibit harsh working conditions such as exposure to the elements and hard physical labor, additional compensation may be required in order to attract qualified people, and we can expect the average salaries of men to be somewhat higher than those for women.

Whether the physical differences between men and women are important enough to cause some occupations to be dominated by one sex or the other is, of course, debatable. Those who argue they are not can point to the Soviet Union, where women can be found in large numbers in most occupations, ranging from street sweepers and construction workers to medical doctors. In fact the majority of doctors in the Soviet Union are women, suggesting some discrimination against men in this occupation. Of course, it is necessary to remember that the "liberation" of women in the Soviet Union probably came more from necessity than design, because of the wholesale dissipation of the male population during World War II.

It is, of course, possible to find occupations in this country where women are doing basically the same work as men but are earning lower salaries. Mainly it is these situations that give rise to charges of discrimination. It is, however, possible to explain at least part of these wage differences without resorting to the discrimination argument. As mentioned in a previous section, employees who are new on the job tend to be somewhat less productive than experienced employees while they're "learning the ropes." If an employer can be reasonably sure an employee will remain, he may be willing to pay the new employee a somewhat higher wage than would be the case if he were less certain the employee would stay. In the latter case, the starting salary of the new employee will likely be lower because the chance of the employer to recoup any early losses will be smaller. There are also some additional costs involved in finding, screening, and breaking-in new employees that have to be met, and these costs mount when employees change jobs relatively often.

In the past, at least, the employment of women has involved somewhat more uncertainty than the employment of men. When single women marry they are more likely than men to change their place of residence and thus to change jobs. Newly married women also have babies, which at least interrupts their employment, if it doesn't halt it. When married men change jobs or are transferred, their wives usually follow. (The opposite is much less likely; men usually do not change jobs because of a change in their wives' employment opportunities.)

This is not to argue that women are any less reliable or stable than men. The increased uncertainty comes about because of our family and social structure. Nor do we want to suggest that discrimination against women in the labor force does not exist. The dominance of men in professions where physical characteristics are not so important, such as law and medicine, is a case in point, although there appears to be less discrimination against women in these occupations than there used to be. The main point of this section is that some wage differences between men and women can be explained on the basis of occupational differences and because of the greater uncertainty involved in the hiring of women.

Labor unions

The primary objectives of labor unions are to obtain higher salaries for their members and to improve working conditions. In this section we will look primarily at the methods that unions use in attempting to raise wages, together with the limitations of these methods.

The discussion of wage determination established that wages are determined by forces of supply and demand similar to the determination of prices in the product market. It is reasonable to believe that in order for unions to modify wages they must in some way modify or change the market for labor. There are three basic ways this can be done.

1. *Increase the demand for labor.* This method is probably the most desirable of all three but the most difficult. It is desirable because it results in both a higher wage and larger employment, as illustrated in Figure 9–7(A) and (B) above. It is difficult because in general unions do not have much influence over the demand for labor.

One means of increasing labor demand is by increasing the demand for the final product. In years past unions utilized advertising urging consumers to buy "union-made" products. But as more and more industries became unionized, it became more difficult to distinguish union from nonunion products.

In recent years unions have been quite active in discouraging imports of foreign-made products by lobbying for protective tariffs or quotas on imports. The success of this kind of program is difficult to gauge because limiting imports has the effect of in turn limiting our exports. If we do not buy from other nations, they understandably limit their purchases from us. As a result there is a decrease in the export demand of union-made products.

Increasing the productivity of labor (or the MPP) will also increase the demand for labor. As a result unions have attempted to improve working conditions and shorten the workweek so as to maximize each man's potential. Unions also have encouraged education and have been active in apprenticeship programs, although, as we will see shortly, apprenticeship programs have been a more effective device for limiting the supply of labor.

Negotiating over job descriptions is another method unions have employed in attempts to increase or at least maintain the demand for labor. A certain job may call for the services of men from two or more unions, each doing a specific part of the job. In building a house, for example, the carpenters dare not infringe on any job the electricians or painters are supposed to do. Related to this is the practice of "featherbedding," which is an attempt by unions to create or maintain jobs that employers claim are not really necessary. The railroad fireman provides a good example. In the days of steam locomotives, this job was, of course, necessary. With the coming of diesel and electric power, railroads argue that the fireman is now redundant, and they maintain that union insistence that this job remain constitutes featherbedding.

Any kind of make-work scheme on the part of unions cannot be very successful, however, because it invariably results in higher than necessary production costs. As consumers substitute other goods and services that are cheaper for the higher priced union-made products, the demand for union labor will decline. Thus the union loses in the long run.

2. *Reduce the supply of labor.*   By and large, unions have been more successful in raising wages by limiting the supply of labor than by increasing demand. This is particularly true among the so-called craft unions representing skilled tradesmen. The prime vehicle for limiting entry into the profession or trade is by controlling entry into the training or apprenticeship program.

In most skilled trades or professions it is virtually impossible for an individual to find employment without a certificate or license bearing witness of successful completion of the training program. Because the power to issue licenses is generally in the hands of the trade or profession itself, it is not difficult to understand why they are generally in short supply.

Shifting the supply of labor back and to the left from what it would be with free entry into the profession increases wages and reduces the number of people employed. Trade unions and professional associations such as the AMA have utilized this technique with a high degree of success because the outcome (higher wages and less employment) does not, at least in the short run, harm established members of the trade or profession. Their wages are high, and they never have to fear unemployment.

The people who are harmed by this technique are those who could obtain higher incomes if they had been allowed to enter the profession and the general public, which ends up paying more for services rendered. If wages and the cost of services become excessively high, however, public opinion may result in governmental pressure to allow more freedom of entry. We are witnessing an example of this in the building trades at the present time. Also, substitute products will begin to show up, as evidenced by "mobile homes" or factory-built housing, which results in a decrease in demand for the services of skilled building tradesmen.

3. Bargain for a union wage. This technique is utilized by unions representing unskilled or semiskilled workers—the teamsters, the steel workers, the auto workers. These are often referred to as the industrial unions, as opposed to the craft unions. Unlike the craft unions, which limit membership, the industrial union's goal is to bring all workers in the industry into union membership. The wisdom of this policy becomes clear when we remember that because the jobs represented by industrial unions require little or no training, there is always a large pool of substitute labor that can easily step in if union labor becomes more costly than nonunion labor. In addition, the success of industrial unions hinges on the condition that all firms in the industry employ union members. When unionized firms pay a higher wage and hence incur higher costs, the lower priced products of the nonunionized firms soon take over the market.

In bargaining for a union wage, unions attempt to obtain a higher wage for their members than would be determined in a free market. As explained earlier in this chapter, this wage corresponds to the intersection of labor's demand and supply in a perfectly competitive market, as is illustrated in Figure 9–8(A) by W_0. The free-market wage in an imperfectly competitive labor market is also denoted in Figure 9–8(B) by W_0. The union wage is denoted by W_u in both diagrams.

In perfect competition, note that the imposition of the union

FIGURE 9–8
Union wages in the labor market
(A) Perfect competition

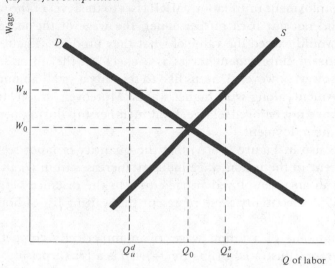

(B) Imperfect competition

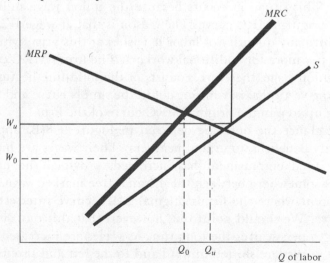

wage reduces the quantity of labor employed in the market from Q_0 to Q_u^d. In order for employers to pay the higher wage they must reduce employment until labor's MRP rises to the level of the wage. If they did not cut back on personnel, the wage of the marginal workers would exceed the value of what they produce. The resulting decline in employment serves as a check on the union's bargaining power, however. Unions like to see only a small amount of unemployment, along with higher wages. Moreover, unions traditionally have not enjoyed a large, loyal membership during periods of high unemployment.

Notice also in Figure 9–8(A) that the quantity of labor seeking employment in the union wage industry increases from Q_0 to Q_u^s, resulting in an unemployed fringe equal to the distance between Q_u^d and Q_u^s. Essentially these represent the waiting list of hopeful employees.

The outcome of a union wage in an imperfectly competitive labor market, illustrated in Figure 9–8(B), is a bit surprising. You will note that in a free market the imperfectly competitive buyer of labor pays W_0 and hires Q_0. But when the union comes in and bargains for a wage, say W_u, the employer increases employment up to Q_u. This situation occurs because the union wage nullifies the firm's original MRC curve. The reason is that at wage W_u, the firm can hire any quantity of labor it wishes at this wage without having to pay more for additional workers. The firm's MRC curve under a union wage, therefore, consists of the solid line beginning at W_u on the vertical axis, running out to the supply curve and then extending up to join the original MRC curve of the firm.

At first glance the outcome depicted in Figure 9–8(B) appears to be highly beneficial to union members: Their wages are higher and their total employment has increased, provided the union wage is set somewhere between the original free market wage, W_0, and the point where the firm's original MRC curve intersects its MRP curve. We should point out, however, that this outcome is not likely to persist over the long run. As wages are increased, the firms' cost curves are shifted upward and to the left and profits are reduced. Those firms making only normal profits to begin with will tend to leave the business, output will decline, and the total demand facing the union for its labor also will decline. So labor still ends up with fewer jobs in the long run than would otherwise be the case. Furthermore, the prevalence of imperfectly competitive employers should not be overemphasized. The vast majority of all employers hire a relatively small proportion of the total labor force in their respective labor markets, which in turn means that they face a highly elastic supply of labor, especially in the long run.

Have unions actually increased wages? At first glance the answer may seem obvious; we continually observe negotiated wage increases in unionized trades or industries. But the question is, would the normal forces of supply and demand result in comparable wage increases? On the basis of empirical studies, it appears that unions have been able to increase wages of their members in the order of magnitude of 7 to 11 percent.[6] These studies also show, however, that wages of nonunion workers are about 3 to 4 percent lower than they would be in the absence of unionism.

It is fairly easy to see why unions have been able to raise wages by collective bargaining and by restricting entry. But why should unions cause other workers to receive lower wages? First it is necessary to recognize that an increase in wages in unionized industries results in fewer jobs in these industries or occupations than would otherwise be the case, that is, there is a movement up along the labor demand income. The people who would have worked in these jobs are forced to find employment in other nonunion occupations. This has the effect of increasing (shifting to the right) the supply of workers to these occupations. When supply increases from what it otherwise would be, price, or in this case, the wage, is lower than it would otherwise be. In other words, farm workers, retail clerks, and other nonunion workers are being forced to work for slightly less because their unionized co-workers are enjoying somewhat higher wages.

This phenomenon is illustrated in Figure 9–9. The increase in wages due to union pressure from W_e to W_u and the resulting reduction in quantity of labor demanded from Q_1 to Q_0 are shown in Figure 9–9(A). (In this case we assume the wage increase is the result of collective bargaining by an industrial union, but the same overall result would occur because of restricting entry into a unionized trade.) The reduction in people working in the unionized industry increases the supply of people in nonunion occupations, as illus-

---

6 See H. Gregg Lewis, *Unionism and Relative Wages in the United States* (Chicago: University of Chicago Press, 1963).

FIGURE 9–9
Effect of union wage increases on union and nonunion occupations
(A) Unionized occupations

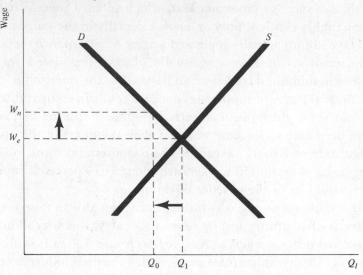

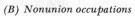

(B) Nonunion occupations

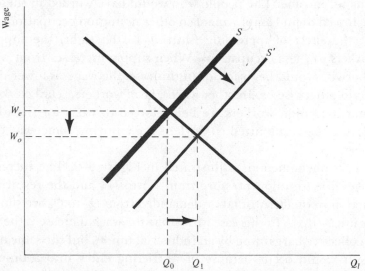

trated in Figure 9–9(B). And, as a result, the wage level in a non-union occupation is lower than would otherwise be the case.

Minimum-wage laws

Society has attempted to ensure itself against employers who pay excessively low wages by the enactment of minimum-wage laws. As the name implies, a minimum-wage law requires employers to pay employees covered under the law a hourly wage at least as high as the stipulated minimum. There is a federal minimum-wage law covering workers in manufacturing and industries engaged in interstate commerce. Many states, particularly northern industrial states, also have minimum-wage laws of their own, especially for employees not covered under the federal law. The stipulated minimum wage, of course, has been steadily increasing in step with inflation and with the rising average level of real wages in the country. The federal law, stemming from the Fair Labor Standards Act of 1938, began with a minimum wage of 25 cents an hour in 1940 and has increased over time to $1.60 in 1968. We can expect it to rise to well over $2 an hour during the 1970s.

The people most affected by such legislation, of course, are those at the low end of the wage scale, mainly teen-agers working on their first jobs and people with relatively few skills, who in large part are members of minority groups. At first glance it may appear that a minimum wage is a boon to low wage earners. After all, if the minimum wage is $2.00 an hour, your take-home pay will be larger than if you had to work for a market-determined wage of, say, $1.60 an hour. The rub comes because even though a minimum wage can guarantee that a worker must receive at least that wage if he (or she) works, it cannot guarantee that a job will be available at that wage. In fact, if the minimum wage is substantially above the equilibrium wage for occupations with low hourly pay, we can expect a decline in the number of jobs available to low-wage people.

This problem can be best illustrated with a simple market demand and supply diagram for labor (Figure 9–10). Assume here that the minimum wage (W_m) is above the market equilibrium wage (W_e). At the minimum wage, the quantity of labor demanded (Q_d)

FIGURE 9–10
Effect of a minimum-wage law on low-income people

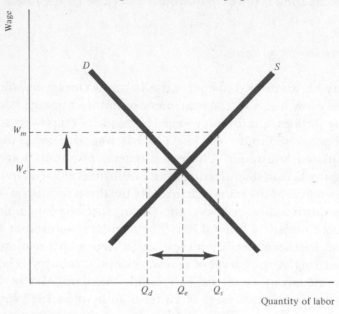

is less than the amount demanded at the equilibrium wage (Q_e). In other words, by imposing a minimum wage, some people, those at the lower end of the wage scale, are faced with a decrease in the number of jobs available. What generally happens is that employers substitute capital or machines for the relatively higher priced labor. At the same time, the higher minimum wage draws an increasing number of people into the market, as illustrated by the increase in quantity of labor supplied from Q_e to Q_s. The gap between Q_d and Q_s, therefore, represents the number of people who would like to work at this wage but cannot find a job (i.e., the unemployed).

The results of minimum-wage laws predicted by our theoretical framework also are substantiated by a number of recent empirical studies.[7] It appears that the impact of minimum-wage laws is felt to

---

[7] See, for example, Douglas K. Adie, "Teen-age Unemployment and Real Federal Minimum Wages," *Journal of Political Economy*, March–April 1973, pp. 435–41, and M. Kosters and F. Welch, "The Effects of Minimum Wages on the Distribution of Changes in Aggregate Unemployment," *American Economic Review*, June 1972, pp. 323–32.

the largest extent by teen-agers, particularly those from minority groups. In view of the relatively high unemployment rates of minorities in general, and teen-agers in particular, one can seriously question whether minimum-wage laws work to the benefit of those most affected. Indeed it has been argued that these laws have been mainly supported by northern industry and unions in order to protect themselves against loss of business and jobs to the South and to rural areas where wages have been lower. It is doubtful, however, that many full-time semiskilled or even unskilled workers in manufacturing would be affected by such laws. It is likely that part-time jobs, particularly those in the service trades, are affected the most.

Main points of Chapter 9

1. The labor market is primarily concerned with the demand for and supply of the services of individuals. The special attributes of labor are reflected in the market.

2. The demand for labor, or any input, by a perfectly competitive firm in the product market is equal to the input's VMP curve. Value of the marginal product (VMP) is equal to marginal physical product (MPP) times product price.

3. If market demand for an input is obtained by holding prices of related inputs constant, then a decrease in its price will bring forth an increase in quantity demanded for two reasons: *(a)* producers will increase output because of lower production costs and, in so doing, will increase the employment of the input in question, and *(b)* producers in many cases can substitute the now relatively cheaper input for other substitute inputs.

4. The demand for labor, or any input, by an imperfectly competitive firm in the product market is equal to the input's MRP curve. Marginal revenue product (MRP) is equal to MPP times marginal revenue.

5. Leisure can be thought of as a good. The more leisure we demand, the less labor we supply. The price of an extra hour of leisure is the income foregone by decreasing labor one hour.

6. The amount of lesiure we take when wages are increased depends on the income and substitution effects. The income effect pulls us toward more leisure because we can afford to "buy" more, while the substitution effect pulls us toward less leisure because it is now more expensive. We will take less leisure (or work more) after a wage increase if the substitution effect more than offsets the income effect.

7. If the income effect more than offsets the substitution effect, the supply of labor will be "backward bending," meaning that less labor will be supplied at higher wages.

8. In a perfectly competitive labor market wages are determined by the interaction of labor demand and supply. An employer will be a perfectly competitive buyer of labor if he hires a small percent of the labor force in his vicinity.

9. Although a perfectly competitive employer faces a perfectly elastic supply curve of labor, he may have some leeway in the wage he pays because labor is not homogeneous.

10. The perfectly competitive employer hires workers up to the point where the wage is equal to the MRP of an additional worker. To stop short of this point would involve an unnecessary loss of profits.

11. Imperfect competition in the labor market occurs if each employer hires a large share of the labor in a vicinity. The imperfectly competitive employer maximizes profits by hiring labor up to the point where labor's MRP is equal to the marginal resource cost (MRC) of labor.

12. The demand for labor, or any input, shifts if there is a change in product price or the MPP of labor.

13. An increase in the use of a complementary input increases the MPP of labor, whereas an increase in the use of a substitute input decreases the MPP of labor.

14. The supply of labor shifts if there is a change in population or in the wages paid in other labor markets. In a given labor market the supply of labor will decrease if there is an increase in wages in alternative employment.

15. The long-run trend toward increasing wages and employment implies that the demand for labor has been increasing more rapidly than the labor supply.

16. In the short run, a decrease in demand for labor by a given firm

or industry tends to result in layoffs rather than a reduction in wages.

17. Wage differences between occupations occur because of differences in demand and supply conditions.

18. Automation, a new term for an old process, results in higher wages for labor. Jobs need not be eliminated if the increase in output offsets the decrease in demand for labor. In an expanding economy the substitution of machines for labor generally takes place by not replacing employees who leave.

19. Although it may appear that employers are largely responsible for discrimination in the labor market, consumers and fellow workers have a strong influence on the actions of employers.

20. Wage differences between men and women exist in part because of occupational differences and because of the greater uncertainty involved in the hiring of women.

21. Labor unions attempt to raise wages of their members by increasing demand, decreasing supply, or bargaining for a union wage. All involve certain drawbacks, although the second, decreasing labor supply, likely has been the most successful.

22. Empirical studies report that unions have succeeded in raising wages of their members in the order of magnitude of 7 to 11 percent, while decreasing the wages of nonunion occupations about 3 to 4 percent. The latter occurs because of the increase in supply of workers to nonunion occupations from what it would otherwise be.

23. Although minimum-wage laws place a floor on wages, they also tend to increase the amount of unemployment of people at the low end of the wage scale, particularly teen-agers looking for their first job and unskilled workers.

Questions for thought and discussion

1. Distinguish between marginal physical product (MPP) and value of the marginal product (VMP). In what units are they measured?

2. Explain, using a diagram, why the VMP curve of labor for a

perfectly competitive seller is also the firm's demand curve for labor.

3. Explain why the quantity demanded of an input in the market increases when its price declines. (Assume prices of other inputs are held constant but their quantities are free to vary.)

4. Suppose you are the owner of a small business and employ ten people. One of your main problems is absenteeism. In order to ease this problem you consider raising wages from $3.00 to $3.50 per hour. Do you think this raise would reduce the number of days missed? Explain the factors that should be considered.

5. Suppose you are the owner of a construction company and you experience a slowdown in business. Which would you prefer to do, lay off part of your employees and cut back on your activities, or reduce the wages of all your employees in order to be able to reduce your bid price so you could pick up more jobs? Explain.

6. If you were an employee of the construction company mentioned in question 5, would you prefer a wage cut or a layoff? Explain.

7. How do perfectly competitive buyers of labor determine the wage they will pay? Utilize diagrams in your answer.

8. Does an imperfectly competitive buyer of labor behave any differently than a perfectly competitive buyer in regard to wages paid and amount of labor hired? Explain.

9. For a number of years a farm labor organization in California urged consumers not to buy California-grown grapes. Assuming that consumers complied with the wishes of the labor organization, what do you expect happened to the demand for grape pickers and the number employed? Would this action likely result in an upward or downward pressure on wages? Explain.

10. Some people argue that automation is good because it increases the productivity and the wages of labor. Others argue it is bad because it throws people out of work. Who is right? Explain.

11. Suppose you are the owner of a small taxicab company and advertise in the paper for a driver; three men and a woman apply. What factors would you consider in deciding whom to hire? Would the chances of your hiring one of the three men be greater than hiring the woman? Explain.

12. Recently there has been much discussion over excessive wage increases in the building trades compared to most other in-

dustries. From what you know about trade unions, can you explain why this has come about?

13. Suppose you are the leader of a craft union representing skilled tradesmen. How would you attempt to obtain higher wages for your members? What would be your limitations?

14. Suppose you are the leader of an industrial union representing semiskilled, blue-collar workers. How would you go about obtaining higher wages for your members? What would be your limitations?

15. Because unskilled farm labor earns relatively low wages, their standard of living is low. Why do they earn low wages? Would a $3.50 per hour minimum wage solve their problem? Why or why not?

10

The capital market

The concept of capital

In the context of business or economics, the word "capital" has taken on two slightly different meanings. The businessman may think of capital as cash or money to carry on a business, as in "working capital." The economist, however, generally defines capital as durable or long-lasting inputs such as machinery, tools, buildings, or land. The quantity of capital employed is generally measured in terms of monetary value, however.

We have separated the study of capital from labor because there are a number of differences between these two inputs. The first and most obvious difference is that capital is an inanimate, non-living input devoid of feelings or preferences. Although the owners of capital are concerned about the wage or return it receives, they do not care at all about its working conditions as the length of its workweek, and seldom whether or not it is employed in a prestigious occupation. Thus many of the factors that are important for labor need not be of concern in our discussion of capital.

A second difference is that capital is generally purchased for use over a relatively long period of time. For example, you may purchase a building this year that will go on producing for you the remainder of your lifetime. Labor, or other inputs such as raw materials, are purchased for immediate or current use only.

Granted there may be an understanding between employer and employee over the length of time they will be associated, but the employer of labor, unlike the employer of capital, does not usually pay the employee a lump sum for all future services. We will see shortly that this difference is quite important.

A third difference between capital and labor is that the purchase of capital may involve an expenditure well in advance of the date it begins to contribute to output. Economists refer to this time interval between the expenditure and the beginning of flow of output as the "gestation period." This time interval is important for capital such as buildings or heavy equipment.

Annual cost of capital

What does capital cost? At first glance the answer to this question may appear obvious. Surely the cost of capital is what buyers pay the people who produce it. But the answer is not quite this simple. To return to the tomato production example, suppose you purchase a $1,000 garden tractor to increase output. It would seem a bit unreasonable to require this year's output to carry the entire $1,000 outlay. After all, the tractor will still be available for tomato production in other years. But at the same time it seems reasonable to charge at least part of the $1,000 toward current production. Thus this year's cost of the $1,000 capital item would be somewhere between $1,000 and zero. Clearly $1,000 is too much, and zero is too little.

It would be reasonable to charge this year's production with at least the amount that the garden tractor had depreciated in value during the year. Suppose the tractor's market value declined to $700 in that period. If you wanted, you could sell the tractor for $700 after using it the first year. Thus the depreciation cost of this capital item for the current year would be $300.

Aside from the normal operating expense, such as gasoline and oil, would the $300 be the total cost of this capital item for the current year? Not quite. Where did you obtain the $1,000 to buy the tractor? If you borrowed it from a bank you must pay interest on the loan. If it were 10 percent per year, you would have to pay the bank $100 per year for the use of their money. Adding up the depreciation plus interest would give you $400 as the cost of this capital item for the current year.

It should not be concluded from this example, however, that the interest charge is only included when capital is purchased with borrowed funds. It would be equally necessary to include an interest charge if your own funds were used to make the purchase, because in this case you would have to forego the interest income of the $1,000 that you could have obtained had you not purchased the garden tractor.

If the $1,000 were your own funds, however, the interest charge probably would not be quite as high as would be the case if you had borrowed the money. The reason is that individuals lend money at "wholesale" but borrow at "retail." Banks and other lending institutions which serve to channel funds of individual lenders into a central location and then screen and loan to borrowers must be paid for their services. The difference between the interest you obtain on savings and the interest paid for a loan constitutes the payment for these services.

To summarize, the cost of capital for a given period consists of two components: depreciation and interest. The use of a capital item also will involve other costs, such as fuel, repairs, and insurance, but these will depend somewhat on the kind of capital under consideration. In this section we are mainly concerned with the two components of capital cost common to most capital items.[1]

The depreciation plus interest cost of a capital item will, of course, vary from one year to the next. In the case of the garden tractor, the depreciation expense for the second year probably will be somewhat lower. For example, suppose it is worth $500 at the end of the second year, resulting in a depreciation charge of $200 during that year. (We will discuss depreciation patterns in more detail in the following section.) Since you have "written off" $300 of the tractor the first year, the interest charge during the second year will be computed on the basis of $700 rather than $1,000, as it was during the first year of ownership. Thus the $200 depreciation plus a $70 interest charge ($700 × .10) gives a $270 annual cost of owner-

---

[1] Land, which in most cases does not depreciate in value, is an exception. In fact, in recent history most land has appreciated in value. We will consider land separately in a later section.

ship for the second year on. If you had purchased the garden tractor as a one-year-old used machine for $700, the cost the first year of ownership would be $270. Although the depreciation plus interest expense will in general decline during the life of a machine, we can expect this to be offset at least in part by an increase in repairs and maintenance as the machine grows older.

Depreciation

Because depreciation accounts for a large share of the annual cost of owning a capital item, it will be useful to examine this phenomenon in a bit more detail. There are two basic reasons why a capital item depreciates: (1) the wearing out or "using up" of the item and (2) obsolescence. In regard to the first reason, it should be kept in mind that the current market value of a capital item reflects the value at the present of its expected future contribution to output. Thus, the older an item becomes, the fewer the years of productive life that remain. For example, a new garden tractor may have ten years of service ahead of it, while a five-year-old machine may have only five years of life remaining. Even if the used machine could do about the same amount of work per day as the new machine, no one would pay as much for the used item because of the smaller number of work days left in it.

In an age of change and technological development, capital also becomes obsolete. If something new comes on the market that reduces production costs or increases efficiency, the demand for the old capital will decline, hence its price will fall. Thus the depreciation of capital depends not only on its own productivity but also on the productivity of the new capital being produced. Because of this it is difficult, if not impossible, to predict in advance how fast an item will become obsolete. Nor is it easy or even useful to attempt to separate how much of an item's depreciation is due to wearing out and how much is due to obsolescence; both have the same effect of reducing its market value.

Because it is necessary to estimate depreciation for income tax purposes, all firms must make an estimate of it. Once a certain pattern of depreciation is selected for a capital item, the same pattern must be followed for as long as the item is kept.

Two widely used methods of estimating depreciation are (1) the straight-line method and (2) the constant-percentage method. The resulting decline in value of the item being depreciated for each of these methods is illustrated in Figure 10–1. The straight-line

FIGURE 10–1
Straight-line and constant percentage patterns of depreciation of a $1,000 garden tractor

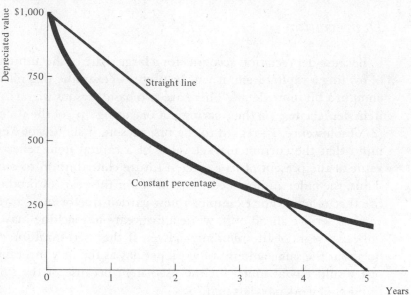

method amounts to decreasing the value of the capital by a constant number of dollars each year. For example, if you were depreciating your $1,000 garden tractor by the straight-line method over a period of five years, you would assess $200 per year as depreciation.

If you employ the constant-percentage method, you would multiply each year's market value by a constant percentage. For example, if you depreciate the garden tractor 30 percent per year, the first year's depreciation would be $300, the second year's $210 ($700 × 0.30), the third year's $147, and so on. You might notice that under this method the annual depreciation is higher when the item is new, resulting in a lower depreciated value during its early years of use. With this method, also, the item does not depreciate to zero. After five years its depreciated value under the constant percentage depreciation is $168. In fact, under this method the depreciated value never completely reaches zero, although it comes close.

The method of depreciation chosen and the length of time involved depend, of course, on the item to be depreciated. The constant-percentage method would seem to be a bit more realistic for most items, since depreciation usually is higher the first few years of ownership. An automobile tends to depreciate between 20 and 25 percent per year, depending on make, model, amount of use, and the care it has received. If you purchase a $4,000 automobile it depreciates $1,000 the first year, where the 25 percent rate applies. In calculating the total cost of ownership the first year, you should also include the interest charge, $400 if taken at 10 percent, together with gasoline, insurance, license fees, and so forth. With normal use, the total annual cost of a $4,000 automobile probably runs in the neighborhood of $2,000 the first year of ownership. Is it worth it?

The marginal product of capital

In deciding whether or not to purchase or keep a machine or other capital items it is necessary to consider both its cost and its returns. In the previous sections we looked at cost; let us now consider the returns of a capital item. In a sense capital is similar to labor or any other input, in that it contributes to the output of goods and services. This contribution to output can be measured either in physical units of output by its marginal physical product (MPP), or in monetary units in terms of its value of the marginal production (VMP)—or marginal revenue product (MRP). Recall from Chapters 4 and 9 that MPP is defined as the additional output obtained from an additional unit of the input, capital in this case. And VMP or MRP, as the case may be, is the value of the additional output obtained from an additional unit of capital. (From now on, to simplify the notation, we will refer only to the MRP of capital.)

The MRP of capital can be visualized as the value of the additional output that is made possible by utilizing a machine, for example, compared to what would be produced if it were not used. Because we are interested in comparing capital's annual MRP with the annual interest plus depreciation charge, we ought to refer to the machine's annual "net" MRP. This would be the value of additional annual output less the added expense incurred by owning and operating the machine, such as fuel, repairs, additional labor, and insurance.

Once the annual net MRP of a capital item has been estimated, it is possible to compare this figure against its annual depreciation plus interest charge in deciding whether or not to purchase it. For example, in the garden tractor example, the first year's depreciation plus interest charge was estimated as $400. If the first year's net MRP of this machine were estimated to be $500, it would pay to purchase it. Anytime you can spend $400 and receive $500 in return, do so. On the other hand, if the estimated net MRP was less than $400, then, of course, the decision would be not to purchase the machine. Thus we can formulate a rule: Purchase a machine as long as its expected annual net contribution to output (MRP) is at least as great as its expected annual depreciation plus interest charge.

Of course, you might ask how it is possible to estimate the net MRP of a machine or capital item. Granted you will probably have to make some rough calculations, but rough estimates are better than no estimates at all. The accuracy of your estimates will in part reflect your ability as a manager of capital.

The rate of return on capital

Because a capital item is generally purchased for use over a number of years, it is common to express its contribution to output during a given year as a fraction of its value at the beginning of the year. The resulting figure is commonly referred to as a "rate of return." We can define the rate of return on capital as the amount each dollar earns each year after all expenses, including depreciation in this case, have been subtracted. It is commonly expressed as a percentage figure. For example, suppose after subtracting depreciation and other expenses from the "gross" MRP of the $1,000 garden tractor, the first year's earnings happen to be $80. During this year its rate of return would be equal to .08 or 8 percent (80/1,000). In other words, each dollar earns 8 cents during the year.

You might have recognized that the rate of return on capital is essentially the same idea as the rate of return on your savings account in the bank. However, unlike a savings deposit in a bank, which goes on earning its stipulated rate of return year after year as long as the money is left in the account, the earnings of a machine or building can be expected to vary from year to year and eventually to come to an end as the item wears out.

There is one kind of capital, however, that does not tend to "wear out" or depreciate with normal care, namely land. In fact, during recent history land has generally appreciated in value. To keep the example simple, suppose you purchase a small plot of land for $1,000 and expect it to remain at this price. Also suppose you can collect $100 per year return from the land for as long as you want to by renting it to a tomato grower. Assume also that there are no other expenses, so the $100 is a net return.

For an asset that can be expected to yield a stream of returns for all time to come, its annual rate of return can be computed as follows:

$$r = \frac{\text{Annual net returns}}{\text{Capital value}}$$

In the land example above, the rate of return would be:

$$r = \frac{\$100}{\$1000} = .10 = 10 \text{ percent}$$

Capitalized value

By manipulating this formula slightly we can derive another formula that is very useful for deciding the maximum price you could afford to pay for a piece of property. To make the formula more manageable, we will abbreviate, letting r represent the interest rate or rate of return, R the annual net return, and K the capital value. Now we have

$$r = \frac{R}{K}, \text{ or } K \times r = R, \text{ or } K = \frac{R}{r}.$$

The resulting formula, $K = R/r$, tells us how much a piece of property is worth if we know its annual return and the interest charge.

Suppose in order to purchase this plot of land you took out a $1,000 loan at 8 percent. Utilizing this formula, we find:

$$K = \frac{\$100}{0.08} = \$1,250.$$

If you were assured of an annual $100 net return on this land and the money to buy it cost 8 percent per year, you could have paid as much as $1,250 for the land. Economists refer to the K in this formula, or the $1,250 in this example, as the "capitalized value" of the property. In a competitive market prospective buyers would tend to bid the price of the property up to this amount. And sellers, knowing this, will be prone to set the selling price at the capitalized value. If you are able to buy a piece of property for $1,000 that has a capitalized value of $1,250 you have made a good deal for yourself.

We should note also from this formula that for a given annual return (R), the capitalized value (K) will vary inversely to the size of the interest rate (r). If the interest rate you had to pay on your loan were 10 percent, K would have been $1,000. A lower interest rate such as 5 percent would result in a capitalized value of $2,000.

Although the relationship between the interest rate and the capitalized value is an algebraic phenomenon—the larger the denominator, the smaller the quotient, and vice-versa—it has an underlying economic rationale. At a relatively high interest rate, say 10 percent, the income that will be forthcoming many years in the future is more expensive to obtain than if the interest rate were lower. At high interest rates the borrower is required to pay more for the distant income, either in terms of an interest charge on borrowed funds or foregone interest from his own funds; hence he cannot pay as high an initial price for the capital.

Cash flow analysis

Most capital that might be considered for purchase, such as buildings or equipment, would not be expected to yield a stream of returns into infinity, however. As years go by capital generally becomes less productive, and its maintenance costs rise. As a result the stream of net returns may exhibit a downward trend, eventually coming to an end when it no longer pays to keep the capital item.

As you might expect, it is somewhat more difficult to compute a rate of return to a capital item in this more common but realistic situation. To facilitate computation of capital's rate of return, economists have devised a technique called "cash flow analysis." As the name implies, this technique involves comparing the cash outflow of a capital item, that is, its purchase price, with the inflow of cash that results from the use of the item.

We can use the garden tractor purchase also to illustrate this technique. Suppose you denote as year 0 the time you purchase the tractor. The first step is to assess, as best you can, the contribution of the tractor to your total production and sales of tomatoes during the years you expect to own it. One way to do this is to estimate your total sales during these years without the tractor and then estimate your total sales with the tractor, less the added expense such as gasoline and repairs. The difference between these two sets of figures gives the net inflow of cash that results from owning the tractor. Your figures might look something like the following:

	Year 0	Year 1	Year 2	Year 3	Year 4	Year 5
Cash outflow	−$1,000	—	—	—	—	—
Gross cash inflow	—	+$350	+$400	+$450	+$475	+$600
Less added expense ...	—	−$100	−$125	−$150	−$200	−$200
Net cash inflow .	−$1,000	+$250	+$275	+$300	+$275	+$400

It is reasonable to assume that the tractor does not begin to pay off at once. Suppose the first payoff comes about one year after you buy it—call this year 1. Also assume that you expect to use the tractor for five years. The net cash inflow figures essentially represent the tractor's net MRP for each year, except for the last year, where net cash inflow also includes the selling price of the tractor.

The added expense figures denote the expenses related to owning the tractor. They include the normal operating expense of fuel and oil, repairs, and the cost of any additional labor that is incurred by operating the tractor. This figure should also include the implicit cost of any additional hours of your own labor utilized. Notice that the added expense figures become larger as the years go by. The main reason for this is the larger amount of repairs that you can expect as the tractor grows older.

The additional expense figures, however, do not include the depreciation expense or a charge for interest on the $1,000. The depreciation is taken into account in the gross cash inflow figure for year 5, the year you expect to sell the tractor. The $600 gross cash inflow figure for year 5 includes both the extra value of production, say $400, and the selling price of the tractor, $200 in this example. The total depreciation over the five-year period of $800 is therefore reflected in the gross cash inflow in year 5. If there had been no depreciation, and you could have sold the tractor for the $1,000 you paid for it, the gross cash inflow would have been $1,400 in year 5.

Probably the main advantage of cash flow analysis is that we do not have to be concerned with the pattern of depreciation of a capital item. For example, if we underestimated the amount of depreciation during an early year, we would overestimate its net returns and therefore overestimate its rate of return. Also many capital items, such as machines in a factory or the factory building itself, may not have a good resale market, making it difficult to estimate their true economic depreciation during their most productive years. With the cash flow technique we need only estimate the depreciated value once, at the end of the time we expect to keep the item. Depending on how long we expect to keep it, this figure may be its scrap value. When its value is low, we are not likely to make a large error in estimating its total depreciation.

Assuming that you are fairly confident in the accuracy of your estimates of the added income and expense connected with the tractor, you still are faced with the question: Should you or should you not buy the tractor? If you add up the net cash inflows over the five-year period, you can see that the $1,000 investment in the tractor enables you to take in a total of $1,500.

Discounted present value

Before you become too optimistic about this investment, however, keep in mind that positive net cash inflows are not available to you until future years. And a dollar that you obtain, say, next year is not as valuable to you as a dollar of income at the present, because you could always loan out or invest the present dollar at a positive rate of interest, enabling you to obtain something more than one dollar a year from now.

How much is one dollar of income forthcoming a year from now worth at the present? In order to answer this question, we must specify the rate of interest that could be obtained by lending the dollar, call it r. The formula for discounting one dollar of future income to the present is given by $1/(1 + r)^n$. The n represents the number of years in the future the income is forthcoming. For example, if r is 5 percent, or 0.05, then one dollar forthcoming one year from now is worth $1/(1.05)$, or 95 cents at the present. Economists would refer to this 95 cents as the discounted present value of one dollar, one year in the future. Notice that if the interest rate increases, the discounted present value declines. At an interest rate of 0.10, the discounted present value of one dollar one year from now declines to 91 cents.

By using this discounting formula you can determine the present value of the future returns of the garden tractor. Suppose that the market rate of interest is 10 percent. The present value of the returns in year 1 is $250/1.10$, or approximately \$227. In year 2 it would be $275/(1.10)^2$ or \$227, and so forth. The discounted present value in year 0 of the net cash inflows from years 1 through 5 is shown below:

Year 1	Year 2	Year 3	Year 4	Year 5	Total
\$227 +	\$227 +	\$226 +	\$188 +	\$248 =	\$1,116

It is interesting to note that the \$1,500 total return from the five years' net cash inflows is only worth \$1,116 at its discounted present value, assuming a 10 percent interest rate. You would, of course, still consider the garden tractor to be a good investment, since the \$1,000 buys \$1,116 of present value. But you would not greet the prospect with quite as much enthusiasm as you might have first thought after seeing the \$1,500 nondiscounted return.

This does not mean, however, that the nondiscounted \$1,500 return to the \$1,000 investment would always be acceptable. Suppose the interest rate you had to pay increased to 15 percent, or you have another use for your funds that would return 15 percent. Discounting the same \$1,500 stream of returns back to year 0, using a 15 percent interest rate, results in a discounted present value of only \$978. Here we find that the present value of the \$1,500 is only worth \$978. Now the tractor would not be an acceptable investment. This illustrates the importance of the interest rate in making investment decisions. The higher the interest rate, the less will future returns be worth. As you might have recognized, the discounted present value is essentially the same thing as the capitalized value discussed earlier. The term "capitalized value" is generally used in reference to capital that does not depreciate or is non-reproducible.

Internal rate of return

Although comparing the discounted present value of the stream of returns with the cost of the capital item is a perfectly acceptable method of judging an investment, economists frequently use another criterion called the "internal rate of return." The internal rate of return is defined as that rate of interest which makes the discounted present value of the stream of returns equal to the cost of the investment.

In the garden tractor example, a 10 percent rate of interest discounted the $1,500 stream of returns down to a present value of $1,116. Thus the internal rate of return is slightly larger than 10 percent. On the other hand, the 15 percent rate was slightly too high; the present value of the $1,500 was reduced to $978. Thus we can conclude that the internal rate of return on the garden tractor is somewhere between 10 and 15 percent.

The only way that we can compute an internal rate of return is by trying alternative interest rates until we find one that makes the discounted present value equal to the cost of the capital item. In the garden tractor example, it turns out to be about 14 percent. Using a 14 percent discount rate, the $1,500 stream of returns reduces down to $1,004 in year 0. Thus the internal rate of return is just a shade over 14 percent, but it generally does not pay to strive for greater accuracy than this.

The meaning of this 14 percent internal rate of return is that the $1,000 investment pays off at the rate of 14 percent per year, or $140 per year, during the five-year payoff period. If you paid, or could have earned, 10 percent on the $1,000, you would reap a 4 percent, or $40 per year, pure profit.

Although the $140 per year net income from this investment may seem somewhat small, we must remember that $1,000 is also a fairly small investment. It does not require a very large business these days to have $100,000 or more invested. And if you obtain 14 percent on $100,000, your yearly earnings from capital are $14,000. If you borrowed the entire $100,000 for 10 percent, your pure profit per year is $4,000. Remember this is in addition to your labor income.

Most of the rich and super rich have gotten to be so by the income from capital. Moreover, most of these people, at least when they started out, utilized borrowed funds. Earning 14 percent on one million dollars returns $140,000 per year. Even if you pay 10 percent for this money, you still clear $40,000 per year for letting the capital work for you. Few people except the top professional athletes, movie stars, and the highest paid executives can obtain an income over $45,000 to $50,000 per year without supplemental earnings from capital. Thus if you strive for a relatively high standard of living in the future, it is never too early to set aside part of your income for investment purposes. You must realize, though, that ownership of capital does not guarantee a high income. For example, if you borrow $100,000 at 10 percent and the capital that is purchased with the money only pays off at 5 percent, you lose $5,000 per year. When playing with stakes this high, it is important to assess rather carefully the anticipated rate of return.

To summarize, we have discussed three ways to assess the profitability of an investment: (1) comparing the annual net MRP of capital with its annual depreciation plus interest expense, (2) comparing the capitalized value or discounted present value of the stream of future returns with its purchase price, and (3) comparing the internal rate of return with the interest rate on borrowed funds or on our own funds. Because of the variability of annual net returns of most capital items, along with the difficulty of accurately estimating the annual depreciation charge, the calculation of the discounted present value or internal rate of return by the cash- flow technique tends to be the most common means of gauging the profitability of an investment.

Ranking of investment opportunities

Most business firms face an assortment of investment opportunities, some more profitable than others, and the criteria for accepting or rejecting an investment opportunity developed above are applied in these decisions. For example, in the tomato-growing endeavor you might estimate that $100 spent on garden tools (hoe, rake, etc.) would pay off at a 20 percent internal rate of return. Adding additional capital such as the $1,000 garden tractor may yield a 14 percent rate of return. Perhaps another $1,000 invested in irrigation equipment (pump, pipes, sprinklers, etc.) might be estimated to yield 10 percent. And so forth.

A convenient way to express such a ranking of investment opportunities is by a diagram. Using the figures from this example we plot the internal rate of return on the vertical axis and the cumulative amount invested on the horizontal axis. To simplify the example, assume that there is a continuous array of investment opportunities. This enables us to connect the points and draw a continuous downward-sloping line, as in Figure 10–2.

Faced with these investment opportunities, you must decide which ones to accept and which to reject for your tomato production ventures. In order to make this decision, you need to know the interest rate that would have to be paid on borrowed funds or that could be obtained on your own funds. If this is 10 percent, you would want to invest in those opportunities that yield 10 percent or above. In the example depicted by Figure 10–2, the total investment for the year would be $2,100.

Stopping short of this amount, say at $1,100, would reduce profits by the value of the shaded area in Figure 10–2. Say you invest $1,101 instead of $1,100. You pay 10 cents per year on this extra dollar of investment and it returns 14 cents per year, so in net it adds 4 cents to your total profits (or it reduces your losses by 4 cents if you are operating in the red). Continuing to add extra dollars of investment will continue to increase profits, or reduce losses, until you reach the $2,100 point. Increasing the investment beyond $2,100, however, would reduce profits because the interest rate of return on this capital would be less than the interest charge on it.

Thus we can formulate a rule: To maximize profits a firm will continue to expand its investments until the internal rate of return on the marginal dollar invested is equal to the interest rate (explicit or implicit) that prevails. We should note, however, that changes in the interest rate will change the profit-maximizing level of investment. For example, if the interest rate were 14 percent, you would invest only $1,400.

FIGURE 10-2
Cumulative ranking of investments

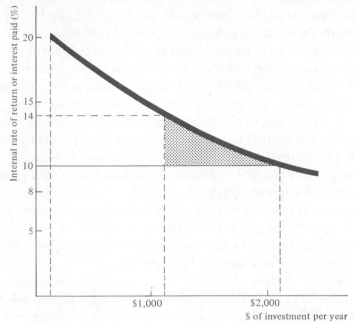

We should stress, in addition, that the cumulative ranking of investments by their rate of return is based on the *expected* profitability of each. No one knows for certain how profitable an investment will be until it has run its course. Thus a change in the degree of optimism or pessimism regarding future business conditions will likely shift the curve shown in Figure 10–2. If investors become more optimistic, for example, the curve will shift to the right, thereby increasing the total investment for a given rate of interest.

Interest rate determination

It should be apparent that the rate of interest that must be paid on borrowed funds or that could be earned on one's own funds is an important consideration in deciding whether or not to invest in a capital item. Recall that as the rate of interest increases, the discounted present value of the income stream from an investment declines. As a result, some investments that would be profitable at low rates of interest become unprofitable at high rates. In other words, as the interest rate increases, the discounted present value of fewer and fewer potential investments will remain above the cost of the investment. Or we can say that as the interest rate increases, the internal rate of return from fewer and fewer investments will remain at least as high as the interest rate. Thus we can expect that the amount of investment which will take place each year in the economy will be larger at lower rates of interest, and vice versa.[2] Of course, as mentioned in the preceding section, the expectations of the business community regarding future sales and profits will have an effect on the level of investment at a given rate of interest.

We might consider here how the rate of interest on loan funds is determined. A complete study of the topic would take us into the realm of macroeconomics in greater detail than is advisable at this point. However, we can say that the rate of interest on loanable funds is determined in the loan market by the demand for a supply of these funds, as illustrated by Figure 10–3.

Viewing the interest rate as the "price" of each dollar of loanable funds, it can be expected that the demand curve for these funds will be downward sloping, like the demand curves for products or other inputs such as labor. If some investments are more profitable than others, at a relatively low rate of interest there will be more opportunities to invest at a profit than if the interest rate were relatively high. As a result we can expect the business community to demand a greater number of dollars for investment purposes when the interest rate is relatively low than when it is high, hence the downward-sloping curve.[3]

Looking at the supply side of the loan market, the question is where these funds come from. In general we can say that the supply of loanable funds is the amount of money that people are willing to divert from current consumption to saving at the various rates of interest.[4]

---

2 Additional discussion on the relationship between the interest rate and investment, and between expectations and investment can be found in Chapter 7 of the companion macro volume.

3 Similarly, an increase in the rate of interest reduces the present value of the service flow of consumer durables such as housing, automobiles, and appliances, thereby making them less attractive as current purchases.

4 Technically speaking, business firms also save by retaining part of their earnings for investment purposes. But, of course, all business firms are owned by people, so the definition still holds.

FIGURE 10–3
Interest rate determination in market for loanable funds

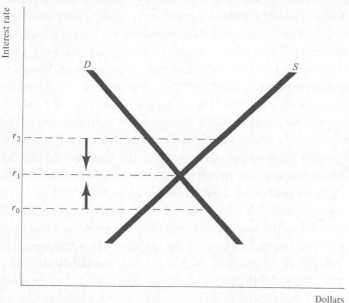

The supply curve of loanable funds in Figure 10–3 is upward sloping, indicating that people will supply a greater number of dollars at relatively high interest rates than at relatively low rates. The degree of responsiveness of savers to changes in the interest rate is still somewhat of an unsettled question in economics. However, if people buy less of an item when its price increases and more when it becomes more expensive, we should expect some increase in the rate of saving (out of a given income) when the interest rate increases. For, as pointed out in Chapter 2, an increase in the interest rate increases the price of current consumption relative to future consumption. That is, as the interest rate rises, a dollar spent on current consumption increases the amount of future consumption given up, because of the greater interest income foregone.

As in any other market, there is one equilibrium price (interest rate) and quantity that will prevail at any one point in time, given the demand and supply curves. This interest rate is illustrated by r_1 in Figure 10–3. At a higher rate, say r_2, a greater number of dollars will be supplied than are demanded; that is, there will be a surplus in the loan market. Borrowers seeing this surplus of funds will press for a rate that is more favorable to them, while lenders will have to agree to the lower rate if they wish to loan out these funds. Similarly, if the interest rate were below the equilibrium, say r_0, there would be a shortage of funds, since a greater number of dollars would be demanded than supplied at this interest rate. As a result lenders will press for a more favorable rate (to them), and borrowers will have to pay the higher rate or go without funds.

As in the product market and the labor market, the demand and supply curves of loanable funds also can be expected to shift from one position to another. The demand for loanable funds will, of course, be closely tied to investment opportunities. If prospects for future profits increase, we can expect some increase in the demand for funds to finance new investment. Or if totally new and profitable investment opportunities arise, perhaps as the result of new technology, the demand for funds also will tend to increase, or shift to the right. Given the supply of funds, the increase in demand will be expected to cause an increase in the interest rate. Of course, changes in the supply of funds also will affect the equilibrium rate of interest. For example, if people decide to increase their rate of saving, the supply of funds will increase, or shift to the right, and as a result the equilibrium rate of interest will decline. Over the long run, both the demand for and the supply of loanable funds are likely to be increasing, or shifting to the right, as the result of population growth and a rising money income in the economy.

Interest rate differences

For simplicity, we have discussed the interest rate as if there were a single rate of interest prevailing in the economy at a point in time. There are, in fact, a number of rates of interest, depending on the loan market under consideration. Banks charge a "prime rate" for their most favored customers and other, higher rates for small business, home, or auto loans. Banks and finance companies charge still higher rates for so-called "personal loans," and "loan sharks" extract rates from their customers that are much higher than that.

What accounts for these differences? Basically we can say that interest rate differences reflect different demand and supply conditions in the particular loan market under consideration. If the supply of funds is large relative to the demand, then the interest rate will be low, and vice versa.

In large part, the differences in interest rates between various borrowers and types of loan are the result of differences on the supply side of the market. The major consideration here is the expected cost of making the loan. Two cost components are important. Perhaps most important is the risk of making the loan. Although lenders can never be 100 percent certain of being repaid, past experience will tell them that certain kinds of loans are much less risky than others. For example, large, reputable companies that have been in business for many years and have built up a good credit rating will likely face a supply curve of funds that lies to the right of that of small, relatively unknown borrowers. The rate of interest charged to the former is often called the "prime rate." As the risk of default increases, lenders are forced to charge a higher rate in order to pay for the money lost through nonpayment of that type of loan. Lenders attempt to segregate potential borrowers by degree of risk in order to give lower rates to low-risk borrowers (mainly to get their business), while making high-risk borrowers pay a larger share of the cost of defaults.

In addition to risk, a second cost component that makes for differences in the rate of interest charged is the administrative cost of making and collecting the loan. On a per-dollar basis, this tends to be higher for small loans than for large ones. For example, the total cost of the paper work necessary to process a $100,000 loan probably is not much different from the total administrative cost of making a loan of $1,000. Thus the cost per dollar is higher for the smaller loan. To recoup these costs, the lender has to charge a higher rate on relatively small loans. The cost of collecting also varies. At the extreme are those lenders who employ a staff of "300-hundred pound field men" to search out and persuade borrowers to pay up, or else. Since these lenders (i.e., the crime syndicate) must pay for these "services," they have to charge a high interest rate. If their rates are above the legal maximum, as they usually are, they also have to be compensated for the risk of getting caught and serving a prison term.

While our discussion of interest rate differences has centered on differences existing in the economy at a point in time, the entire structure of interest rates tends to fluctuate over time. During certain periods, particularly times of inflation, there are relatively high rates, while at other times interest rates are more favorable to borrowers. Again, these differences over time also can be explained by changes in demand and supply conditions. For example, during times of strong demand for loans the interest rate will tend to rise to a relatively high level. The amount of inflation that borrowers and lenders expect in the future has a significant impact on the demand for and supply of loan funds and therefore affects the rate of interest in the market. To see why this occurs, we need to distinguish between the so-called "money rate" and the "real rate" of interest.

The money rate versus the real rate of interest

The interest rate we have been discussing can be termed the "money rate." The "real rate" is defined as the money rate adjusted by the rate of change of the general price level, that is, the rate of inflation. A simple example will illustrate the effect of inflation on the interest cost and returns of a loan. Suppose you lend someone $100 at 6 percent interest, to be paid back with interest one year from now, and the rate of inflation during this year happens to be 4 percent. At the end of the year you would receive $106. But the 4 percent inflation rate means that it now takes $104 to buy the same amount of goods and services that the $100 could have purchased at the beginning of the year. Thus you've gained only $2 in real purchasing power by making the loan. In other words, you received a 2 percent real rate of interest on the loan. Assuming that the borrower spent the $100 on something that increased in value with the price level, say a typewriter, the $4 increase in value of the asset over what it otherwise would have been in part offsets the interest paid. In this case, $6 interest is offset by the $4 increase in value of the typewriter, so the real rate paid by the borrower is 2 percent. The formula for finding the real rate is given below:

Real rate = Money rate minus annual percent change in price level.

Now it is possible to see why demanders of loan funds are willing to pay higher money rates of interest if they expect inflation to occur during the term of the loan. If they expect inflation to increase the value of assets purchased with the loan and thereby offset part of the interest charge, they will be willing to pay a higher money rate of interest than if they expect prices to remain stable in the future. In other words, the demand for funds will increase or shift to the right with the expectation of inflation in the future.

On the supply side, the suppliers of loan funds, that is, savers, can be expected to be less willing to save and to offer funds on the loan market if they believe that inflation will erode the purchasing power of their savings. To compensate for the loss of purchasing power of their savings, suppliers of loans will be willing to place a given amount of funds on the market only at a higher rate of interest. In other words, the supply of loan funds will tend to decrease or shift to the left with the expectation of inflation in the future. Both the increase in demand and the decrease in supply of loan funds have the effect of increasing the money rate of interest.

If there were no restriction on the level of the money rate of interest, the loan market would establish an equilibrium money rate of interest high enough to compensate for the expected inflation. In reality, upper limits on money rates of interest as set by usury laws may restrict the money rate of interest from rising to its free market equilibrium. In developing nations the rate of inflation may be so high, 50 to 100 percent, that the real rate turns out to be negative, that is, the money rate is smaller than the rate of inflation. One might ask why savers offer any funds at all under such circumstances. Of course, lending even at a negative real rate is better than not lending at all and having inflation diminish one's cash even more rapidly.[5] Also, if negative real rates prevail, loans are likely to be selectively rationed to "good friends" of the lending agency or institution, usually large, low-risk borrowers.

Rationing and allocating functions of the interest rate

Market price serves as a rationing device whereby people voluntarily limit the use of goods and services that are not free, as noted

---

[5] Further discussion on the affect of inflation on the value of assets is contained in Chapter 2 of the macro book.

in Chapter 6. Price also allocates scarce resources to the production of the goods and services that are most highly valued by society. The interest rate, being the "price" of investment funds, also serves to ration and allocate these funds.

It goes without saying that the potential amount of investment that could conceivably be undertaken during a given year far exceeds the resources available to undertake it. As a result, the available funds have to be rationed and allocated to their most valuable uses. Since, in the private sector, investment will not be undertaken unless the expected rate of return is at least as large as the interest rate, the available investment funds are in a sense rationed or made unavailable to low-payoff, unprofitable investments.

Moreover, the interest rate also has the effect of allocating the available investment funds to the areas where the expected rate of return is the highest. The greater the expected rate of return in relation to the interest rate, the more incentive investors have to allocate funds to these areas because of the expected profits. Thus the interest rate not only serves to keep funds from being invested in low-return areas, but it pulls the funds to more highly productive investments; that is, it allocates funds.

A great deal of investment also takes place with public funds in which profit is not a major consideration. Yet public planners also need to consider the interest rate. For a public investment to be socially profitable, its contribution to the output of society should be large enough to yield a rate of return at least equal to the prevailing interest rate, or the marginal rate of return on alternative private investments.[6]

The stock market

A large share of the total annual investment in the United States is financed by the sale of stock. Although the loan market and the stock market are similar in economic terms and are closely related, there is a legal difference in that the people who provide the funds in the stock market (i.e., those who save) become part owners of the

---

6 An example of valuing the output of a public investment is discussed in the section on agricultural research in Chapter 12.

business they "invest" in. Although relatively few stockholders actively participate in the management of the companies in which they invest, they nevertheless are the owners. Thus money raised by the sale of stock is sometimes called "equity capital," while money raised by borrowing is known as "debt capital."

The procedure of raising money by the sale of stock can be illustrated by a simple example. Suppose you decided to form a corporation to raise $1,000 to purchase your garden tractor for your tomato production venture. After receiving a charter for your corporation, you proceed to issue 100 stock certificates, each having a face value of $10. The fact that each stock certificate carries a $10 face value does not guarantee that the 100 shares would raise $1,000, however. If prospective buyers of your stock were pessimistic of your chances for success in growing tomatoes, they might not be willing to pay the $10 price. If you were able to sell them for, say, $8 a share, the remaining $200 would have to be provided by your own funds or by borrowing. At any rate, the price of your stock would closely reflect the market's evaluation of your earning and growth potential. If you were fortunate enough to enjoy a profitable year and could pay an attractive dividend, the price of your stock would likely rise. There is no legal limit on how high (or low) it could go; the determining factor would be the market's evaluation of your profit and growth potential.

Essentially the price of existing stock is determined by the forces of demand and supply. If the demand for stocks increases relative to the supply, their prices will increase, and vice versa. Many of the short-run fluctuations in the stock market stem from changing expectations of future business conditions and/or changing expectations on the future value of the stock itself. For example, if many people who own stock believe stock prices will fall in the near future, they may attempt to sell, thereby increasing supply and lowering stock prices. Thus the "psychology" of the market can be rather important in the short run. Over the long run, however, the value of each firm's stock will tend to reflect the dividends paid and the growth in value of the firm's assets.

Although people who own stock receive dividends, as opposed to interest, the meaning is virtually the same. For example, if you paid the owners of your $100 stocks an annual dividend of $5, they would in effect receive a 5 percent rate of interest on their money (assuming the stocks sold for $100). It is common in the stock market to quote the interest return in terms of the stock's price/earnings ratio. In the above example, the price/earnings ratio is 20—$100/$5. The interest return on stocks is simply the reciprocal of the price/earnings ratio. If a stock has a high price/earnings ratio, say 33, its interest return would be only about 3 percent.

Many stocks which have been selling for 30 to 40 times their earnings nevertheless have been quite popular in recent years. The reason is that instead of paying high dividends on their stocks, many companies have been "plowing" their profits back into business, and as a result the value of their stocks have been increasing. Stocks which pay a small dividend but increase in value each year are often called "growth stocks." Stockholders have shown a preference for growth stocks because of the favorable tax treatment they receive under the "capital gains" provision of our income tax law. For example, if you're in the 30 percent tax bracket and receive an extra $100 in dividends, you pay $30 of it in income taxes. But if your stock instead increases in value by $100 and you sell it for this gain, you pay a tax on this realized capital gain at only one half the rate that you pay on ordinary income. In this case, the tax on the extra $100 of realized capital gains is only $15. Thus it is not difficult to see why growth stocks have become popular.

Main points of Chapter 10

1. Capital, as used in the context of this chapter, refers to durable or long-lasting inputs such as machines, buildings, and land, rather than cash or money.
2. The annual cost of capital is made up of two components: depreciation and the interest charge.
3. Capital depreciates for two reasons: wearing out and obsolescence. Two common methods of estimating depreciation are the straight-line method and the constant-percentage method.
4. The marginal product of capital is the additional output obtained by adding one more unit of capital.

5.   One method of gauging the profitability of an investment is to
     determine whether or not capital's annual net VMP or **MRP**
     is greater than its annual depreciation plus interest charge.

6.   The rate of return on capital is the amount of income that
     each dollar invested earns each year after all expenses, includ-
     ing depreciation, have been subtracted. For example, a 6 per-
     cent rate of return means that each dollar earns 6 cents per
     year.

7.   The capitalized value of nondepreciable capital is obtained
     by dividing the annual net return by the interest rate.

8.   Cash flow analysis is a technique used to compare the cash out-
     flow of a capital item, i.e., its purchase price, with the addi-
     tional net cash inflows or net returns resulting from the use of
     the item.

9.   The discounted present value of one dollar to be received n
     years in the future is equal to $1/(1 + r)^n$, where r is the rate
     of interest.

10. A second method of assessing the profitability of an invest-
     ment is to compare the purchase price of the capital with its
     capitalized value or the discounted present value of its stream
     of future returns.

11. The internal rate of return on a capital item is that rate of
     interest which makes the discounted present value of the
     stream of returns equal to the purchase price or total cost of
     the capital.

12. The third method of determining the profitability of a capital
     item is to compare its internal rate of return with the rate of
     interest that has to be paid on borrowed funds or that can be
     earned on equity funds.

13. To maximize profits a firm should invest in capital until the
     internal rate of return on the marginal dollar invested is
     equal to the interest rate.

14. The rate of interest on loan funds is determined by the de-
     mand for and supply of these funds.

15. Differences in the interest paid on various types of loans are
     due in large part to differences in the expected cost of making
     the loan. These cost differences are due mainly to differences
     in risk and the per-dollar administrative cost of making and
     collecting the loan.

16. The real rate of interest is equal to the money rate less the rate of inflation. During times of inflation or expected inflation, the money rate of interest tends to rise to offset the cost-reducing effect of inflation on loans.

17. The interest rate rations and allocates investment funds by making it unprofitable to invest in low-return activities, while drawing funds into high-return areas.

18. A major share of investment funds is raised by the sale of stock certificates. The value or price of each certificate also is determined by their demand and supply in the stock market.

Questions for thought and discussion

1. Suppose you bought a new typewriter at the beginning of your freshman year for $100. How would you determine the cost of owning the typewriter during your freshman year?

2. Suppose farm land in a community sells for $500 per acre. If the net rent (after real estate taxes) that can be obtained from the land is $20 per year, what is the annual rate of return on the land?

3. Consider a new garden tractor that sells for $1,000. The same model of this tractor that is three years old may sell for $400, yet it is likely that the used tractor can do about the same work as the new one. Why should the used tractor sell for $600 less?

4. Estimate the annual cost of owning and operating a new $4,000 automobile the first year of ownership. Assume a 25 percent depreciation rate on interest rate of 10 percent and that the car is driven 20,000 miles.

5. What is the discounted present value of $100 forthcoming two years from now if the interest rate is 8 percent? What is the economic rationale behind the fact that one dollar forthcoming two years in the future is worth less than one dollar at the present?

6. If the interest rate is 8 percent, what would be the capitalized value of the land referred to in question 2? Why do you suppose it sells for $500 per acre?

7. Referring to question 1, set up a cash flow analysis for this

typewriter for four years of college. Use some actual figures. Assume you could sell the typewriter at the end of your senior year for $40. (Hint: Estimate each year's gross cash inflow by letting it be equal to the amount you would have to pay to have your typing done. Let each year's added expense figure be equal to the value you would put on the time you would have to spend to do your own typing.)

a) Is the sum of the net cash outflow and inflow figures negative or positive?

b) If the sum is positive, should you definitely buy the typewriter? Why or why not?

c) How would you determine the discounted present value of the typewriter's services?

d) How would you determine the internal rate of return on the typewriter?

8. How does the interest rate influence the profitability of an investment?

9. Differentiate between the discounted present value of an investment and its internal rate of return.

10. Why can large corporations borrow money at a lower rate of interest than individuals?

11. Why would anyone borrow from a loan shark or the syndicate at a 50 to 100 percent rate of interest if banks are lending at 10 percent? What does one pledge as collateral when borrowing from the syndicate?

12. Differentiate between the money rate and the real rate of interest. Why does the money rate tend to rise during periods of inflation or expected inflation?

13. If the price/earnings ratio of a stock is 40, what is its annual rate of return? Why would anyone choose to purchase such a stock if other stocks were selling at a price/earnings ratio of 15 to 20?

14. Why do some stocks increase in value over time, while others decline in value?

11

The economics of education

The concept of human capital

In our discussion of the capital market in Chapter 10, we defined capital as durable or long-lasting inputs, such as buildings and equipment, that contribute to the production of goods and services. We noted that capital inputs are expensive and that the present value of their stream of returns must be greater than their purchase price in order for them to yield a net positive contribution to total output.

In recent years there has been a growing awareness that the acquisition of knowledge and skills by human beings also results in the creation of capital—human capital. At the same time there has been a reluctance on the part of some educators to regard education and training as a kind of capital formation. Their rationale is similar to those who have argued that labor, the services of human beings, should not be treated as an input of production subject to economic analysis. They believe it is dehumanizing to think of boys and girls learning to read and write, or of young men and women acquiring a knowledge of mathematics, history, and economics as a process that results in the formation of capital.

Surely the psychological and sociological aspects of human beings must be considered. As we pointed out at the beginning of the labor market chapter, there is no reason why economists who work in the area of labor economics or human capital need to be less "human" than anyone else. Indeed, the separate study of the labor market or the economics of education allows us to take into account the uniqueness of people, as compared to nonhuman inputs such as machines, tools and raw materials. The fact that we identify human capital as a separate field of study denotes its uniqueness. While the special characteristics of human beings are recognized, there are a number of similarities between nonhuman capital and human capital, or skills and knowledge acquired through education or training.

First, both kinds of capital, human and nonhuman, enhance the productive capacity of society. Man without tools and without knowledge is a very unproductive creature. Moreover, even a cursory study of history will reveal that human capital must exist before nonhuman capital can be produced. For example, the wheel came into being when man learned that a round object rolling along the ground encountered less friction and took less power to move than a flat object being dragged. We could point to innumerable examples of new applications of knowledge that have led to the production of new nonhuman capital.

A second similarity between the two kinds of capital is that they both pay off over a long period of time. Indeed, the stream of returns to education for most people covers 30 to 40 or more years. We will discuss shortly the kind of returns that human capital provides. For the moment it is sufficient that we become aware of the consequences of this long payoff period. First, it precipitates a great deal of uncertainty. Students are faced with the nagging question of whether the job that is being prepared for will be available when they graduate, to say nothing of 10 to 20 years in the future. At the high school and undergraduate level of training, it is virtually impossible to predict what kind of employment will be forthcoming. Since a person's job can be expected to change several times during a lifetime, it is important that training, particularly at the college level, will facilitate learning new jobs and adjusting to new environments. Another consequence of the long payoff is the need to discount future returns, as in the garden tractor example of the preceding chapter. For instance, one dollar forthcoming 40 years from now discounted back at a 6 percent interest rate is worth less than 10 cents today. With the demands of the present upon a young person's resources, such as for car, clothes, and travel, the decision to invest now for a payoff far into the future is difficult to say the least.

Third, human capital, like some nonhuman capital, requires a lengthy building period. With human capital, this period is generally a good deal longer. Eight years is the least amount of time that can be devoted to the process, and it may run up to 18 or 20 years for people who obtain a Ph.D. or professional degree. We will see later in the chapter that this long gestation or building period, coupled with the long payoff period, makes the discounting factor especially important in the case of human capital.

A fourth similarity between the two kinds of capital is that both tend to depreciate. The ultimate depreciation for human capital, of course, is growing old and passing from the scene. But there is a more immediate depreciation that begins the minute after we learn something new—forgetting. Educators tell us that a large part of what we learn is forgotten in a relatively short time. How much do you recall of a book you read or a course you took last year, or even last quarter? Depreciation of human capital also occurs because of obsolescence. Each year new knowledge is being produced that reduces the value of existing knowledge. Skills such as the ability to repair a steam locomotive or fly a propeller-driven aircraft are no longer in demand because new knowledge and technology that has come on the scene. Because of obsolescence, it is necessary for most people to continue learning throughout their lifetimes. This is particularly true for those in the professions or skilled trades. A college professor who wants to keep abreast of new knowledge in his field, for example, probably should spend about 20 to 25 percent of his time learning.

HUMAN CAPITAL FORMATION

The major part of all human capital is the result of formal schooling provided by elementary schools, high schools, trade and vocational schools, and colleges and universities. Not all schooling, of course, needs to be of this type. A good deal of learning takes place on the job, either through apprenticeship programs or through learning by doing.

In addition, some learning takes place through individual study, although the truly self-made man, Abraham Lincoln, for example, always has been a rare case. In spite of the criticism levied against the traditional student-teacher arrangement in learning, it is the rare individual who can master a field or body of knowledge by himself. Most of us require someone who can tell us what is important or what to study. In fact, this may be the most valuable function of a teacher. Of course, different teachers have different ideas of what is important. The ability to identify and teach the important material just might be the crucial characteristic of a "good" teacher; a teacher who allocates the time of his students to material that only he considers important, and that in fact turns out to be trivial, cannot be "good" no matter how lucid or entertaining he might be. The ability to foresee and identify the important, high-payoff material seems to be a rather rare talent, however.

Personal returns to education

What does an individual obtain from education? Essentially there are two components of the return to education: investment and consumption. The investment component of the returns to education refers to the future years of increased earning power that can be obtained with additional years of schooling. This increased earning power comes largely from one or both of two factors: (1) an increase in the productive capacity of the individual and (2) the ability to conceive of and produce new goods or services that are valued more highly by society.

The contribution of education to increased productivity appears to stem, at least in part, from an increased ability to organize and use resources efficiently, including the very scarce resource, time. Surely no one appreciates the importance of time more than the student. With two or three exams coming up and a term paper to finish, the student is forced to make each minute count. The experience gained in allocating time efficiently is one of the most important advantages of a college education, at least from the standpoint of productivity of the individual. Education also enhances productivity by enabling the individual to more readily accept new technology and use it effectively. Education is particularly important with regard to technology that requires new or different skills. The more educated person seems to possess a greater capacity for self-teaching and adapting to new situations.

The effect of education on the kinds of goods and services produced is demonstrated clearly by comparing the output of a modern industrialized society that has a high proportion of educated people with that of a traditional society. The traditional society's choice of goods and services tends to be limited to a rather narrow array of low-quality items, most of which are considered necessities. The output of the more highly educated society is of a higher quality and much more diverse in nature. The world would be a dull place for the educated man if education only resulted in greater output of the traditional necessities, such as food, clothing, and shelter. Thus the monetary rewards of additional education stem at least in part from an increased ability to conceive of and produce new and different goods and services that are demanded by a more productive society.

Of course, when considering the monetary rewards of increased education, it is always possible to point out exceptions: self-made men with an eighth-grade education who have built up fortunes in the business world, or high school dropouts who made it big in show business. But if we look at large numbers of people, we find that high school graduates, on the average, earn more than people with an eighth-grade education, and people with college training earn more than high school graduates. Thus, an individual who does not achieve a high school or college education is not necessarily doomed to a life of poverty, but the chances that he will remain poor are substantially higher than if he would have received the schooling.

For most people the returns to additional education exceed the investment component, that is, the monetary value of increased earnings over a lifetime. The consumption or nonmonetary returns to education include: (1) the immediate utility or satisfaction that a person receives during the time of his schooling and (2) the long-run stream of increased satisfaction that accrues during his lifetime because of the educational experience.

Although few students think fondly of exams or assignments, most derive some satisfaction from being in an educational environment. The friends that are made, the dances and parties, the dates, the sporting events, the good books that are read, even the pleasure of learning all provide immediate satisfaction that is not measured in monetary terms.

But the nonmonetary rewards to schooling are not limited to the immediate time spent in school. Many friendships that begin in school endure over a lifetime. Many girls acquire husbands, and many fellows find their wives during their school years. It would seem also that education enhances the quality of life by facilitating an awareness and greater understanding of the world around us. The lives of educated people are ruled less by superstition and fear and more by rational thought and deliberate choice. Although we do not have adequate quantitative measures of happiness, psychological studies seem to indicate that people with more education are on the average happier and find greater fulfillment in life than those with less education. Perhaps education is even more important than money in finding that elusive and nebulous quality called happiness.

At any rate, it is fairly certain that individuals obtain more from education than just the monetary rewards reflected in a higher income. One can think of these nonmonetary rewards to education as a consumption good. It provides utility, hence people are willing to pay a positive price for it. It appears also that education is a superior good; as incomes rise, the demand for education also rises. It is reasonable to believe that as incomes continue to rise, the nonmonetary rewards to education will grow in importance relative to the monetary returns. Young people will come to school more to enrich their lives than to "make a bundle." We see more and more evidence of this, particularly among young people from upper income families.

If in fact education is becoming more of a consumption good, we might expect as well that students will demand more voice in the courses being offered. If courses are taught primarily to increase earning power, the professional in the field (i.e., the professor) wins hands down as far as knowing what to teach. But when it comes to offering courses for consumption or nonmonetary purposes, it must be admitted that the student has a better idea of what "turns him on" than the professor or school administrators. This does not imply that courses need be less scholarly or the intellectual demands less rigorous, but we can expect to see greater emphasis placed on the relevance of the course and its interest to the student. With the increased emphasis on the consumption component of education, we might also expect to see a decreased emphasis on grades. If the student is not particularly concerned with the effect of courses on his earning capacity, there is less incentive to master the fine points of the course for an A or B.

The fact that we are observing these trends is evidence that the monetary return to an education is becoming slightly less important. However, the monetary return still represents the major reason for attending college, and even more so for graduate or professional school attendance.

Social returns to education

The returns to education are not limited to those realized by the individual. Society as a whole also gains. Economists often call these gains "social returns" or "externalities," that is, the benefits that are external to the individual receiving the education.

At the family level, the education of the parents, particularly that of the mother, should have some beneficial effects on the children. For one thing it tends to broaden the children's cultural background and opportunities. Children of college-educated parents are more likely to attend college than those whose parents stopped at the grade school or high school level, although this may be less important now than it used to be because of the accessibility of community colleges. There also would seem to be a tendency for at least a part of the knowledge gained by parents during their school years to be transmitted to their children. Children who gain an appreciation for the importance of knowledge have gained a great deal.

At the community level it could be argued that the education of individuals makes the community a better place to live for all. For example, one's chances of getting "mugged" appear to be somewhat greater in neighborhoods where people are poorly educated and have low incomes than in those where the majority is highly educated and affluent. Granted the income level may be the important factor in this difference, but, as we will see shortly, education has an important bearing on income. An increase in the educational level of people also seems to reduce the amount of fear and suspicion that people have of one another. Because education usually acquaints us with people of different backgrounds and tastes, it may help us become a bit more tolerant of those who happen to be different in one way or another.

It might be expected that different kinds of education would provide different degrees of social returns. It is often argued that education which imparts purely technical skills, such as programming a computer, repairing an automobile, or setting a broken bone, primarily benefits the person receiving the education because of the larger income he can earn by selling these skills.[1] Social returns may be greatest in education, which provides a better understanding of people and society such as the liberal arts and social sciences.

The amount of social return derived from the education of individuals is an important point because it bears on the financing of education. If social returns are important, then society ought to pay at least part of the cost of educating the individual, as is now done in public schools, colleges, and universities. The argument is that if society receives some benefit from education over and above that received by the individual, it will have to pay part of the individual's educational expense in order for him to be willing to invest an optimum amount in himself from the standpoint of society. On the other hand, if the individual receives all the benefits of his education, then it might be argued that the individual should be willing to buy the amount that provides a return equal to other investments he could make. We will come back to the problem of financing education in just a bit, but first let us look at the costs of education.

Personal costs of education

Needless to say, education is not a free good. Indeed, it is becoming more expensive each year, as every student and parent is well aware. It will be useful at this point, therefore, to itemize the major costs that a student or his parents bear for education. These include: (1) foregone earnings, (2) tuition, and (3) books and supplies.

It is a temptation to exclude foregone earnings (the money you could be earning if you were not in school) as part of the cost of an education because this cost is not paid by check or cash. It must be admitted, however, that a person who decides to go to work after high school gives up a college or technical school education. It is just as logical to argue that a person who decides to go to school

---

[1] Of course, the people who purchase the goods or services made possible by education also benefit.

gives up full-time employment earnings during the college years.

In the more developed countries of the world, foregone earnings are negligible for the elementary and junior high school student but begin to be a factor as the student finishes high school and enters college or some other kind of advanced training. In developing countries, where educational attainment is usually low and children enter the labor force at a relatively young age, foregone earnings are relatively important even in the lower grades.

Although the average student may not feel the pinch of foregone earnings as much as the out-of-pocket costs of tuition, books, and so forth, it is necessary just the same to take this money into account when deciding how far to go in school. Considering the relatively modest salary that a high school graduate can obtain the first few years out of school, say five to six thousand dollars per year, it becomes clear that even a modest amount of income foregone is relatively large when viewed as a cost.

The foregone earnings expense can be reduced substantially, however, by taking part-time employment while attending school. For example, if you could be earning $5,500 per year on a full-time job were you not in school, but you work part time for $2,000 per year, your foregone earnings are reduced to $3,500 per year. Of course, part-time work means that something has to be given up—study time, school activities, or leisure. Thus the reduction in foregone earnings by working part time will be offset at least in part by the value of what is given up. It should also be remembered that the further one goes in school, the higher the earnings that have to be given up to remain in school.

Any scholarships or financial aid received by students also would be deducted from foregone earnings. In the example above, a $500 scholarship would further reduce earnings foregone, down to $3,000 per year.

The other two cost components—tuition and books and supplies—are familiar enough that we need not go into detail here, though we should note that tuition generally does not cover the full educational costs of colleges and universities. We will consider this part of the cost in the next section.

One cost item that is conspicuous by its absence is board and room. Surely, you might argue, a student who pays $1,000 during the school year for a room and meals at the college dormitory should include this amount as a logical part of college costs. But bear in mind that everyone has to be somewhere, so if the student did not pay the $1,000 for living on or near campus, he would have to pay as much or more to live wherever he worked. Thus the cost items listed above include only the extra costs involved in attending college as opposed to doing something else. Costs are measured in this manner so they can be compared with the extra income that is obtained by furthering an education.

Public costs of education

From the viewpoint of the total society, all of the private costs that we considered in the previous section would, of course, be a part of the total educational cost that society must bear. The operation of schools and colleges financed in part by tuition, the production of books and supplies, and the loss of earnings during school years all involve a using up of real resources that could have been used to produce something else, had they not been used to produce education.

In the majority of our educational institutions, however, tuition does not come close to covering the cost of operating the schools. In the public elementary and high schools, tuition is zero, so the entire cost is borne by the taxpayers. In colleges and universities tuition varies a great deal; some city or community colleges set tuition at zero or close to it, while the more exclusive private schools try to cover a larger share of their operating costs by tuition. Most of the high-tuition private schools, however, must rely on endowments to make ends meet. The main point is that the total cost of education for most students is substantially greater than the cost borne by the student himself.

Financing education

The relative increase in the cost of providing educational services in recent years has prompted considerable discussion on the optimum methods of paying for these services. In the United States and most other countries of the world, a substantial share of the cost of operating educational institutions has been provided by public funds, that is, taxes. The popularity of this method of finance probably stems from a rather special characteristic of the education service: People who buy this service, namely students, have had little or no opportunity to earn and save enough to pay for it. It could be argued that many other goods and services, such as pablum and the services of pediatricians, also exhibit this characteristic, although their benefits tend to be somewhat more certain and immediate than the returns to education. By using public tax funds to finance a large part of the cost of education, we are in essence spreading its current cost over several generations, as opposed to concentrating it on one or two generations, that is, the parents of the students or the students themselves.

One alternative to public payment of tuition is for parents or families to pay for the education of their children. Among upper middle- and high-income people, this is frequently done. However, for a large segment of our population the cost of purchasing 12 to 16 years of quality schooling for their children would be prohibitive. It is argued that children of poor parents would continue to be doomed to a life of poverty because of an inability to buy a means of escape through education.

A second alternative to public support of education is for students to borrow to pay for it. This alternative has not enjoyed much popularity, even among students in professional and graduate schools, to say nothing of elementary and high school students. Indeed, students seem more willing to go into debt for an automobile than for schooling. It is not clear why, but one possible explanation is the uncertainty of the future. The automobile provides immediate and certain utility, whereas the payoff to education is both uncertain and far off. It is also true that lending agencies have not been especially eager to promote educational loans compared to auto loans, for example. No doubt, risk or uncertainty is also a prime consideration for the lender. If a person who borrows for an automobile defaults on his payments, the lender always can repossess the car. But if a person who borrows for an education defaults, it is not possible to repossess the person—or the education. Granted there are devices such as wage garnishment, but these have not been popular and involve added legal expense and effort.

At any rate, if society desires its young people to continue to achieve 12 to 16 years of quality schooling, then it probably will have to continue to use public tax funds to finance at least a part of the cost of education. Whether such funding leads to a so-called "optimum" amount of education is a question that is being debated at the present time. It has been argued that such funding provides a strong incentive to overinvest in education because the full cost is not borne by the individual. That is, when the cost of something is subsidized, the individual has an incentive to buy more of it than if he had to bear the full cost on his own.

On the other hand, it can be argued that the uncertainty faced by the individual who must pay for his entire education leads him to purchase less education than would be desirable from the standpoint of society. The argument here is that the individual faces a great deal more uncertainty regarding the payoff to education than would a large group of individuals, that is, society. Thus each individual will be inclined to invest less in education than would be the case if he faced the same uncertainty as society as a whole. Therefore, it is argued, society will have to bear a part of the individual's education cost in order to make him willing to purchase as much education as he would if he were faced with the same uncertainty as society. The existence of any so-called "social returns," as mentioned previously, also implies the use of public tax funds for education. However, this argument has lost some of its appeal in recent years because of our inability to quantify the magnitude of such returns or even to demonstrate their existence.

An argument for using public funds to support education also can be made on the basis of achieving a more equal distribution of income. If only the rich could "afford" to buy education for their children, the children of poor parents would likely remain poor. It should be kept in mind, though, that students at the high school and college level will continue to bear a substantial share of the cost of schooling, regardless of how tuition is financed, because of their foregone earnings. And these foregone earnings probably loom larger in the minds of poor students than those from high-income families.

The common method of using public funds to finance education is by allocating the funds directly to the educational institutions. An alternative to this procedure would be to provide grants in the form of vouchers directly to the students or to their parents, allowing them to spend the vouchers at the school of their choice. The school would then turn in the vouchers and receive money from the government. A major advantage of this approach is that it would give people more freedom of choice and promote competition between schools. As mentioned previously, public schools now enjoy substantial freedom from competitive forces and therefore have little incentive to innovate and improve the quality of their services or to strive for greater efficiency. For example, there is a tendency on the part of educators to treat students' time as if it were a free good.[2]

Returns to investment in education

Although the returns to education are reflected in more than just monetary rewards, it is helpful to obtain measures of both the costs and returns to investment in human capital or education. If education turns out to be a good investment strictly from a monetary point of view, then we can be sure it is an even better investment when nonmonetary returns are considered. We will look first at the monetary returns to education.

MEASURING MONETARY RETURNS

The figures in Table 11–1 provide an indication of the monetary value of various levels of education. These are the median incomes of male persons (all races) for the year 1968 classified by age and education, as published by the U.S. Department of Commerce, Bureau of the Census.

The most obvious difference in the income streams of people with different levels of education is the increased size of income as education increases. Secondly, a person with an eighth-grade or even a high school education cannot look forward to as large an increase in his income as he grows older as he could if he were a college

---

2 For further discussion of the problems of financing education, see the report of the "Investment in Education: The Equity Efficiency Quandary," workshop at the University of Chicago, June 7–10, 1971, sponsored by the Committee on Basic Research in Education of the National Research Council, T. W. Schultz (ed.), *Journal of Political Economy,* Vol. 80, pt. 2 (May–June, 1972).

TABLE 11-1

Median incomes of full-time employed males by age and education, 1968 ($ per year)

Level of school completed	Age span			
	25–34	35–44	45–54	55–64
Eighth grade	$ 5,994	$ 6,702	$ 6,815	$ 6,787
High school	7,762	8,826	8,686	8,194
One to three years over high school	8,409	10,076	10,009	9,400
Four years' college	10,132	12,596	12,910	13,063
One or more years' postgraduate work	10,538	13,508	14,401	14,634

Source: U.S. Department of Commerce, *Current Population Reports*, Series P-60, No. 66, (December 1969), Table 41.

graduate. People with relatively less schooling tend to reach their peak income years during the 35–54 age span, whereas college graduates and those with postgraduate work by and large continue to enjoy increased incomes until they retire. With overall economic growth occurring, there has been a tendency, in the United States at least, for most everyone to enjoy some income growth, but people with more education tend to enjoy more income growth in an absolute sense than people with less education.

In order to use these figures to calculate the monetary returns of achieving a given level of education, we must compute the differential in earnings between the various levels of schooling. For example, the monetary value of a high school over an eighth-grade education during the 25–34 age span is $7,762 − $5,994, or $1,768 per year. These income differentials are presented in Table 11–2.

TABLE 11-2

Income differentials for various levels of education ($ per year)

Differences in educational level	Age span			
	25–34	35–44	45–54	55–64
High school over eighth grade	$1,768	$2,124	$1,871	$1,407
One to three years' college over high school	647	1,250	1,323	1,206
Four years' college over high school	2,370	3,770	4,224	4,869
One or more years' postgraduate over college	406	912	1,500	1,571

Source: Computed from Table 11–1.

Assuming a 40-year working life, we can obtain a rough idea of the extra income that a person can expect if he completes a given level of schooling. For example, during the 10-year 25–34 age span a person can expect to earn about $17,680 more by completing high school than by stopping at the eighth grade. Total lifetime earnings differentials for various levels of schooling are presented in Table 11–3.

TABLE 11–3

Total lifetime earnings differentials for various levels of education

Level school completed	Additions to income
High school over eighth grade	$ 71,700
One to three years' college over high school	44,260
Four years' college over high school	152,330
One or more years' postgraduate over college	43,890

Bear in mind that the figures in Table 11–3 are *additions* to income because of additional years of schooling, not total income. For example, the total lifetime income of a high school graduate is in the neighborhood of $334,680, as obtained from Table 11–1, whereas lifetime earnings of a college graduate are $487,010.

There are some interesting contrasts in these differentials. Notice that by investing in four years of high school, total lifetime earnings increase by $71,700. But by investing in four years of college, the extra income over high school increases to $152,330, or just about double the payoff in the four high school years.

However, before we can evaluate the payoff to different levels of schooling, we must consider two additional factors: the cost of the schooling, and the present value of future income, or the internal rate of return.

MEASURING COSTS

Recall that the three major cost components of education are (1) foregone earnings (less earnings from part-time work, scholarships, and financial aid); (2) tuition; and (3) books and supplies. As an example, we will consider the investment in a four-year college education.

To obtain a measure of foregone earnings while attending college, we need to estimate what a person could earn on a first job immediately out of high school. Unfortunately the figures in Table 11–1 do not help us a great deal here. The $7,762 median earnings figure for the 25–34 age span would be more representative of a person with a high school education who has worked about 10 years, rather than a new graduate. Therefore, we will assume that a high school graduate could earn about $5,500 per year for the first two years out of school and $6,000 per year for the next two years. We will also assume that while attending college the student does not hold down a part-time job during the school year but earns $1,200 on a summer job. His net foregone earnings would be $4,300 per year ($5,500 − $1,200) for the first two years of college and $4,800 annually for the last two years.

Assume also that the student pays resident tuition at a large state university, say $500 per year. This figure would increase up to around $2,500 to $3,000 or more per year at the more exclusive private schools, of course. But in some cases private school tuition also includes a charge for board and room, and that sum should be subtracted.

Books, supplies, and so forth, may seem expensive when they are purchased, but they actually constitute a relatively minor part of total costs. A rather liberal figure of $250 per year would represent that cost for most students.

These three cost items for the four years of college are summarized in Table 11–4. The figures indicate the importance of foregone earnings in the total cost of a college education. In this example they comprise about 85 percent of the total costs. The further one goes in school, the larger foregone earnings become. This undoubtedly explains why students become more and more anxious to join the

TABLE 11–4

Summary of costs for a four-year college education

	Freshman	Sophomore	Junior	Senior
Foregone earnings*	$4,300	$4,300	$4,800	$4,800
Tuition	500	500	500	500
Books and supplies	250	250	250	250
Total	$5,050	$5,050	$5,550	$5,550

* Assuming a $1,200 per year summer job.

labor force as they approach the end of their schooling. Some, particularly Ph.D. candidates, leave school before they are finished, hoping to complete their requirements on the job. Some never do.

If we add up the total costs of four years of college in this example, the total is $21,200. It is unlikely that most college students realize how much they invest in themselves during their college years. Comparing this $21,200 cost figure with the $152,330 additional-income figures from Table 11–3, would, however, make it appear that the investment is well worth the cost.

Before we become too optimistic, we should remember that the $152,330 additional income is spread out over an entire lifetime. One dollar forthcoming 30 to 40 years from now is not worth much at the present. Therefore, we need to compute the present value of this extra income stream, just as we did in the garden tractor example. In the process we can estimate the internal rate of return to a college education. First let us set up the problem in terms of cash flow analysis, as we did with the garden tractor.

CASH FLOW ANALYSIS APPLIED TO EDUCATION

In the context of cash flow analysis we can view the costs of going to school (Table 11–4) as the cash outflow and the added income over a high school education (Table 11–1) as the cash inflow. The configuration of these cash flows for a college education is illustrated in Figure 11–1.

The net cash outflow increases slightly after the first two years because of the increased earning potential of people with two extra years of schooling. The level of cash inflows is illustrated in a stepwise fashion because of the age groupings given by the census data on earnings. Although it may be more realistic to show earnings differentials rising in a smooth line, the stepwise procedure will not alter the results greatly. We assume a 43-year working life starting at age 22 and extending up to age 65.

ACCUMULATING COSTS

There is an important difference in this investment compared to the garden tractor example of the previous chapter. The cost of a

FIGURE 11–1
Cash outflows and inflows from investment in a college education

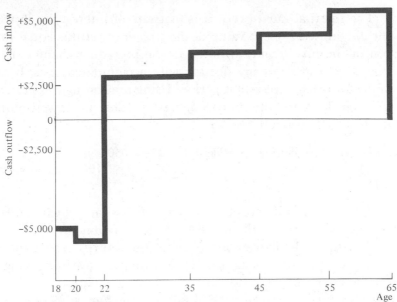

college education is incurred over a four-year period, rather than taking place at a single point in time. As a result, we need to introduce the idea of accumulating costs.[3]

Costs must be accumulated because the cost today of one dollar spent a number of years ago is larger than one dollar. This is because of the interest that the dollar could have earned had we not spent it on the investment in question. The formula for determining the accumulated cost of one dollar spent n years ago is $(1 + r)^n$ where r is the rate of interest employed. For example, in computing the accumulated cost of $1,000 invested two years ago using a 10 percent rate of interest, we would obtain $1,000 $(1 + .10)^2 = 1210. With this procedure in mind, we can compute the internal ráte of return to a college education.

---

[3] Actually the internal rate of return could be computed by discounting both the returns and costs back to the freshman year. In this case the costs would enter the calculation as negative numbers. The same answer is obtained, regardless of the point of reference used. We set the point of reference in the education problem at the end of the senior year in order to separate the costs from the returns more clearly.

INTERNAL RATE OF RETURN TO A COLLEGE EDUCATION

The internal rate of return is that rate of interest which makes the discounted present value of the stream of returns equal to the cost of the investment, as noted in the preceding chapter. In the case of education we are dealing with accumulated costs, because of the four-year investment period. Using the cost figures presented in Table 11–4 and the returns figures of Table 11–2, we would set up the problem as follows:

$$5050(1+r)^4 + 5050(1+r)^3 + 5550(1+r)^2 + 5550(1+r) = \frac{2370}{(1+r)} + \frac{2370}{(1+r)^2} + \cdots + \frac{4869}{(1+r)^{43}}$$

The internal rate of return is that interest rate which makes the sum of the figures on the left side of the equation (the costs) equal to the sum of the figures on the right (the returns). (Bear in mind that only 3 of the 43 figures representing a 43-year working life are shown on the right side in the preceding equation.)

Choosing a 10 percent rate of interest, the four years of expenditure for a college education accumulates to a total of $26,910 if we take each year up to the point where the investment starts paying off (age 22 in this example). If we discount each of the 43 years of returns back to age 22 by an interest rate of 10 percent and add them up, we obtain a cumulative figure of $27,860. Thus the internal rate of return to investment in a four-year college education is just slightly over 10 percent.

In view of the fact that the total undiscounted extra earnings of a college education over that of a high school education came out to be over $152,000 or over seven times the $21,200 unaccumulated expenditure, we might have expected the internal rate of return to be somewhat higher. But we must remember that with a 10 percent rate of discount the extra $4,869 forthcoming at age 65 is only worth about $97 at age 22. It is not surprising, then, that young people do not consider the extra earnings forthcoming much later in life to be very important.

As an alternative procedure, we could have simply discounted the future returns back to age 22, accumulated the costs forward to this date, and then observed if the discounted returns were greater than the accumulated costs. If they were, then the investment would have been worthwhile. The interest rate that would be used to discount returns and accumulate costs should reflect the rate of return on the best alternative use of these funds, such as investment in the stock market or municipal bonds.

We utilize the procedure for determining the internal rate of return here because much of the work of evaluating the cost and returns to education also utilizes this procedure. Also, in other methods the interest rate used may determine whether or not the discounted present value is greater than the accumulated costs. With the internal-rate-of-return procedure we need not concern ourselves with the choice of the "correct" interest rate to use in the accumulating and discounting procedure. Much excellent statistical work has been done recently on the cost and returns to education at all levels.[4] The procedure used in most of these studies is basically the same as the one utilized in the example above, and the results of these studies are of a comparable order of magnitude to the results obtained from this example.

PART-TIME EMPLOYMENT

Because earnings foregone represent such an important part of the cost of a college education, the case where the student holds down a part-time job during the school year calls for some special attention. Choosing some plausible figures, suppose as a freshman the student earns $100 per month, $150 per month as a sophomore, and $200 per month during his junior and senior years. These earnings could be obtained if the student worked about 10 to 15 hours per week during his first two years and 15 to 20 hours per week during his junior and senior years, which is not uncommon.

If we assume that other costs remain the same, as shown in Table 11–4, we can obtain the revised costs by subtracting the above part-time earnings from these figures, obtaining:

Freshman:	$5,050 − $ 900 =	$4,150
Sophomore:	5,050 − 1,350 =	3,700
Junior:	5,550 − 1,800 =	3,750
Senior:	5,550 − 1,800 =	3,750

---

[4] See, for example, T. W. Schultz, *Investment in Human Capital* (New York: Free Press, 1971); T. W. Schultz, *The Economic Value of Education* (New York and London: Columbia University Press, 1963); and W. Lee Hansen, "Total and Private Rates of Return to Investment in Schooling," *Journal of Political Economy*, Vol. 71 (April 1963).

Adding up these figures for the four years yields a total cost for a four-year college education of $15,350, compared to $21,200 when the student did not work during the school year. Assuming the same stream of returns and following the same procedure as before, where we accumulate the 4 years of costs up to the end of the senior year and discount the 43 years of returns back to this point, we obtain approximately a 13 percent internal rate of return. At this rate of discount accumulated costs add up to $21,208, and discounted future returns total $20,561. Thus the internal rate of return to a four-year college education with a total of $5,850 part-time earnings for the four years is just slightly less than 13 percent.

Although it cannot be disputed that part-time earnings are very important to a college student during his time in college, it is a bit surprising to find that they do not drastically alter the rate of return to a college education. Granted, of course, 13 percent is better than 10 percent. But even with substantial part-time earnings, foregone earnings still constitute the largest part of the cost of attending college.

One problem we have not considered in regard to part-time employment is its effect on the quality of education, in terms of both nonmonetary returns and future earning power, or its effect on the time required to finish the degree. We have assumed the same monetary returns and the same four years of time in college in the above calculations. However, virtually no quantitative information exists on the effect of part-time employment during college. Does it hamper a person's future earning power or enhance it? How much, if any, does it delay a student's graduation date?

By subtracting the value of part-time earnings from the total costs of attending college and then calculating a rate of return, we are implicitly assuming that whatever is given up in order to work part time has a zero value to the student. Even if leisure is the only thing given up, this assumption is admittedly extreme. To be strictly correct, we should have also reduced the returns by the value of leisure given up or other nonmonetary returns to education that are not obtained because of a part-time job. However, any estimate of these items would be a pure guess and would vary considerably between individuals. At any rate, the more important these items are, the closer will be the estimated rate of return with part-time earnings to that without it, as presented in the previous section. We can be sure, in any event, that the value to the student of whatever is given up to work part time is less than the value of the earnings from the part-time job, or the student would not elect to work part time.

RETURNS TO WOMEN

In our discussion of the monetary returns to education we have assumed that the graduate will work 40 years or more. Most girls who attend college do not remain in the labor force all their lives, however; many get married shortly after college and foresake occupational pursuits to raise a family. Further, women's salaries have tended to be lower than men's. For these reasons, if we were to estimate the monetary returns to a college education for women they would be somewhat less than those for men.

This is not to say that college is a bad investment for girls. Increasingly, women educated for the professions devote as much time to them as men do, although they probably will not make as much at it. From a personal point of view, a college-educated girl may enjoy more purchasing power during her life simply because she will be more likely to marry a college-educated man, who has the potential of greater lifetime earnings. The girl who attends college to obtain her MRS. degree knows this very well, although few girls in college now would admit to this motivation. Such a girl also buys security with college because if she wants to or must enter the labor force she is better prepared to do so. Many women now combine homemaking and a career or voluntarily reenter the labor force when their children are older, primarily to supplement the family income. These earnings (over and above the amount that could be earned with a high school education) would, of course, be counted in the monetary return of a woman's college education.

THE COLLEGE DROPOUT

Not all students who enter colleges and universities come out with a four-year bachelor's degree or equivalent, however. In 1964, 1,224,840 freshmen enrolled in U.S. institutions of higher learning.

Four years later, in 1968, 671,591 received a bachelor's degree or equivalent.[5] Thus of all students entering college, almost one half drop out somewhere along the way.

Part of the gap between freshman enrollment and the number of bachelor's degrees granted four years later is taken up by junior college students who decide to terminate their studies with the two-year degree. Enrollment in junior colleges has increased substantially in recent years. In 1960 for example, there were 451,333 students in junior colleges, whereas by 1968 this figure had almost tripled, to 1,289,993.[6] Some of these students, of course, transfer to four-year institutions and obtain a bachelor's degree.

At any rate, because almost half of all college students either stop at the two-year degree or drop out of four-year institutions, it is important that we know something of the return to this schooling. Let us take as an example a student who invests in two years of college. Assume that the annual cost of attending college during these two years is equal to the freshman- and sophomore-year costs shown in Table 11–4: $5,050 for each year.

Tables 11–1 and 11–2 above provide an indication of the monetary returns to investment in one to three additional years of schooling beyond high school. Assume that these figures are representative of the earnings forthcoming from two years of college. As shown in Table 11–3, the total lifetime earnings differential for one–three years of college is about $44,000.

In order to correctly evaluate the two-year college investment as opposed to the four-year investment, we must both consider costs and discount the future returns back to their beginning. If we use a 10 percent rate of interest to accumulate the two years of costs and discount the 45 years of returns, we obtain $11,665 for the costs and only $7,372 for the returns. Hence the internal rate of return to two years of college is somewhat less than 10 percent. It turns out that the discounted return just about equals the accumulated costs when a 7 percent rate of interest is used. Thus the internal rate of return to two years of college as opposed to stopping at high school is about 7 percent. Although this is a bit more than one can obtain from a savings account, it isn't spectacular.

---

[5] *Statistical Abstract, 1965*, p. 132, and *1970*, p. 131.
[6] *Statistical Abstract, 1970*, p. 126.

Of course, the two-year student also can work part time, so we should compute the rate of return in this situation too. Assume in this case that the student earns $900 during the first year of college (in addition to the $1,200 summer job) and $1,350 the second year, resulting in total costs of $4,150 and $3,700, respectively for these two years. Accumulating these two years of costs and discounting the 45 years of returns (assuming the same returns as the previous case), we obtain an internal rate of return of about 9 percent.

SUMMARY OF RETURNS TO INVESTMENT IN EDUCATION

We have covered a variety of different situations in computing the rate of return on an investment in education. It will be useful to summarize these rates of return, as is done in Table 11–5.

Keep in mind that these figures represent the private rate of return to a college education. Because society pays a substantial share of the cost of operating most colleges and universities, the public return would be somewhat lower. With relatively low rates of return to one to three years of college, we might at least raise the question of whether it is wise for society to encourage the entry of students who will likely drop out after one or two years of college. Perhaps the technical institute or trade school is a more profitable alternative both for these individual students and for society. It is very difficult to predict in advance, however, which students will successfully complete the four-year program.

TABLE 11–5

Summary of internal rates of return to investment in a college education

	Rate of return (percent)
Four-year degree, full-time school	10
Four-year degree, part-time earnings	13
Two-years college, full-time school	7
Two-years college, part-time earnings	9

Future returns to education

In estimating the returns to education we have to use data that show the present income differences between groups with different educational levels, high school versus college, for instance. But it is reasonable to ask whether a person who invests in education today can expect these differentials to continue into the future. The depressed state of the job market for college graduates in the early 1970s has led many to question whether a college education is still a good investment. Although the increased joblessness among college graduates during this time is a factor to consider, a student should not allow a temporary downturn in economic activity to change the course of his entire life. He should base his decision on the conditions expected to prevail over the next half century, rather than on what has happened over the past few years.

Although no one can predict the future with certainty, especially 40 to 50 years hence, we might be able to obtain some idea of future income differentials by looking at long-run trends. Table 11–6 presents differences in mean income for various levels of edu-

TABLE 11–6

Mean annual income differentials of males 25 years old and over for selected years by years of school completed, 1968 dollars

	1949	1956	1961	1968
High school over eighth grade	$1,395	$1,987	$2,018	$2,681
One–three years' college over high school ...	934	1,042	1,627	1,249
Four years' college over high school	3,496	3,448	4,490	4,790
Four years' college over one to three years' college	2,562	2,406	2,863	3,541

Source: Calculated from *Statistical Abstract, 1970,* p. 111. Mean income figures deflated by Consumers Price Index, 1968 = 100, before calculating differentials.

cation for selected years over about a 20-year period. It is clear from these figures that the long-run trend in absolute income differentials is upward. For example, the added mean income differential of four years of college over high school was $3496 in 1949 (1968 prices) and $4790 in 1968.[7] It appears, therefore, that present investment in education will likely pay off at a higher rate in the future than our current data would indicate.

With the substantial increase in the proportion of young people going to college since the end of World War II, it is some-

---

[7] In estimating the returns to education, the relevant returns figures are the absolute differentials, as opposed to relative differences.

what of a puzzle why these income differentials show an upward trend. With the large increase in supply of people with greater skills, we might have predicted just the opposite to occur. However, bear in mind that the wages or earnings of people with various levels of education depend on both the supply and the demand for people with these skills. If, for example, the demand for people with a four-year college degree is growing (shifting to the right) more rapidly than the supply of these people, their earnings will rise. Moreover, if the demand for college-trained people is increasing faster than the demand for high school graduates, the income differential of college over high school will increase. This appears to have been happening. Why? We can only speculate. One explanation is that new technology is a complement to skills, and as our society advances technologically, the demand for highly trained people increases relative to the demand for unskilled and semi-skilled labor. It seems likely that technology will continue to advance and, as it does, so will the demand for skills.

Additional considerations

In order to keep the analysis as simple as possible, we have throughout the discussion on the returns to education neglected to mention a number of factors that could affect the outcome. One important consideration is taxes, particularly income taxes. Since our calculations have been based upon differences in income rather than absolute levels, there is a tendency for taxes to cancel out because everyone, regardless of the amount of schooling they have, must pay them. However, to the extent that tax rates are higher for higher income people, there will be a slight reduction in the private returns to education if income taxes were first deducted from everyone's income. The public or social returns to education are, of course, not affected by taxes; society can enjoy the entire increased output due to education.

A second consideration is the innate abilities of people. It has been argued that the procedure we have used to estimate the returns to education result in an overestimate because it applies to education alone. It is argued that the more capable people obtain more education and, as a result, part of what we attribute to education is in fact a result of superior innate intelligence. The degree of upward bias in the income differentials due to innate ability is still an open question. The evidence up to this time would indicate that the bias may not be as serious as first supposed, probably on the order of 10 percent.[8] It appears, therefore, that acquired ability is considerably more important than innate ability when it comes to earning money. This is reasonable when we consider that education opens doors to occupations that are otherwise closed, regardless of an individual's innate intelligence. Education in a sense enables him to exploit his capabilities to a much greater extent.

A third consideration is a difference in nonmonetary rewards relating to jobs that require more education. As a rule an increase in the amount of education results in an increase in job satisfaction, as well as income. Jobs available to people with relatively little education tend to be menial and routine in character and do not pay off much in terms of personal satisfaction.

There is also less security in less skilled types of work. In times of high unemployment, it is usually the unskilled workers who are first to be laid off and last to be hired. Increased job security has some psychological benefits as well as the advantage of a more certain income, since it lessens the necessity to be so concerned about whether a man's family will be provided for in the future.

Main points of Chapter 11

1. Economists have come to regard the skills and knowledge acquired through education as human capital.
2. A number of similarities exist between human and nonhuman capital: *(a)* both contribute to the real output of society, *(b)* both pay off over a long period of time, *(c)* both require a building period, and *(d)* both tend to depreciate.
3. Most human capital formation takes place as the result of formal schooling. A critical role of the teacher is to point out the important, high-payoff material to be learned.

---

8 See Zvi Griliches and William M. Mason, "Education, Income, and Ability," *Journal of Political Economy* Vol. 80, pt. 2 (May–June 1972), pp. S74–S103.

4.   The returns to education for the individual consist of two components: investment and consumption. The investment component refers to the increased earning power that results from additional education, whereas the consumption component refers to the utility that students derive out of being in school and the increased satisfaction that life brings because of the educational experience.

5.   Social returns to education refer to benefits derived over and above those obtained by the individual receiving the education. In part these benefits accrue to children in the home.

6.   The cost of education for the individual includes three main items: foregone earnings, tuition, and books and supplies. Foregone earnings is by far the largest cost. Board and room is not included because it must be paid regardless of what one does; it does not represent a special cost of going to school.

7.   There is a temptation not to include foregone earnings as a cost of education. But giving up earnings from a full-time job to attend school is in the same category as giving up an education to go to work.

8.   The public cost of education that is borne by society is, for most education, greater than the cost to the individual, because tuition generally does not cover the full cost of building and operating schools.

9.   A large share of the cost of education is financed by tax funds, which tends to spread the current cost of educating society's young people over several generations. However, because the individual does not have to bear part of his educational expense, he has an incentive to overinvest in education. Offsetting this is the uncertainty faced by the individual regarding the payoff to his education.

10. Income data collected by the U.S. Bureau of Census reveal that additional education results in higher incomes at every age level.

11. Monetary returns to education are measured by the differences in earnings of people with varying educational achievements.

12. In order to correctly evaluate the payoff to investment in education it is necessary to accumulate costs and discount future returns by an interest charge.

13. Choosing plausible cost figures and using the U.S. Census data on income by educational level, we can compute an internal rate of return to investment in education. The internal rate of return is that interest rate which makes the accumulated costs equal to the discounted returns.

14. The internal rate of return to a college education for a student who attends school full time during the school year but earns $1,200 during the summer is approximately 10 percent. The rate of return increases to about 13 percent if the student holds down a part-time job during the school year because of the reduced foregone earnings cost.

15. About one half of all college students who enter the freshman year do not graduate with a bachelor's degree. The rate of return to investment in two years of college is substantially lower than that for four years; 7 percent for a full-time student without part-time earnings and 9 percent with part-time earnings during the school year.

16. Over the past 20 years the absolute income differential for additional years of schooling has been increasing, indicating that the demand for people with more highly developed skills has been increasing more than the demand for people with fewer skills. From this we might conclude that our current figures understate the future returns to present education.

Questions for thought and discussion

1. Education is sometimes referred to as investment in human capital. In what respects is this investment similar to investment in nonhuman capital?

2. Distinguish between the investment and consumption components of education. Would you be in college if there were only a consumption return? Be honest.

3. Estimate the cost of your schooling this term. How much is this course costing you?

4. How would you set up a cash flow analysis to determine the internal rate of return to your investment in a college education?

5. Do we have to have public schools in order to have publicly supported education? Explain.
6. Would you be in favor of the voucher plan for funding education? Why or why not?
7. Do you think our society would be any different if all education had been funded privately by the student or his family? Elaborate.
8. Can you envision any advantage to a system where colleges charge a high tuition but provide scholarships covering all or most of the tuition for all students who could maintain passing grades? Explain.
9. As shown in Table 11–3, the total lifetime earnings differential for students with one to three years of college education is less than one third the added earnings of a four-year college education over high school. What reasons might be given for this rather large difference in earnings?
10. What do students who work part time give up during their college years?
11. "Because many women do not remain in the labor force for very long after graduation, a college education should provide a higher return to men as a group than to women." Do you agree? Why or why not?
12. Do you think the monetary rate of return to a college education will be as large in the future as in the past? Why?

12

The economics of
science and technology

The production of new knowledge

In the preceding chapter we developed the idea that the process of education, the transfer of knowledge from books and teachers into the minds of students, is akin to an investment involving both a cost and a return. In this chapter we will probe a bit deeper into this process, seeking an understanding of the production of knowledge itself.

At the beginning of history the stock of knowledge that existed in the minds of men was indeed small as measured by today's standards. Hunting and fishing skills and the ability to transform nature's bounty into food, clothing, and shelter about constituted the complete body of existing knowledge. Somewhere along the way man acquired the ability to communicate by sound. Although we now take this skill for granted, as somewhat akin to the instincts of animals or birds, a little reflection will suggest the tremendous advance in knowledge that the introduction of verbal skills represented. Every object, action, or thought became associated with a sound. Moreover, there had to be common agreement, at least within an area or tribe, as to the meaning of sounds produced by a human's vocal cords. Anyone who has studied a foreign language appreciates the difficulty of learning correct sounds and the advance in knowledge that this skill represents.

As the verbal skills were mastered, it became possible to pass on from one generation to the next important information that otherwise would have to be relearned anew by each individual through trial and error. Equally important, of course, was the introduction of written language, which is more efficient as a permanent means of communication and has a more far-reaching effect on the transfer and acquisition of knowledge.

A common characteristic of knowledge produced during the dawning of recorded history is that most of it came into being as the result of happy accident. In the process of sustaining himself, man learned new things about plants, animals, and the environment. In the era of the Greek and Roman civilizations, scholars and philosophers began to pursue knowledge as a full-time occupation. And in the Middle Ages the early Church emerged as a center of learning. (Mendel, one of the Church's best known monks, discovered the principle of hybridization while experimenting with peas.) Although the pursuit of knowledge by gifted individuals had important consequences, the "knowledge industry," that is, the employment of people for the sole purpose of advancing knowledge, was relatively unknown. Indeed, during the Dark Ages, the overall stock of knowledge appeared to decline rather than grow.

Research as a production activity

In the course of history, it became apparent that if certain people could devote themselves to the full-time pursuit of knowledge, a much greater intellectual output per unit of effort was possible than when knowledge came as a by-product of daily activities. Obviously people with special talents in the development of new knowledge could accomplish more if freed from other tasks. Galileo, Newton, Edison, Franklin, and Einstein could hardly have accomplished what they did had they been required to toil as full-time farmers or shopkeepers.

Thus the production of new knowledge through research began as a by-product of daily activities and gradually emerged as the domain of a select few. Now it has become established as a full-fledged industry. In the United States during recent years, research has been one of the most rapidly growing industries. In 1955 the resources devoted to all research (basic and applied) and development in the United States amounted to about $10 billion (1970 prices); by 1970 this figure had grown to over $30 billion, a threefold real increase in 15 years.[1]

We refer to research as an industry because it has much in common with more traditional types of production. Essentially research is a production activity. Inputs consist mainly of scientists and engineers, laboratories and testing facilities; output consists of new knowledge. The same concepts we employed in our discussion of producer choice and product supply—such as marginal and average product, marginal and average costs, diminishing returns, and economies of scale—apply also to the production of new knowledge.

At the same time there are some unique characteristics of research. First, there is the difficulty of measuring output. Knowledge does not come in easy-to-measure units like bushels, pounds, or dollars. Economists have found ways of measuring knowledge indirectly, however, but we will postpone until later in the chapter our discussion of this problem.

A second unique characteristic of research is that there is reason to believe that in the aggregate it may not be subject to the law of diminishing returns. Recall that the law of diminishing returns refers to a situation where the addition of a variable input to one or more fixed inputs after a point results in a diminished marginal physical product to the variable input. It is conceivable to view scientists and their supporting personnel and facilities as the variable input and nature's secrets or the potential stock of knowledge as the fixed input in the production of new knowledge (that is, research).

Will the addition of more scientists result in a diminishing and eventually a zero marginal product of scientific research? If nature's secrets or the potential stock of knowledge were finite, then we would reasonably expect diminishing returns to set in at some point. But if all knowledge, both known and unknown, is infinite, then research need not be subject to the law of diminishing returns.

The question is, as we acquire more knowledge, will it become more or less difficult to add to the stock of knowledge? For those who believe that the potential stock of knowledge is finite and that we already have discovered nature's most accessible secrets, it fol-

---

1 *Statistical Abstract, 1970,* p. 519.

lows that the acquisition of new knowledge will be increasingly difficult. On the other hand, it can be argued that knowledge, like the universe, is boundless and that previously discovered knowledge only scratches the surface allowing us to be even more productive in our future quest.

Unfortunately, we are not likely to be able to measure the limits of knowledge, at least within the confines of our finite lives here on earth. No one will be able to say, "We have now discovered all the knowledge there is to be known; nothing else remains to be discovered." When we consider that no two people who have lived or are living on earth are exactly the same, or that no two snowflakes have exactly the same form, we can begin to appreciate the boundlessness of nature.

We should be aware, also, that knowledge is more than having information or facts. In large part it is the ability to know what to do with information. Prehistoric man, for example, knew that fire was hot and that water moved swiftly in rivers, but he did not know that these phenomena could be transformed into sources of power. Even today the libraries filled with information do us little good unless we can apply that information.

It will be useful to probe a bit more deeply into the activity we call "research." It encompasses a fairly wide array of endeavors, ranging from what scientists call basic research to the more applied and developmental types of activity.

BASIC RESEARCH

Basic research can be thought of as activity concerned strictly with unlocking the secrets of nature without being directed at solving a particular problem. This does not imply, though, that the output of basic research is of little use. Indeed some of the most useful research results have come out of basic research.

A relatively small proportion of all research and development funds is spent on basic research. In 1970 expenditures for basic research totaled $3.9 billion, or about 13 percent of all research and development expenditures.[2] It is not difficult to understand why basic research has remained relatively small. An industrial firm in-

---

2 Ibid., p. 519.

vests in research for the purpose of increasing profits. If the firm has virtually no guarantee that the research results can be applied to the firm's operation, as is true for basic research, it has little incentive to pay for it. Some of the large firms allow their scientists a relatively small amount of free time for basic research, but this is mainly a fringe benefit for the scientists.

As a consequence, most basic research is carried on by colleges and universities or by the federal government. But even here there has been a reluctance to "turn scientists loose." In part this might be due to a fear by the public that the funds would be squandered on scientists' pet projects, with little chance for any payoff to society. Basic research is also a very risky business. Perhaps one project out of ten really adds something significant to the fund of knowledge.

This is not to say, however, that the high degree of risk associated with basic research necessarily implies a low return to this research. The one or two successful projects out of ten can well pay for the failures. From the standpoint of risk, research is much like drilling for oil. In oil exploration, roughly one well out of ten produces a significant find, but as a rule the gushers more than pay for the dry holes.

APPLIED RESEARCH

As the name implies, applied research is concerned with solving a particular problem or finding out a specific unknown. For example, the problem might be finding a way to reduce air pollution caused by automobiles or a way to curb the noise of jet engines.

As a rule both industry and public institutions have been more willing to finance applied research than basic research. Understandably, the business firm is more certain that a return will be forthcoming if the research is centered on a problem of concern to the firm. Much the same holds true for publicly sponsored research. Society feels somewhat more certain that it is getting its money's worth from research if scientists work on a recognized problem.

DEVELOPMENT

The activity referred to as development is the almost exclusive domain of the large industrial firm or the federal government. Development activities include such things as building prototypes of new products and testing them before their introduction on the market. However, it is rather difficult to separate development from applied research. In a sense, development is a kind of applied research because it is directed at finding out the unknown of a product or production technique. In fact, most industrial research is lumped together in one category and called research and development (R&D).

There is even some difficulty in distinguishing between the basic and applied categories of research. An applied research project can bring forth unexpected knowledge totally unrelated to the problem at hand. In this sense applied research has the same characteristics as basic research. It is best, therefore, to view these three categories of research as a continuum ranging from pure basic research, to applied research, to the development type of activity on the other end of the scale.

Research by industrial firms (R&D)

Research by industrial firms tends to be concentrated towards the applied and development types of activity. The overall motivation for a firm to carry on R&D is to improve its profit position. Research and development can increase profits for the firm by (1) the development of new or improved products, which has the effect of increasing the demand for the firm's products, or (2) the development of new cost-reducing techniques of production, which reduce average and marginal cost for the firm. The production of new or improved products resulting from R&D is illustrated in Figure 12–1 (A) and (B).

Figure 12–1(A) illustrates the situation for an imperfectly competitive firm before it undertakes the development of a new or improved product. If the R&D program is successful and a new product is developed, the demand facing the firm shifts to the right, shown by D_1 in Figure 12–1(B). This might depict a petroleum company that has developed a new additive for its gasoline which results in better gas mileage. Understandably, the demand for the company's product shifts to the right as customers switch from brands that do not contain the additive.

FIGURE 12–1
**The effect of new and improved products resulting
from R&D**
(A) Before R&D

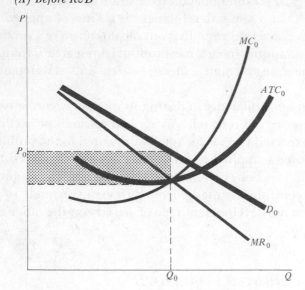

(B) After R&D

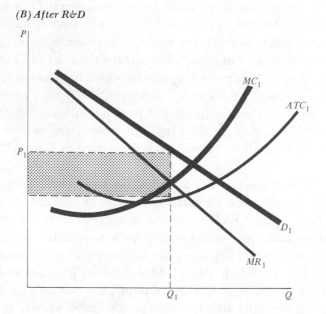

We must keep in mind, though, that R&D is a costly activity. Hence the R&D program will have the effect also of increasing the firm's average total cost (ATC) and marginal cost (MC) from what they would otherwise be. Thus ATC_1 and MC_1 in Figure 12–1 (B) are drawn in slightly higher than their original position in Figure 12–1(A). In this particular example, total profits, depicted by the shaded areas, are higher after the R&D than before, indicating that the additional revenue brought in by the increase in product demand more than offsets the additional cost of the R&D.

The second possibility for increasing profits through R&D is to reduce production costs through the discovery and adoption of new cost-reducing techniques. For example, a petroleum company might develop a new, more efficient method of refining crude oil. This would have the effect of shifting ATC and MC down and to the right, as illustrated in Figure 12–2. Here we assume that the product remains the same, so that the demand and marginal revenue curves are the same in both diagrams.

In this example we have assumed also that the cost saving obtained through the new technique was more than enough to offset the increase in costs brought on by the R&D. Total profits, denoted by the shaded areas in Figure 12–2, therefore increase as a result of the increased R&D expenditure.[3]

RETURNS TO INDUSTRIAL R&D

Conceptually, the decision on whether or not to carry on R&D is rather straightforward; it should be carried on as long as expected revenue increases more than expected costs. But in an actual decision-making situation, the main problem is to assess the returns to R&D. The firm has no guarantee, of course, that demand will shift right or costs will shift down.

The usual procedure for a firm is to begin with a rather modest R&D program, perhaps hiring an engineer to spend full time thinking up new ways of doing things. If total revenue increases more than his salary and expenses, the firm may add another R&D person, and so on. In other words, decisions to do or not to do R&D

---

[3] For further discussion on the economic aspects of research by industrial firms, see Edwin Mansfield, *The Economics of Technological Change* (New York: W. W. Norton & Co., 1968).

FIGURE 12–2
**Effect of new cost-reducing techniques resulting
from R&D**
(A) Before R&D

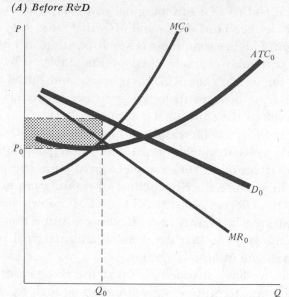

(B) After R&D

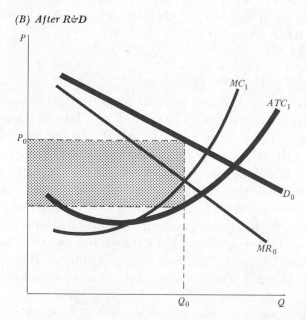

tend to be of a marginal nature. Because of the substantial increase in R&D during recent years, we can only infer that most firms have found it very profitable, hence they are doing more.

The decision by a firm to engage in R&D may be motivated as well by the desire to simply maintain a profit position. If other firms in the industry are investing in R&D to create new or improved products or to lower production costs, the firm that does not keep up soon will find itself with few customers or excessively high costs and eventually will be forced out of business. Even in this context, the effects of R&D still can be illustrated by Figures 12–1 and 12–2. Profits after R&D are higher than they would otherwise be.

In deciding whether or not to engage in R&D the overriding consideration by the firm must be whether or not it will be possible to capture a return to its investment. If the new knowledge that is produced by R&D is readily available to competing firms, the firm that originally produced the knowledge will not be able to gain any special advantage. For example, the petroleum firm that develops a new gasoline additive will naturally guard its secret very closely. If other firms should find it out and duplicate the additive, they could gain all of its advantages without paying any of the cost. No doubt this explains why some firms find it profitable to employ industrial spies.

One alternative for the firm or individual who discovers or develops something new is to take out a patent with the U.S. government patent office. Patent laws forbid the duplication of the patented item or process by other firms or individuals for a period of 17 years. Without these laws or protection, it is argued, there would be little incentive to invest in R&D.

In reality, however, patent laws probably have not offered the protection that might be supposed. Although a patented item cannot be duplicated exactly, in many cases a close substitute can be developed by making a few minor changes. Patenting certain products or processes, then, may actually hasten their discovery and adoption by competing firms. For this reason it is not unusual for firms to deliberately not patent something they have developed; rather, they try to keep it a secret. The decision whether or not to take out a patent depends mainly on the nature of the product or process. If it is something that is relatively easy to keep secret, such as an additive or minute ingredient, it might be best not to patent.

But if it is something like a machine or gadget that will be widely used, then patenting provides some protection, although rarely complete protection, against copying by other firms.

Another important factor that bears upon whether or not a firm will invest in R&D is the absolute size of the firm. Understandably it will not pay for a small firm to engage in any sizable R&D effort. Consider, for example, your tomato-growing endeavor. Even if you were to assume that no one would copy your research results, it would not pay you to spend several thousand dollars attempting to increase tomato yields. Even if you could double the yield of each tomato plant, the return would be small compared to the probable cost of doing so.

On the other hand, a very large firm, Standard Oil, for example, can find it profitable to spend a great deal on something that may improve its product only a small amount, say one penny per gallon. If this penny per gallon is multiplied by the millions of gallons of gasoline the company sells each year, we can see why it pays for the firm to engage in substantial R&D. In general, the larger the firm, the more profitable it is to invest in research and development to achieve a given increase in demand or decrease in costs.

Thus far we have considered only the private returns, that is, extra profits, of industrial R&D. But keep in mind that R&D can still be a good investment from the point of view of society even if it does not provide higher profits for the firm doing the R&D. What generally happens is that the extra profits coming from a new product or a new technique of production are eventually eroded away as more and more firms copy the product or technique.

But the fact that the individual firm's extra profits from R&D eventually disappear does not mean that society's benefits from R&D disappear also. Society continues to enjoy a return from R&D long after its profits are eroded away because of the resulting new or improved products that continue to be consumed and/or the reduced costs brought about by new technology. In other words, R&D makes it possible for society to obtain a greater value of output from its limited resources. Economists refer to this benefit as a "social return."[4]

---

[4] For estimates of the rates of return on industrial R&D, see Edwin Mansfield, *Industrial Research and Technological Innovation* (New York: W. W. Norton & Co., 1968).

Publicly sponsored research

An industrial firm will not choose to invest in research unless it has a reasonable assurance that it will add to profits, and the relatively small firm will not engage in research because the expense is too great to be borne by the relatively small output. However, society can benefit greatly from research that may not be profitable for an individual firm or that affects the output of industries made up of firms too small to do their own research, such as agriculture. For this reason the federal and state governments either sponsor research or carry it on in their own laboratories or institutions.

Most publicly sponsored research is done in colleges and universities. Because of the risk involved and the small chance of capturing a profit on the knowledge produced, much of the country's so-called basic research is done in these institutions. With the exception of market research on individual products, most economic research is done in institutions of higher learning. This is true as well for the humanities and other social sciences.

The decisions on what kind of and how much public research should be done are even more difficult in this area than for industrial research. The decision-making process is slow, cumbersome, and often based on very inadequate information. Someone, of course, must make these decisions, regardless of the information available. The basic decisions are made by society's elected representatives in the state and federal governments. They must decide how much of the taxpayer's money is to be devoted to research. Usually the amount that is allocated to research for a current year is based on what was allocated the year before, plus a little extra for new problems, increasing expenses, and the like.

Once the funds reach the research institutions, more decisions are required to further allocate the money. How much goes to physics, how much to chemistry, economics, agriculture, and so forth? Again the current allocation is made mainly on the basis of past allocation. Marginal changes come about with changes in personnel or with the emergence or recognition of new and pressing problems such as pollution.

Ideally, public research allocation should be made on the basis of the highest payoff to the research, but the main problem is to identify and measure the returns to public research.

RETURNS TO PUBLIC RESEARCH

The returns to public research, like those to education, can be classified into investment and consumption components. In the consumption area, society is willing to pay something to gain information about itself or about the universe, even though this knowledge may not lead to an increase in value of real output of society. For example, society has been willing to pay a sizable amount to develop a means of getting to the moon and back. Society also considers it worthwhile to find out more about man's origin and about his behavior, both past and present. Even though knowledge of this sort may not add to the monetary value of real output, it presumably does add something to the utility of society.

Aside from the space program, most public research is aimed at increasing the value of output of society, that is, an investment or monetary return. People value good health or the avoidance of the "grim reaper" before their time; hence they are willing to pay for medical research. Society places a value on a clean environment, so it supports research on ways of achieving this goal without giving up the goods and services that contribute to the pollution. Most of the basic research that is carried on, such as the work in physics, chemistry, biology, and mathematics, may not be aimed at a specific problem, but it is anticipated that the knowledge produced will somehow have a monetary value.

Measuring the monetary value of public research is indeed a difficult problem, and a great deal of work remains to be done in this area. Until some quantitative measures can be found, decisions to allocate public research will have to be made from purely subjective criteria or historical precedence, neither of which guarantees that society is getting the most for its money.

Agricultural research

We include a separate discussion of agricultural research for two reasons: (1) it is an area where some progress has been made in estimating social returns and (2) there seems to be widespread misunderstanding about who benefits from this research.

The major outcome of agricultural research is to increase the productive capacity of farmers. These include new, higher yielding crop varieties; breeding and disease-control advances to make livestock and poultry more efficient converters of feed; completely new inputs such as herbicides and pesticides; and new and improved management practices for farmers.

As we pointed out in the chapter on product supply, the effect of new technology is to increase, or shift to the right, the supply curve of individual producers and the industry, as shown in Figure 12–3.

FIGURE 12–3
Effect of agricultural research and resulting new technology that shifts agricultural supply

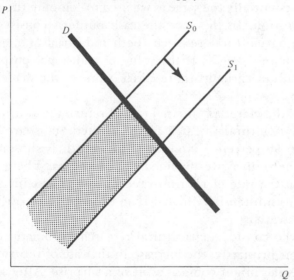

For a given price producers are willing to put more on the market or will sell a given amount for a lower price because their unit costs are lower.

The increase in productive efficiency, hence the increase in product supply, brought about by agricultural research in effect increases the total value of agricultural output for a given amount of traditional resources such as land, labor, and capital. In other words, by producing knowledge and new, more productive inputs, society obtains more output from its scarce resources. The annual value of this additional output to society is illustrated in Figure 12–3 by the shaded area lying between S_0 and S_1, bounded on the top by the demand for agricultural products.

Supply curve S_0 in Figure 12–3 represents what the supply of agricultural output would be without the new technology. By measuring the increase in productive efficiency of agriculture, economists have been able to determine the location of S_1 for a given year. The difference between these two curves, therefore, represents the annual value of output attributable to agricultural research.

By comparing the annual expenditure on research with the value of extra output attributable to research, economists have been able to obtain estimates of its social internal rate of return. The procedure used is essentially the same as we used to compute the rate of return to education. In this case the cash outflows consist of expenditures on agricultural research (both industrial and public), and the cash inflows consist of the value of additional output obtained as a result of agricultural research (value of the shaded area in Figure 12–3).

Estimates of the *marginal* internal rate of return to *additional* investment in agricultural research in the United States are in the range of 40 to 50 percent.[5] Note that this return is substantially higher than the returns we obtained for education. There is evidence also that the rate of return to recent investment in agricultural research is substantially higher than the return to past investment in this research.[6]

To those who consider agricultural research as something that benefits farmers primarily, the increase in the rate of return to agricultural research might come as a bit of a surprise. After all, the farm population has declined from about 32 million people in 1920 to about 10 million people at the present. During this period the farm population as a percent of total population declined from about 30 percent to 5 percent.

This brings us to our second major point. The long-run beneficiaries of agricultural research tend to be consumers of farm products rather than farmers. Of course, farmers benefit as consumers, along with everyone else. Consumers benefit from agricultural re-

---

5 Willis Peterson, "The Returns to Investment in Agricultural Research in the United States," in Walter Fishel (ed.), *Resource Allocation in Agricultural Research* (Minneapolis, University of Minnesota Press, 1971), p. 160.
6 Ibid.

search because the resulting increase in productive efficiency shifts the supply of agricultural products to the right, thereby increasing food output and reducing food prices below what they would otherwise be.

Many people, particularly housewives, would argue, though, that food prices are not cheap, judging from the prices in supermarkets these days. But one must look at the real cost of food—the proportion of a country's resources that is devoted to food production. At the present time Americans spend about 15 percent of their income on food. Contrast this to Nigeria, for example, where food accounts for 70 percent of a family's budget.[7]

Even in the United States at the turn of the century, people spent almost 40 percent of their income on food. A nation with a relatively unproductive agricultural sector must devote a relatively large share of its resources to food production. As agricultural productivity increases, more and more people leave agriculture to produce other things that make life more interesting and enjoyable. If 70 to 80 percent of a nation's population is required to produce food, modern conveniences such as reasonably priced automobiles, adequate medical care, and the host of labor-saving appliances that make life more enjoyable cannot also be produced. Life might have been simpler in the "good old days" when most people were farmers, but few people today would accept the inconveniences that our forefathers had to contend with.

This is not to say that agricultural research can take sole credit for economic development. Other knowledge is required as well to produce the variety of modern goods and services that raise the standard of living. But as developing nations are learning, little progress can be made without technological advance in agriculture.

Social costs of new technology

There is a growing concern in the United States and other highly developed nations that the true cost of research that produces new knowledge and technology may exceed the expenditures for re-

---

[7] Marguerite Burk, *Consumption Economics: A Multidisciplinary Approach* (New York: John Wiley & Sons, Inc., 1968), p. 41.

search. One of the concerns is the movement of people between occupations and areas. If new technology makes a job obsolete, what
is the social cost of having the person who held this job move to another occupation in another location?

It is fairly easy to measure moving costs, but there are other
things to consider. People who move must leave family, friends, and
familiar ways of living for the unknown. Some find moving an ex-
citing experience, others dread it. The largest case in point is the
huge rural to urban migration that has taken place in the United
States. Most would agree that the increased concentration of population in urban areas has contributed to many present-day problems: air and water pollution, congestion of transportation systems
and of housing, and increased tension and unrest.

Without the new technology would these problems disappear?
Perhaps some would. But we must remember also that problems
have always plagued mankind. Consider the disease, isolation, long
hours of drudgery both in the home and on the job, and ignorance,
with which our forefathers had to contend. Even pollution existed
in those days. Imagine the smell in the cities when vehicles were
horse drawn, or the smoke and soot that came forth when coal was
the main source of heat and power. Indeed some of the worst pollution in the world today exists in countries that have experienced
relatively little advance in technology. When dealing with present-
day problems we tend to visualize things as we would like to see
them, without regard to their historical background.

Main points of Chapter 12

1. The introduction of a spoken and written language early in
   history represented a significant advance in knowledge for
   mankind.
2. At the dawning of history new knowledge came mainly as a
   by-product of everyday activities.
3. During the course of history man learned that output of
   knowledge could be increased if certain people devoted full
   time to its production. Today the production of knowledge is

a large and growing industry expending billions of dollars per year in the United States alone.

4. We can think of research as a production activity in which inputs consist of such things as scientists and engineers, laboratories, and testing facilities, and output consists of new knowledge.

5. Unlike more traditional types of production, we cannot be sure that the production of new knowledge is subject to the law of diminishing returns. If the potential stock of knowledge is infinite there is no reason why diminishing returns must set in.

6. Knowledge is more than having information or facts; in large part it is the ability to know what to do with information.

7. Basic research is concerned with unlocking the secrets of nature without having a preconceived idea of how the knowledge might be used.

8. Applied research is concerned with solving a particular problem or finding out a specific unknown.

9. Development is an extension of applied research concerned with finding out the unknown about new products or production techniques and testing them before their introduction on the market.

10. Industrial firms are motivated to carry on R&D by the prospect of increased profits. Research and development can increase profits by the introduction of new and improved products, which shifts the demand facing the firm to the right, or the development of new cost-reducing techniques of production, which shifts the firm's cost curves down and to the right.

11. The type of research carried on by a firm will be governed by its ability to capture a return to the research.

12. Patent laws are intended to help firms or individuals capture a return from new products or techniques. The ability of competitors to develop close substitutes for patented items limits their protection, however.

13. In general it does not pay a small firm to engage in organized R&D because the cost cannot be spread across a large enough output.

14. Even though the private profits from R&D may decline or be nonexistent, expenditures for it can still be a good investment

for society because R&D makes it possible for society to obtain a greater value of output from its limited resources.

15. Because society can benefit greatly from research that is not profitable for individual firms, the federal and state governments sponsor or carry on research of their own. Most public research is done in colleges and universities.

16. The allocation of public research is a difficult problem because knowledge does not come in easy-to-measure units like bushels, pounds, or dollars.

17. The value to society of agricultural research has been estimated by measuring the value of the increased output brought about by the increase in productive efficiency of farmers.

18. Contrary to popular belief, the main benefits of agricultural research flow to consumers rather than to farmers. As agriculture becomes more productive, a larger share of a nation's resources are devoted to the production of things other than food.

19. There has been a growing awareness in recent years of problems associated with new technology. What is often overlooked, however, is the quality of life that existed in years past and the problems that confronted people before the advent of modern technology.

Questions for thought and discussion

1. How might the work of a medical researcher in developing a cure for cancer be considered a production activity? What are the inputs and the outputs?

2. What kind of research would you expect to be carried on by business firms? Why?

3. What kind of research would you expect to find in universities? Why?

4. How does research benefit society?

5. Do you believe that auto makers have much incentive to carry on research that will lead to safer vehicles? Explain.

6. "Farmers should pay for all agricultural research because they're the ones who benefit from it." Do you agree? Explain.

7. Agricultural scientists in California recently developed a variety of tomatoes that can be picked by a machine. Who benefits from this research? Is anyone harmed by it? Explain.

8. Knowing what you do about the relationship between price elasticity of demand and total revenue (Chapter 3), what effect would you suppose agricultural research has on total revenue going to farmers as a group if the demand for food is highly inelastic? Illustrate with a supply-demand diagram.

Index

This book has been set in 11 point and 10 point Baskerville, leaded 2 points. Chapter numbers are in 30 point Baskerville italic and chapter titles are in 24 point Baskerville. The size of the type page is 26 x 45 picas.